EXPLORING COMPOSITION STUDIES

EXPLORING COMPOSITION STUDIES

STUDIES

Sites, Issues, and Perspectives

KELLY RITTER AND PAUL KEI MATSUDA

UTAH STATE UNIVERSITY PRESS
Logan, Utah
2012

Published by Utah State University Press
An imprint of University Press of Colorado
5589 Arapahoe Avenue, Suite 206C
Boulder, Colorado 80303

The University Press of Colorado is a proud member of

The Association of American University Presses.

AAUP '93/ 2012

The University Press of Colorado is a cooperative publishing enterprise supported, in part, by Adams State College, Colorado State University, Fort Lewis College, Metropolitan State College of Denver, Regis University, University of Colorado, University of Northern Colorado, Utah State University, and Western State College of Colorado.

ISBN: 978-0-87421-882-4 (hardcover)
ISBN: 978-1-60732-629-8 (paper)
ISBN: 978-0-87421-883-1 (e-book)

Library of Congress Cataloging-in-Publication Data

Ritter, Kelly.
  Exploring composition studies : sites, issues, and perspectives / Kelly Ritter and Paul Kei Matsuda.
    p. cm.
  Includes bibliographical references and index.
  ISBN 978-0-87421-882-4 (hardcover) – ISBN 978-1-60732-629-8 (pbk.) – ISBN 978-0-87421-883-1 (e-book)
1. English language–Rhetoric–Study and teaching. I. Matsuda, Paul Kei. II. Title.
  PE1404.R524 2012
  808'.042071–dc23

                           2011048144

CONTENTS

FOREWORD
Defining Composition Studies . . . Again, and Again

Andrea A. Lunsford

Some fifteen years ago, Lynn Bloom, Don Daiker, and Ed White published *Composition in the Twenty-first Century: Crisis and Change*, a collection of essays from a conference by the same name that had been, according to the editors' preface, three years in the making and that had a strong impact on the field. Their volume still makes for instructive reading, perhaps especially with fifteen years' hindsight. Hoping to chart a "new geography of composition" (2), the editors and writers of this volume (including Stephen North, Shirley Brice Heath, David Bartholomae, Linda Flower, James Berlin, Anne Gere, James Slevin, and Peter Elbow) took on a number of then-pressing questions, as indicated by a selection of section titles:

- "What Is Composition and Why Do We Teach It?"
- "What Have We Learned from the Past and How Can It Shape the Future of Composition?"
- "Who Will Assess Composition in the 21st Century and How Will They Assess It?"
- "What Issues Will Writing Program Administration Confront in the 21st Century?"
- "Who Should Teach Composition and What Should They Know?"
- "What Direction Will Research in Composition Take and How Will Research Affect Teaching?"
- "What Political and Social Issues Will Shape Composition in the Future?"
- "What Will Be the Meaning of Literate Action and Intellectual Property?"

In closing the volume, Lynn Bloom notes that conference attendees approached the new century "far from complacent about the past, uncomfortable with the present, uneasy about the future." Taken together, she says, the essays in the volume recognized this state of mind and, in addressing the questions above, demonstrated "the need for a new map to provide direction through territory that superficially looks like familiar terrain" but that is, in some important ways, still "terra incognita" (273). Bloom signs off with a haunting image of the "map of the universe of composition at the emergence of the 21st century" as an echo of "Escher's engraving of one hand drawing another hand. At first glance, the hands look like mirror images of one another; they are not. Nor is either image finished, though initially it appears to be. The process of conceiving, constructing, changing any field is ongoing, dynamic; it represents a world of hope, a world without end" (277).

As the Bloom, Daiker, and White volume demonstrates, composition or writing studies has been working on maps of its territory for a long time, often in ongoing and dynamic ways. In fact, a search of the literature will turn up dozens of attempts to map the field along with its theories, objects of study, methods, and pedagogies, at least from the 1960s through the end of the twentieth century. We have been, and perhaps continue to be, much like that one hand attempting to draw another.

In *Exploring Composition Studies: Sites, Issues, and Perspectives*, editors Ritter and Matsuda are in intertextual conversation with these earlier mapping expeditions and particularly with Bloom, Daiker, and White's 1996 volume. Certainly they continue the search for definitions—of the nature of first-year writing (Downs and Wardle), of basic writing (Adler-Kassner and Harrington), and of writing across the curriculum (Malenczyk). And this collection also addresses methodological issues (Chiseri-Strater; L'Epplantenier and Mastrangelo; and Hawisher and Selfe) as well as concerns related to support for and assessment of writing and learning (Donahue; Fitzgerald; Estrem and Reid; Gunner; Yancey; Matsuda; Peeples and Hart-Davidson). Yet while this volume explores a number of the same issues and asks some of the same questions as those posed by Bloom, Daiker, and White a decade and a half ago, Ritter and Matsuda's volume focuses much more specifically on the role of research in responding to such questions. As a result, *Exploring Composition Studies* aims to map a scholarly agenda for writing studies in the coming years. While all the essays here provide nutritious food for thought, to my mind several offer particularly compelling challenges to long-held assumptions. In "Teaching Composition in a Multilingual World: Second Language Writing in Composition Studies," Paul Matsuda points toward the global linguistic and cultural turn that composition *must* make—and is indeed slowly beginning to make, with his leadership. A second essay highlighting the challenges of literacy and globalization is Gail Hawisher and Cynthia Selfe's "Studying Literacy in Digital Contexts: Computers and Composition Studies," which outlines how "multimodal digital research . . . allows for the increasingly rich representation of language and literacy" and in doing so not only troubles traditional assumptions but sketches in the outlines of a whole new country in the map of writing studies. And in "Reimagining the Nature of FYC: Trends in Writing-about-Writing Pedagogies," Doug Downs and Elizabeth Wardle continue to push against traditional definitions of first-year writing, showing how that "service" course can and should be reconceived with a strong disciplinary focus.

Read together, this collection of essays issues a set of challenges to the field in terms of the research questions we ask (or sometimes fail to ask), the methods we use to pursue them, the material sites they occupy, and—at least in a few cases—the ideological baggage they entail. Behind all these essays, however, lie several meta-questions that need our undivided attention now that the rhetorical triangle of text, writer, and reader has exploded or splintered into additional elements and the three key terms have blurred significantly: What *is* writing in the twenty-first century, and why does it matter? What *is* reading in a time when texts are verbal, vocal, and visual, and how can we expand reading repertoires and theories to accommodate and account for these practices? The essays in this provocative collection offer some tantalizing hints in response to these questions: my hope is that our ongoing project of mapping will increasingly turn toward these last two meta-questions, for how we approach them will have lasting implications for our theory, practice, and pedagogy.

EXPLORING COMPOSITION STUDIES

INTRODUCTION
How Did We Get Here?

Kelly Ritter and Paul Kei Matsuda

Composition studies—an important subset of the larger field of rhetoric and composition—is an intellectual formation that draws insights from various related fields in order to address issues in the teaching of writing. Due to its inherently interdisciplinary nature, composition studies draws its students and prospective scholars from many areas inside and outside English studies. These new members of the composition studies community are often trained to varying degrees in the pedagogy of composition through teaching practica or proseminars. While many of them have been exposed to some of the major theories of the field in addition to other specialized topics in which they or their faculty mentors happen to have interests, others may not have been introduced to the discipline through a broader articulation of how (and why) its members undertake research that is not only pedagogical but also historical, theoretical, and social scientific in nature. Relative newcomers to composition studies who are not familiar with the broad scope of the field—including its allied sites of research such as professional and technical writing, writing-across-the-curriculum programs, writing centers, and writing program administration—may struggle as they try to understand its diverse and growing constituencies and enduring questions in various subareas of composition studies. This collection aims to provide that understanding, through a detailed exploration of the field.

As editors, and as teachers, we recognize that such an exploration requires first the presence of a road map. As such, we feel it is helpful here to briefly sketch a modern history of composition studies that might then put the concerns of this book's thirteen essays in a larger context. While origin stories of composition studies abound, historians of the field seem to agree that there are two branches to the "beginning" of composition as a subject of interest in the university. The first branch would be the study of the cultural history and practice of rhetoric, which has existed in various permutations from antiquity through the present; rhetoric as a field and a practice is critical for many of the undergraduate and graduate programs in composition studies (or composition and rhetoric or rhetoric and composition, depending upon local nomenclature) today. The second branch, arriving in force in the nineteenth century, would be the institutional imperative to inculcate in students the principles of composing—specifically, to create in students the proper markers of taste and, arguably, class, as exhibited in written compositions, usually based on the analysis of literary works. The intertwined beginnings of this field have been articulated, and debated, by a variety of scholars (see, for example, Gage; Andrea Lunsford; Crowley; Connors; Berlin; Susan Miller; and Thomas Miller); we recognize the complex politics and interests surrounding the intermingling of rhetoric with composition, and composition with rhetoric. But for the purpose of this book, we will focus specifically on the scholarship of writing and composing—and, as such, limit our history to a brief discussion of research and inquiry that focuses on composition studies per se. We have, however, included a brief list of recommended comprehensive field histories of rhetoric and composition at the conclusion of this introduction for those who would like to learn more about the ongoing debates over the field's trajectory and mission.

Different historians of the field will position the "start" of composition studies at different points. Some will argue that U.S. college composition was born at Harvard in the 1890s; others will argue that it was not truly born until the beginning of the 1970s. Still others will position the birth of the field at various points in between, including 1911, when the National Council of Teachers of English was formed, or 1949, when the first Conference on College Composition and Communication took place, or 1950, when the journal *College Composition and Communication* debuted. The date one chooses has much to do with what one insists is being born. Is it the first-year course that one sees as the origin of things? If so, then the 1890s sounds about right—though some forms of writing at the introductory level were offered in colleges several years before this, and extra-institutional writing collectives existed even earlier in the nineteenth century as well. Is it the emergence of a collective recognition that writing is an important aspect of education, and thus an organization needs to be formed to unite its teachers? Then 1911 would be the best date to choose, and is in fact the date we feel is the best start for a modern "origins" story of composition studies. Or is the issue the birth of composition studies as an academic field? If so, then the 1970s sounds about right, since this decade gave us the first doctoral programs in rhetoric and composition, and a series of prominent studies about writers and writing, significantly using cognitive scientific approaches and arguing for the field as a site of *research*. But readers can see how even in retelling its history, composition studies becomes a tricky entity to narrate in any agreed-upon way.

So, we must choose one way to provide a series of snapshots, that road map we mentioned earlier. A tangible way to do this, especially for readers new to the field and also perhaps new to the teaching of writing, is through that first-year course—its history and its pedagogies. While recent pedagogies have called for a "revival" of rhetoric and rhetorical studies in the first-year composition course, at the critical era in which composition as a *course* became relatively standardized in American colleges and universities (circa 1880–1910), the division between the study of rhetoric as an *art* and composition as a *skill* was acute, both in pedagogical design and in pedagogical labor. As an all-male enterprise, the first-year composition course was primarily a course taught *by* men *for* men. It is true that composition also existed at both elite and public women's colleges (and in those settings women instructors did teach). Yet, from a socioeconomic point of view, the larger, broader imperative in the composition course nationwide, one might argue, was to produce learned *men* for deployment into professional roles in society. Women, in contrast, were taught the principles of composition in order to grow as teachers, or as mother-teachers, to borrow a term from Eileen Schell—those who would educate their children and grow a literate family. Only since the post–World War II era have we been able to argue that coeducational writing spaces have existed as the norm rather than the exception in American colleges and universities.

Two factors led to a shift in this pedagogical landscape for composition (and other subjects). First, the successful enterprise of land-grant universities, following the Morrill Act of 1862, meant that young men no longer had to travel to the eastern seaboard for a quality college education. Many large public universities began to siphon away enrollments from Harvard, Yale, Princeton, and other elites typically seen as inevitable schools of choice for men with the money and ability to enroll. They also admitted women, in contrast to the practices of the Ivy League. As a result, the applicant pool for eastern colleges in particular was dropping dramatically from a near-guaranteed group of educated, wealthy (or at least upper-middle class) men. Second, after World War I, there was a sizeable loss of young men (due to death as well as serious injury) who would have otherwise been target students in colleges and universities. Simply put, the casualties of the war left many seats unfilled; this was also a glaring problem in post–World War II classrooms. To collapse some of the finer details of this shift into a summary point here, elite colleges began facing economic realities in the early twentieth century that would lead them to admit students who were "less" in both educational preparedness and social class. No longer were colleges such as Harvard and Yale able to limit their admissions to men of "taste"; as a result, these colleges lost some of their territorial control, if not cultural capital, over higher education, and the way in which courses that exemplified taste and breeding were taught changed—by necessity, not by choice—in response.

Each time our nation has witnessed a significant cultural event—a world war, a "baby boom," a civil rights movement—higher education responds to that event in kind. As well-educated, upper-class men began to choose public universities in equal numbers to private ones, and as the number of eligible male students dramatically diminished due to wartime casualties, admission standards were altered to allow for an economic reality of vacated seats; as some of these students were not prepared in ways that were expected of traditional college students, the discourse of "remedial" English emerged in our field journals and in our writing program discourse on all types of campuses. The conclusion of World War II brought a large number of nontraditional students on G.I. Bill. The conclusion of the war also brought an influx of international students (then called "foreign students"), and the United States replaced Germany as the leading destination for international students.

Women began to fill seats alongside these other new student types, both as part of a social movement valuing a broader definition of women's education and in response to the sudden welcome of colleges and universities that were now in competition for bodies—male or female—to stay afloat. As a result, writing instruction shifted yet again to address the coeducational student experience and, as Robert Connors would argue in *Composition-Rhetoric*, to diminish the previously confrontational basis of instruction in writing and rhetoric. And finally, as the civil rights protests of the 1960s led to the open admissions movement, colleges such as the City University of New York, among others, began to welcome a new group of students—which included adult, lower-income, and minority students, many of whom spoke the dominant variety of

English as a second language or a second dialect. This shift revived the discourse surrounding basic writing, and also invigorated composition's ongoing attention to the relationship between language and power, and the position of first-year writing as a "gatekeeper," in Sharon Crowley's terms (*Composition in the University*), limiting entrance to the university community to those able to pass its requirements.

Alongside these social movements that were affecting higher education in general and writing education in particular, composition studies has gone through various waves of pedagogical theory, each providing a view of the student, his or her audience, and the written product in different relation to one another. These waves, like the history of composition studies itself, are viewed differently by different scholars. In *Rhetoric and Reality*, James Berlin created a taxonomy based in epistemology as a means of organizing these waves historically, via differing theories of rhetoric (objective, subjective, and transactional). Robert Connors, in contrast, singled out social and material phenomena in cataloguing this pedagogical history—such as the entry of women into postsecondary classrooms, which shifted rhetoric from a space for heated debate and speaker challenges to an "irenic" rhetoric that de-emphasized conflict and privatized the space for study. Such a social shift, in Connors's view, changed rhetoric (chiefly oratory) to "composition-rhetoric" (chiefly writing). Connors also cites the emergence of the writing textbook industry as a material condition for the standardization of writing instruction, a move created to fill the need for a freestanding vehicle of instruction to aid the growing number of frequently untrained, contingent faculty in the teaching of writing. Still others, such as Susan Miller (*Textual Carnivals*) and Sharon Crowley, would characterize the pedagogy of composition as having a normalizing, "gatekeeping" function in the university, secondary to the primacy of literary study and the need for students of nonelite social groups to be inculcated into the space of higher education. Both Miller and Crowley would also argue that composition as a course has been significantly *feminized*, by its predominantly women labor force and by its lower position on the institutional hierarchy of subjects of study.

Sitting behind all of these historians' views are multiple questions related to the most appropriate way of teaching writing. Some of these questions are structural. For example: How should a teacher approach the balance between instruction in grammar and mechanics and instruction in content and rhetorical effectiveness? What strategies are best for addressing these two areas, particularly in classrooms consisting of students with diverse learning needs? Should students read published literary texts, expository texts, or localized student texts in the composition classroom? Should students be placed into writing courses based on levels of preparedness or on language backgrounds, or should such populations be "mainstreamed"? How does one assess what types of learning have taken place? Should writing instruction be the sole province of first-year composition, or should it be diffused across the curriculum?

Other questions pertain to the philosophy of instruction itself. For example: How much should a teacher emphasize a student or student group's cultural and/or political conditions in the teaching of writing? Should the teacher teach his or her students that writing is a vehicle for self-awareness? Should the teacher go further, and promote writing as a means of social liberation? Or should writing be instead taught as an expressive and informative skill that always responds to existing community expectations that are further dependent upon local context? Still deeper questions pertain to the delivery and very nature of the course— and writing—itself: Who teaches writing, and under what labor conditions? How are teachers of writing trained, and within what institutional parameters? How do writing courses bridge the gap between academic literacy and other sites of literacy practices, such as professional writing? These are just a sampling of the questions and question types that continue to occupy scholars of composition studies' research agendas, as readers will see in this collection.

Most, if not all, teachers of writing have, at one time or another, found themselves in the position of employing bits and pieces of many different theories and approaches; it would be unnecessarily limiting for a writing teacher to feel that he or she must "fit" into one particular model, or seek to answer only one of the above questions in creating his or her writing course. New teachers in particular often take some time to find their pedagogical "voice" and may return to a particular theory sometime after studying it, only to find it offers new ideas.

The most important thing we might suggest that readers take away from this brief historical overview of writing students and writing pedagogies is that composition studies is a dynamic field that, perhaps more than any other area of academic study, mirrors the institutional and noninstitutional forces within which it operates. A longer history of this field would include writing outside the first-year classroom, including how writing in corporate, nonprofit, and other communal nonacademic settings has affected the ways in which we view literacy acquisition and the value of the written word in our culture at large. It would also include a greater attention to the subfields of composition that have made it such a force in the university, and the theoretical positions underpinning these subfields. In many ways, we hope that the essays in this collection will provide readers with those valuable, alternate looks at the history and practice of composition *outside* the trajectory of the first-year course we have just outlined, and thus provide a much-needed supplement to the narrative of this field, its slippery boundaries and layered stories included.

* * *

The twenty seasoned contributors who lend their expertise to *Exploring Composition Studies: Sites, Issues, and Perspectives* have designed their chapters with the above histories of, and questions about, writing and the teaching of writing in mind, and in doing so, have collectively created what we believe to be a comprehensive and thoughtful exploration of the enterprise of composition studies as it stands in the twenty-first century. Given the overwhelming growth of this field, and the changes to its research and, by extension, pedagogical agendas over just the past ten years, as we have just illustrated—especially noting composition studies' basic endeavor that its theories should inform its practices—we believe this multivocal collection is long overdue.

The thirteen essays in *Exploring Composition Studies* concentrate on diverse yet specific areas of research and scholarship—such as writing assessment, ethnography, technologies of composing, basic writing, archival research, second language writing, writing centers, and writing assessment—in order to provide a succinct overview of the purpose and relevance of these areas of inquiry to composition studies as a multifaceted discipline. Each of the essays (1) defines a particular area or site of scholarship and inquiry within the field as it stands today; (2) discusses its specific importance to the field of composition studies; (3) examines its relation to other areas of research; and (4) reflects on its intellectual issues and controversies. As a final reflection on these individual investigations, Deborah Holdstein, former editor of *CCC*, offers an afterword. *Exploring Composition Studies* presents current perspectives of important scholarly voices in this field, speaking on the key accomplishments and central debates of composition studies research and scholarship today. The book provides the reader with a foundation for better understanding the various constituencies within this field—hopefully so as to someday stake one's own scholarly place in it.

We bring these voices together to not only introduce and overview the current research and scholarship trends in composition studies, but also to put those areas in dialogue with one another in productive ways—dialogues that we hope will spark classroom conversations and lively debates. Readers will also see insightful profiles of contested sites within the field—such as basic writing and second language writing— put in important historical and theoretical perspective. In general, students and scholars who are new to the work of composition studies will gain a broader perspective on what lines of inquiry are possible, what research agendas inform others, and how the field has grown to include the study of various writing communities beyond the first year, and beyond the university itself.

Exploring Composition Studies is divided into two sections: "The State of the Field(s)" and "Innovations, Advancements, and Methodologies." Grouping these essays by first, a sense of the locations of writing research and pedagogy and second, the methodologies employed in researching and explicating these various sites allows readers a grounding in both the specific spaces housing the work of the field and the broader theories and practices—and controversies—that inform it. Because the field has become highly interdisciplinary—as many of these essays note— these two sections of the book are, we believe, a way to fairly represent the diverse work that goes on in composition studies without privileging any one practice or approach.

Section 1 discusses seven key "locations" wherein composition studies happens. The first two of these discussed—basic writing, second language writing—are traditionally positioned by those outside the field as singularly classroom-based. Linda Adler-Kassner and Susanmarie Harrington in the first chapter and Paul Kei Matsuda in the second make clear, however, that each of these pedagogically defined groups also has roots in the community outside the university as well as within other areas of academia beyond English and the humanities. The next four sites discussed—professional and technical writing, the writing center, the writing-across-the-curriculum program, and writing pedagogy education programs—each point to the other physical locations wherein the work of composition studies takes place, and challenge the boundaries of composition studies as typically defined through its first-year pedagogies alone, or its historical "service" function within the university. Tim Peeples and Bill Hart-Davidson, Lauren Fitzgerald, Rita Malenczyk, and Jeanne Gunner call attention to the intellectual work of professional writing and technical writing, writing centers, WAC programs, and writing program administration Their essays debunk the commonplace view of composition studies as being limited to introductory coursework and rote classroom approaches. This first section of the book thus poses several key questions for new scholars of the field, including: What is "composition" and who is composing (and under what conditions)? What does composition tell us about writing and research in areas outside the traditional classroom (and vice versa)? How can we reenvision first-year composition as a *study of* writing, rather than a (pedestrian) requirement? Why and how are extra-institutional sites of writing—such as commonly employed in professional and technical writing as a practice—critical to the sustainability and growth of composition studies as a field?

Section 2 attempts to bring into focus select questions and methodologies that go toward characterizing current research and inquiry in the field. These seven chapters illustrate many questions that currently inform composition studies, particularly concerning the place of history, the role of the community, and the work of theory—both as pedagogical framework and program assessment tool. Doug Downs and Elizabeth Wardle contemplate a revision of the framework of first-year composition via their " writing-about-writing" approach; Christiane Donahue investigates whether composition "carries" by presenting an overview of transfer theory; Kathleen Blake Yancey recovers the recent history of writing assessment in our colleges and universities; Elizabeth Chiseri-Strater details the history and currency of ethnography; and Barbara L'Eplattenier and Lisa Mastrangelo illustrate the resurgence of archival histories in the research on composition and composing.In addition, Heidi Estrem and E. Shelley Reid detail the advances in teacher education in composition studies and writing pedagogy more generally. This second section therefore raises questions about methodologies in composition studies, such as: Do ethnographic and historical studies find their way often enough into practice-based research agendas? How do we define "community" in a field so clearly populated by a diversity of interests, identities, and agencies? What happens when students leave composition—does their knowledge "transfer"? How might we better define and extend the theories driving composition studies if they were no longer housed—or were responsible for—the first-year composition course?

This book is intended, ultimately, to serve as a conversation starter, a research primer, and a reference text for those who are on the verge of entering our field, who want to understand it from the inside out. We welcome these emerging voices, and look forward to seeing their own articulations of what composition studies, in all its many roots and branches, truly is.

RECOMMENDED FURTHER READINGS IN THE HISTORY OF COMPOSITION STUDIES

Berlin, James. *Rhetoric and Reality: Writing Instruction in American Colleges, 1900–1985.* Studies in Writing and Rhetoric Series. Carbondale: Southern Illinois UP, 1987. Print.

———. *Writing Instruction in Nineteenth-Century American Colleges.* Studies in Writing and Rhetoric Series. Carbondale: Southern Illinois UP, 1984. Print.

Brereton, John C., ed. *The Origins of Composition Studies in the American College, 1875–1925: A Documentary History.* Pittsburgh: U of Pittsburgh P, 1995. Print.

Carr, Jean Ferguson, Stephen L. Carr, and Lucille Schultz, eds. *Archives of Instruction: Nineteenth Century Rhetorics, Readers, and Composition Books in the United States.* Pittsburgh: U of Pittsburgh P, 2005. Print.

Connors, Robert. *Composition-Rhetoric: Backgrounds, Theory, and Pedagogy.* Pittsburgh: U of Pittsburgh P, 1997. Print.

Crowley, Sharon. *Composition in the University: Historical and Polemical Essays.* Pittsburgh: U of Pittsburgh P, 1998. Print.

Hawk, Byron. *A Counter-History of Composition: Toward Methodologies of Complexity.* Pittsburgh: U of Pittsburgh P, 2007. Print.

Miller, Susan. *Textual Carnivals: The Politics of Composition.* Carbondale: Southern Illinois UP, 1993. Print.

Miller, Thomas. *The Evolution of College English: Literacy Studies from the Puritans to the Postmoderns.* Pittsburgh: U of Pittsburgh P, 2010. Print.

———. *The Formation of College English: Rhetoric and Belles Lettres in the British Cultural Provinces.* Pittsburgh: U of Pittsburgh P, 1997. Print.

North, Stephen M. *The Making of Knowledge in Composition: Portrait of an Emerging Field.* Portsmouth, NH: Boynton/Cook, 1987. Print.

Phelps, Louise Weatherbee, and Janet Emig. *Feminine Principles and Women's Experience in Composition and Rhetoric.* Pittsburgh: U of Pittsburgh P, 1995. Print.

Tate, Gary, and Erika Lindemann. *An Introduction to Composition Studies.* New York: Oxford UP, 1991. Print.

I

The State of the Field(s)

1

CREATION MYTHS AND FLASH POINTS
Understanding Basic Writing through Conflicted Stories

Linda Adler-Kassner and Susanmarie Harrington

By now there is a well-developed literature attesting to the importance of stories—of narrative—for the development of institutional, cultural, and organizational identities. Texts from a diversity of fields, from organizational behavior and management (e.g., Brown et al. 2005) to historiography (Noble) to documentary studies (Coles) to our own field of composition (Rose, *Lives on the Boundary*; *The Mind at Work*; Ede, *Situating Composition*), document the power of stories to shape peoples' understandings. This includes (but is not limited to) understandings of a number of relationships: between people and their articulation of understandings; between different ideas about a common subject; between understandings and larger issues of interest or relevance for the subject(s) under discussion.

As a field, basic writing is in many ways defined by the stories that researchers, teachers, and institutions have told about teachers and the students that populate basic writing classes. These stories are located not only in the anecdotes shared at conferences, on e-mail discussion lists, or in teacher lounges, but also in the scholarship of basic writing itself. Scholarship, as well as public discussions in the news and among policy makers, promotes narratives about students and teachers. Academic studies depend on assumptions about the roles students and teachers play, their motivations, and their backgrounds. To understand the scholarship, we must understand the narratives the scholarship conveys. Student placement, for instance, extends from (and tends to perpetuate) a combination of narratives about what literacies they should have developed before arriving at college and what they will be expected to do upon arrival. The content of basic writing courses tends to reflect stories about what students should know to be ready for "regular" composition classes (just as the content of first-year composition more generally tends to reflect stories about what students should know to succeed in more advanced courses across campus). The relationships between definitions of basic writing and basic writers, institutional contexts, and local systems (such as placement and classes) are themselves situated within broader narratives about the purpose of higher education in American culture.

In some situations and circumstances, these identity-forming narratives are relatively stable. When they are connected to basic writing, however, they are considerably less so. Reviewing the literature in basic writing published in the last thirty years reveals a series of break points in stories that have been told about students, instructors, and the purpose of basic writing classes. At each of these points, there is tension in the scholarship about the narrative of basic writing, and these tensions have considerable consequence for the field's very meaning. Basic writing, however defined and however situated, is always a political act, and the stories that shape it have significant implications for students, the institutions they attend, and the culture(s) in which those students participate and, ideally, make greater contributions to once they graduate.

Here, we focus on two overarching themes in basic writing that reverberate in these break points: political sensitivities and origin myths. Specifically, we examine three moments of tension around stories that are seen as central to basic writing's identity and purpose: the discussion, in the early 1990s, about Mina Shaughnessy's work as a founding figure and icon in basic writing; the debate, from the early 1970s forward, about the purpose of basic writing and the movement toward mainstreaming efforts; and recent revisions to the presumed history and origins of basic writing. Each of these moments of tension addresses the fundamental nature of the field, and thus the study of these moments provides a comprehensive overview of the themes that have driven basic writing forward. For a more exhaustive summary of individual works in the field, we refer readers to Laura Gray-Rosendale's *Rethinking Basic Writing*; our own *Basic Writing as a Political Act*; and Kelly Ritter's *Before Shaughnessy*. We focus here on these break points in order to provide a framework for understanding key moments in the movement of conceptions of students, instructors, and programs that extend from the notion of "basic writer" and "basic writing."

As we look at basic writing through these particular moments in time, we emphasize the ways each break point involves competing frames of the story of basic writing. In each break point, conflict emerged because differing viewpoints constructed alternative narratives about basic writing and basic writers. These passionate narratives, complete with villains and heroes, victims and oppressors, locate basic writing in different settings. They differ in the agency assigned to writers and teachers, and thus describe the problems basic writing addresses. Conflict over these narratives emerged as scholars sought to define basic writing. While it is a running academic joke that faculty conflicts are so impassioned precisely because the stakes are so low, in basic writing scholarship, there is an acute awareness of the high stakes. Basic-writing programs are seen as crucial to the success of the academy's most vulnerable writers, and those vulnerable writers often emerge from underrepresented social groups. For the advocates of mainstreaming basic writing, for the advocates of separate basic-writing and tutoring programs, for the advocates of basic writing via enhanced or innovative curriculum structures, the stakes were seen as very high: the promise of higher education for the nation.

BASIC WRITING'S ORIGIN STORIES

Any creation story addresses questions such as "Who am I? "Who made me?" and "Why am I here?" for the purpose of providing inspiration or guidance in the present. Fractures in the story, then, create problems: the past becomes an unreliable guide for current actions. In the same way, stories about basic writing's purpose and its intended audience (especially in the context of institutional and political turbulence) disrupt the flow of a steady story about progress. If there is dissensus about purpose and audience, how can we see that we have moved from X to Y to accomplish goal Z? Indeed, these break points reflect tensions in basic writing—and tensions in the larger society about the purpose of higher education—regarding the very purpose of basic-writing programs. Those associated with basic writing, often working in marginalized parts of the university, have an enormous investment in creating basic-writing stories that offer them—and us—a role that makes a difference. Precisely because of the personal investment in these stories, disruptions are threats. Basic writing, however practiced and theorized, sees itself as the protector of students who are beginning careers as college writers, seeking to create better personal opportunities. Threats to the basic-writing narrative thus become threats to basic-writing students. At each break point, then, fears for students dominate. Without the safety offered by a coherent and successful story, basic writers' access to instruction is threatened.

Swirling around the political sensitivities work is the sense of origin. Creation myths serve, in part, to empower those who come after, and basic-writing creation myths have served to inspire generations of teachers (often working in poor material conditions). Debates about Mina Shaughnessy's role in basic writing have been fierce. First represented as the brave leader in the establishment of basic writing, Shaughnessy was transformed from a scholar-teacher to an icon. Following that transformation, Shaughnessy-as-icon became the subject of critique in work by Min-Zhan Lu and Jeanne Gunner. These critiques of Shaughnessy have opened up debates on the function and history of the basic-writing movement in America.

Shaughnessy is remembered as the founding editor of *Journal of Basic Writing* and the CUNY faculty member who led the writing program through CUNY's open admissions experience. Even today, almost fifty years after that movement, she remains the best-known figure in basic writing. Shaughnessy's prowess as a teacher, administrator, and colleague had a powerful influence on the emerging field of basic writing. Her *Errors and Expectations* (1977) articulated a powerful argument on behalf of CUNY's basic-writing students. Adrienne Rich (then an adjunct faculty member at CUNY) called *Errors and Expectations* a "moving" book. In her blurb on the back of the book, Rich notes that Shaughnessy's work "reminds us, as we may still need reminding, that student and teacher in a Basic Writing course are not adversaries but natural allies, joined in a common cause against the waste of intelligence."

Shaughnessy's career, cut short by her early death, has come to symbolize basic writing itself. Shaughnessy became a symbol or icon of the passionate teacher working in the trenches. *Errors and Expectations* was cast as the text that founded the field of basic-writing studies, and by extension Shaughnessy herself came to function as an authorial icon. As Jeanne Gunner explained, the actual Mina Shaughnessy transformed into "Mina Shaughnessy" (the author figure), "someone who is 'not just the author of [her] own works [but someone who has] produced something else: the possibilities and the rules of formation of other texts'" ("Iconic Discourse," 28). Shaughnessy's authorial status has held up over time. Although her popularity in the larger field of composition studies has waned somewhat—of the roughly 380 references to her work in JSTOR since 1960, about 40 percent occurred between 1980 and 1989, and they have markedly fallen off since 2000—Shaughnessy remains a touchstone for basic-writing references. Most issues of *JBW* still contain several articles citing Shaughnessy. As Jeanne Gunner notes, though, references to Shaughnessy "speak of the field as having been founded, developed, popularized by, or identified with Mina Shaughnessy." *Errors and Expectations* is typically cited "foundationally, rather than noted for particular conceptual attribution" (29). Shaughnessy's assertions about students and teachers, articulated in a particular moment in CUNY history, have to some extent become a foundational philosophy of the field.

Errors and Expectations, along with other publications by Shaughnessy such as "Diving In," a 1976 article published in *CCC* and reprinted in Victor Villanueva's *Cross-Talk in Comp Theory* (both first and second editions, 1997 and 2003 respectively), made several assertions about students in basic-writing classes. As Shaughnessy's work circulated after its publication, these rapidly moved from assertions to assumptions, essential elements of the story of basic writing about students in these classes and the instructors who taught them.

The first of these assumptions was that

> basic writers write the way they do, not because they are slow or non-verbal, indifferent to or incapable of academic excellence, but because they are beginners and must, like all beginners, learn by making mistakes. These they make aplenty and for such a variety of reasons that the inexperienced teacher is almost certain to see nothing but a chaos of error when he first encounters their papers. Yet a closer look will reveal very little that is random or "illogical" in what they have written. And the keys to their development as writers often lie hidden in the very features of their writing that English teachers have been trained to brush aside with a marginal code letter or a scribbled injunction to "Proofread!" (Shaughnessy, *Errors and Expectations* 3)

Errors and Expectations moved from this assumption to take a long, slow look at students' writing, analyzing the domains of error that may confound readers. Shaughnessy offered readers a combination of teaching strategies, attitude adjustments, and commentary on the attitudes that students bring to basic-writing classes that affect their responses to writing instruction. In the process, the book also established advanced additional assumptions that rapidly became part of basic writing's fundamental story: that students entering the academy are coming to a new land with which they are unfamiliar, and that the job of the basic-writing instructor is to diligently help students find their way in this strange new world. Shaughnessy famously characterized basic writing as "very much of a frontier, unmapped, except for a scattering of impressionistic articles and a few blazed trails that individual teachers propose through their texts" (4). Shaughnessy's vision argued for the settlement of this frontier territory by students and teachers who would essentially remake higher education. The closing chapter of *Errors and Expectations* brought together the two pieces of this story, cautioning readers that writing is always in progress. "Few people, even the most accomplished of writers, would say that they always write as well as they can. Writing is something writers are always learning to do" (276). The book noted that basic-writing students are "a unique group from whom we have already learned much and from whom we can learn much more in the years ahead" (291). Most importantly, Shaughnessy contended that the presence of basic writers calls on higher education to reexamine itself. "Colleges must be prepared to make more than a graceless and begrudging accommodation to [bw students'] unpreparedness, opening their doors with one hand and then leading students into an endless corridor of remedial anterooms with the other" (293).

Working from assumptions about students, *Errors and Expectations* outlined practices for teachers to follow. Shaughnessy's approach to language was partly social—she conceded that students had to navigate "different pressures and codes" as they navigated through different situations. In the story constructed through her writing, she expressed her belief that the presence of errors in students' written texts propelled misperceptions of those students. Thus, Shaughnessy says in the introduction to *Errors and Expectations* that she chose to focus on formal elements of writing as a step toward disrupting those larger, socially constructed, misconceptions (6). Her work suggests that while she did not perceive academic language to be superior to other registers, she believed that students needed to participate in the dominant language of the academy if they were to be seen as successful (10, 121). This accounts for the focus of *Errors and Expectations*—readers who approach the book now may be surprised to find how many chapters are devoted to what might seem like surface features of writing.

Shaughnessy's interest in error and its reception did not overly narrow her focus on language, for she further assumed that that an attention to form should be accompanied by an attention to the emotional and psychological aspects of writing. She acknowledged the potentially enormous psychological leap involved in participating in this language as well, noting that "by the time he reaches college, the BW student both resents and resists his vulnerability as a writer. He is aware that he leaves a trail of errors behind him when he writes. He can usually think of little else while he is writing. But he doesn't know what to do about it" (*Errors and Expectations* 7). Shaughnessy noted that the BW student may start in a "linguistically barren situation," having been "systematically isolated as a writer both from his own response as a thinker and speaker and from the resources of others" (82). Language and thinking can be separated for Shaughnessy, in a way that would seem problematic for theorists two decades later.

[handwritten margin notes: Is language and thinking separate? – NO – for me – Socratic seminar]

While *Errors and Expectations* acted as a seminal text for basic-writing instructors, in the mid- to late 1980s teacher-researchers began to question elements of the story reflected in Shaughnessy's assumptions about students and writing and the practices she outlined extending from those assumptions. Min-Zhan Lu, in two separate articles (one in *College English*, "Conflict and Struggle," and one in the *Journal of Basic Writing*, "Redefining the Legacy of Mina Shaughnessy") argued that Shaughnessy, self-consciously involved in a struggle to establish basic writing as a legitimate field of inquiry and basic writers as legitimate college students, was naturally drawn to narratives that cast basic writers as students who are ambivalent about college culture. Thus Lu explains Shaughnessy's interest in formal aspects of language could be controlled and managed as part of an assimilationist project that would move basic writers into the academy.

Lu's work reflects her acknowledgment that her analysis of basic writing proceeded from a very different point in time. Working in a moment of fierce opposition to open admissions and fighting against critics who warned that basic writers would destabilize the institution, Shaughnessy, Lu said, was drawn to a story about writing that emphasized calm over conflict. Lu argued that in another era, another story about basic writing was necessary. The late '80s/early '90s saw the rise of the cultural turn in the humanities generally and writing more particularly (Harrington and Adler-Kassner.) A year earlier, in 1990, Mary Louise Pratt's "The Arts of the Contact Zone" had articulated a challenge to notions of community that had previously informed approaches to writing and language. Pratt challenged such notions that emphasized sameness and harmony of expectations, calling for exploration of "unsolicited oppositional discourse, parody, resistance, critique in the imagined classroom community" (39). An engagement with multiculturalism and the curriculum

led to a reconception of academic communities, highlighting the importance of maintaining productive tensions between different cultural
spaces—while using classroom space for the intellectual work of bridging cultural spaces to create learning. Shaughnessy, working twenty years
earlier, had a considerably more cognitive view of language, as well as
a view of academic discourse that was considerably more assimilationist
than Lu would later develop. Different eras prized different values, and
the scholarship reflects that.

Through this revised narrative, Lu argued that rather than understanding students in basic writing classes as ambivalent writers, they
should be understood as writers who could successfully struggle with the
transition from home to college, who could directly confront whatever
emotional or psychological strains the move to college causes. Drawing
on Gloria Anzaldúa, Lu used a different metaphor for this tale: basic
writing not as a frontier but as borderlands. In the borderlands, "teachers can and should draw upon students' perception of conflict as a
constructive resource" ("Conflict and Struggle" 889). Such approaches
would promote better learning because centralizing conflicts would
help students reposition themselves as language learners and language
users, crafting new identities in the complex modern politics of literacy.
In Lu's estimation, language flowed from "one's need to deliberate over
and decide how to reposition oneself in relationship to conflicting cultures and powers" (906).

Lu offered new propositions, most importantly this: basic writing
should embrace two key notions of border-crossing literacy. First, that
writers work at sites of conflict, rather than at clear and comfortable
positions inside (or outside) the university; and second, that innovative writing moves across and between issues of race, class, gender,
and disciplines. Lu's vision of basic writing took actual and perceived
conflicts between students' home and academic worlds as a generative
point of departure for writing and exploration. It promoted writing that
cuts across issues of race, class, gender, and disciplines ("Conflict and
Struggle" 888). Lu ultimately concluded that basic writing must embrace
the everyday politics of language, for language was always political, and
linked to identity. Thus Shaughnessy's approach to the project of basic
writing proceeded from a very different frame than did Lu's.

Lu's critique of Shaughnessy recast some of the fundamental stories
about who basic-writing students were, what was the role of language
in their education and in the academy more generally, and thus what

basic-writing instruction should do. Basic writing, ever a political enterprise, concerned not simply students' growing language proficiency and increasing comfort with academic roles, but students' negotiation of identity. Lu assumed that "reading and writing take place at sites of political as well as linguistic conflict" ("Conflict and Struggle" 888). Calling into question tenets that had become accepted as commonsensical among many basic-writing instructors, many of whom saw themselves as advocating for the academy's most vulnerable student population, Lu's critiques of Shaughnessy led to a strong, almost visceral reaction in the field. The way she questioned Shaughnessy's approaches created a flash point around conceptualizations of basic-writing teachers and students that had extended from *Errors and Expectations*. For those who had come of age in basic writing with Shaughnessy, or considered themselves working in her tradition, basic writing held the moral high ground as the part of composition studies—indeed, as the part of the university—that stood up for students who needed advocates. Basic writing was home to the teachers who worked bravely on the frontier, figuring out how to work with students they were coaching into success with formal academic language. Shaughnessy's frontier metaphor described a project of domestication and settlement. Lu's borderlands metaphor described a project of conflict and negotiation.

Even as it was published, Lu's critique signaled the emergence of an alternative to this fundamental tenet of basic writing's story; there were many who still endorsed and participated in that earlier narrative. The December 1992 issue of *College English* in which Lu's piece appeared, for instance, also included an essay by Terry Collins and Paul Hunter, "'Waiting for an Aristotle': A Moment in the History of the Basic Writing Movement," which also examined Shaughnessy's presence as a central figure in the construction of basic writing's foundational story, and both examined the social and cultural context in which this presence was constructed. A rhetorical examination of the narrative running through pieces in a special issue of the *Journal of Basic Writing* entitled "Toward a Literate Democracy" published as a memorial to Shaughnessy after her death, much of Collins and Hunter's article is devoted to examining how pieces in that 1980 journal reflect components of the epitaphios logos. But their analysis propels an argument that Shaughnessy's work might seem conservative on its surface, but in fact it was carefully calculated to advance a case for students who occupied a precarious space in a charged historical moment. Far from trying to preserve the status quo in this context, Collins and Hunter wrote, Shaughnessy was a pragmatist, not a formalist. "The experience of a 'worn urban classroom', not a 'politics of linguistic innocence,'" they write, "underlay [Shaughnessy's] respectful assumptions about her students. . . . And the voice of the revolutionary, not the voice of 'the Liberal tempered,'" propelled her work (926).

The pairing of these two essays in the same issue of *College English* reflected the uncertain narratives about basic writing that were in play at the time. Even while Lu was continuing to develop a critique of the ways Shaughnessy figured in the basic-writing narrative, Collins and Hunter's piece, comparing the tributes to Shaughnessy to those offered in ancient Rome, continues the tale of Shaughnessy's central and inspiring role for basic-writing teachers. The following issue of *College English* revealed just how high tensions between these two narratives were when a symposium on basic writing was presented in order to contain and present responses to Lu's challenge. Patricia Laurence (Laurence et al.) responded that Lu failed to appreciate the true context at CUNY, with its 80 percent minority student population and a built-in capacity for conflict given the varied demographics of the student body. Shaughnessy's "language of understanding, caring, exchange, and reciprocity" was just what was needed in the moment. Laurence argued that the role of faculty was to "help us find clarity of mind and common ground in our institutions and classrooms, and nourish, as Adrienne Rich says, 'the dream of a common language'" (882). Laurence, then, believed that an instructor's role was to draw students into a common vision; Lu believed it was to draw people together in class for the purpose of interrogating cultural conflicts. Peter Rondinone, another CUNY faculty member included in the symposium, also argued that radical reforming was indeed what he (and many of his students) aspired to in higher education. But this reforming was directed to a place not on the borders, as Lu imagined it, but across the border into a new culture reflected by higher education. Rondinone's quite personal response to Lu concludes with the assertion, "Unless someone offers to pay my rent and to put shoes on my little girl, no one is going to convince me that hovering between the two worlds (educated and uneducated) is the place for me" (Laurence et al. 885).

In Rondinone's narrative, the conflict between home and school impeded learning; in Lu's frame, the conflict between home and school should promote learning, for the role of basic writing should be to explore "Basic Writers' efforts to grapple with the conflict within and among diverse discourses" (Laurence et al. 910). This response, like Laurence's, went beyond simply discussing the position of Mina Shaughnessy to address the function of writing in the university and the story that basic-writing instructors might tell about their work in the classroom and about the students who populated their classes. As such, it raised questions about what were appropriate ways to frame, and tell, this story. Could basic writing be understood through post-structural theory? What did it mean to reinterpret the Shaughnessy years in light of later theory? How could basic writing tell a coherent, unfolding story in keeping with theoretical shifts in the field?

The conflict about representations of Mina Shaughnessy, then, was not just about one person. Instead, it was about what constitutes the history of basic writing. Can we tell that history through the stories about and by individuals—courageous teachers like Shaughnessy, working with individual students who might not have access to education if not for classes like those taught by CUNY basic-writing instructors? Or should we tell the story as one about and shaped by larger social forces, those that affect Lu's notion of the borderlands, to take one example. These are the questions that arise through the fissures outlined in this debate. The notion that basic writing's history is a cultural/political one has been powerfully explicated by Mary Soliday in *The Politics of Remediation*. As she notes, the label "basic writers" grows from a "discourse of student need" that was invoked in order to make the case that institutional standards are stable, but that students (and their abilities) change. Through this frame, basic writing is always fundamentally conservative, because it shifted the focus away from institutional issues and focused it on individual students. The problem, in this discourse, was that students didn't come to college equipped with the right skills and thus required the development of basic writing (or basic math or basic reasoning) courses and programs. These crises, she said, "help[ed] to justify the institutional decision to stratify by admissions, curriculum, and mission" (107).

Soliday identifies conflict between Lu and Shaughnessy as a clash of frames: language emerges from identity politics for Lu and Gunner, but from access politics for Shaughnessy (*Politics of Remediation* 25). Shaughnessy, in this telling, was someone who aimed to change the student body first and the curriculum second. Tom Fox notes that Shaughnessy's defining achievement was that she "created a space called 'Basic Writing.'" Fox's reading of *Errors and Expectations* highlights the tensions between access and exclusion that have always been at the center of debates about basic writing. Shaughnessy's formalistic impulses—what Fox terms her "microscopic attention to form" (*Defending Access* 46)—can be seen as calling for careful, compassionate close reading of student work or as calling for rigid and prescriptive pedagogies. Depending on the frame, discussions of basic writing through stories of CUNY and references to Mina Shaughnessy generate different roles for students: foreigners in a strange land; travelers seeking to cross a frontier; residents of borderlands; lazy or ignorant slackers. One role of basic-writing scholarship has been to create a coherent story for the field itself, about itself.

TIDY HOUSE, TIDY STORIES: THE DEBATE ABOUT THE PURPOSE OF BASIC WRITING

The debate surrounding Mina Shaughnessy's work began a discussion about some of the fundamental assumptions underscoring basic writing: what the intention of classes were, how they should be taught to enact those assumptions, and how students might be changed (or not) as a result of their work with writing in these classes. Contested visions of the fundamental purpose of basic writing became a more overt part of the scholarship on basic writing during another critical flash point in the late 1990s. Once again, CUNY was the center of the flash point, as top-down plans to phase in admissions requirements and eliminate remedial courses from all the senior colleges threatened to eradicate much of the basic writing then in place across the CUNY system. In this context, exchanges between Karen Greenberg, Terry Collins, and Ira Shor—in the pages of the *Journal of Basic Writing* and in the pixels of two professional electronic discussion groups—reflected sharp divisions about the place of basic writing in higher education.

Shor, a teacher-scholar at CUNY's Staten Island campus, kicked off this conflict with his provocatively titled "Our Apartheid: Writing Instruction and Inequality," which appeared in *JBW* in 1997. Shor's piece opened by connecting basic writing and crisis, referencing the story that basic writing emerged in order to protect students in times of trouble: "Basic writing as a field was born in crisis nearly thirty years ago. It has grown in crisis amid declining conditions for mass education" (91). But tracing the development of composition and basic-writing classes through the nineteenth and twentieth centuries, Shor recasts both this origin story and the implication that basic writing is an access point for students labeled underprepared. Instead, he tells a story about the economic implications of basic writing's creation and the function of basic-writing classes, saying that composition generally and basic writing specifically were not meant as entry portals but as a site for separating students as they entered the academy. "Basic writing," he said, was "an extra sorting-out gate . . . a curricular mechanism to secure unequal power relations in yet another age of instability . . . a containment track below freshman comp, a gate below the gate" (92–94).

Shor further characterized basic writing as a practice that "helps slow down the students' progress towards the college degree" (94). And by the 1970s, Shor charged, basic writing had also become a means by which economic stratification was not only preserved but advanced. Basic writing teachers, many of them "underpaid, overworked, (female) adjuncts," were segregated from the pool of mainstream instructors (95). More significantly, the separation of students into basic-writing classes ensured the existence of an economic underclass that would both sustain and support an economic divide inherent in America's structure (92–93). With this analysis, Shor took direct aim at the moral center of basic writing that was established by instructors who read what Jeanne Gunner has called the "iconic teacher figure" in Shaughnessy's work as a mentor for students entering the academy ("Iconic Discourse" 41). This set up an argument about the structure and purpose of basic-writing programs. Using metaphors of obstacles, he linked the problems for students with labor problems for faculty, hooking into a long line of arguments about the poor status of writing faculty more generally.

Shor's essay caused a sharp reaction almost immediately. In a post to the writing program administrators' listserv (WPA-L), fellow CUNY faculty member and basic-writing instructor Karen Greenberg suggested that Shor's abolitionist arguments had played a role in the CUNY administrative decision to eliminate remediation on CUNY's senior campuses. On the Conference on Basic Writing listserv, CBW-L, the exchange took an even more personal turn, with Shor and Greenberg debating Shor's qualifications as a basic-writing teacher/scholar. A more tempered debate about this issue of structure took place in the pages of *JBW* in articles authored by Shor, Greenberg, and Terence Collins, the University of Minnesota's General College director of curriculum (and former WPA). (Shor had visited the General College's cutting-edge basic-writing program in 1995 and used anecdotes from his visit as part of the analysis in "Our Apartheid.") Both Greenberg and Collins took issue with what they viewed as Shor's monolithic construction of "basic writing." From their different perspectives, they advanced alternative narratives about the structure of basic-writing programs that pointed back to the earlier narrative of basic writing as an element of open access to higher education. Greenberg's response stressed the ways basic writing "helps students acquire the knowledge and 'tools' they need to empower themselves" (92), and Collins drew on institutional research at the University of Minnesota's General College to show that basic writing was an effective means of helping students progress toward degrees.

Basic tools

Echoing earlier narratives about basic-writing courses, Greenberg refuted both Shor's charges against basic writing and his conceptualization of the education system more broadly. While Shor cast the system as one that perpetuated socioeconomic division, Greenberg argued that education "empower[ed] students to use language fluently and authoritatively to transform their lives." In this sense, basic-writing courses were neither a gate nor a blocking mechanism but the "beginning of an integrated sequence of required English courses. . . .The goal in these courses is often the same as the goal in upper-level courses" (91). Where Shor focused on barriers and separation, Greenberg emphasized student movement over time. Echoing Rondinone (Laurence et al.), Greenberg contended that basic-writing courses were tickets out of one class and into another (as well as tickets out of one sector of the university curriculum and into another). Greenberg reached back to Shaughnessy's legacy to buttress her position, underscoring both the historical origins of CUNY's basic-writing courses and illustrating the stakes in the moment. Referencing Shaughnessy's efforts to fight back in another period of retrenchment, Greenberg asserted that when "colleges accept for admission students with serious basic skills deficiencies, then they are morally obligated to provide them with the developmental instruction that they need to succeed in their college course. To deny this instruction implies a 'right to fail'—that students should have the freedom to take college-level courses of their choice, even if there is a low probability of their succeeding in these courses" (93–94). For Greenberg, as for Peter Rondinone in his contribution to the *College English* symposium, basic writing was synonymous with the goal of higher education itself.

Writing Power

Collins, meanwhile, questioned specific aspects of Shor's analysis, some of which was based on claims made about the General College writing program directed by Collins. (In the interests of full disclosure, we should note that Adler-Kassner also taught in this program.) Some of Shor's claims raised issues about working conditions for instructors that Collins noted did not hold true in the General College program. Collins also noted that Shor's own citations—which reference "the work of Soliday and Gleason, Fox, Grego and Thompson, Glau, and others, all of whom have built on knowledge generated by research in Basic Writing programs to build creative local solutions to the situation of inexperienced writers on their varied campuses" (98)—convey the richness of basic writing as implemented in diverse local contexts, a richness that is at odds with the oversimplified vision of basic writing that Shor critiques. The diversity of approaches to basic writing suggests the health of the field. Collins crafted a story about basic writing in which local innovation provides assistance to inexperienced writers—a somewhat different frame from Greenberg's suggestion that basic writers are those with "basic skills deficiencies." Collins resisted Shor's imposition of a single story for all basic-writing programs. Rather, he concludes, "there are any number of situated, institutionally constrained iterations of things like 'Basic Writing,' some more fortunately located than others, some more successful in resisting pariah status than others, some formed with more authentic educational purposes than others" (99).

This moment of fracture is striking for the deeply personal nature of the discourse surrounding basic-writing courses and the structure of basic-writing programs. The threats to basic writing at CUNY were quite real (and since then, top-down directives from the CUNY system have indeed instituted a variety of changes that have prevented students from accessing education at the senior colleges). A significant piece of the rhetorical context was simply the stress under which CUNY colleagues were operating, looking at programs that took decades to build being dismantled by administrative fiat, against faculty advice. Basic-writing programs often operate on the margins—and are clearly vulnerable to budget cuts and reforms aimed at changing the nature of open-access policies. The stress of the marginalized political position creates strong personal bonds among faculty and administrators working in basic-writing programs. Particularly for those working within the frame that stresses personal transformation as a key goal of basic writing, the line between professional commitment and personal commitment is close. Basic writing is easily personalized and personified. George Otte's public discussion of the Greenberg-Shor debate noted that anger at the political context played a role in the debate itself. Only recently has composition scholarship seriously begun to examine the importance of connecting with public-policy audiences directly. But the lived reality of basic-writing programs has meant that basic-writing scholar-administrators have always been involved with the impact of public policy. Hence the highly politicized stories of what it means to have basic-writing programs in the academy. For Shor, basic-writing programs supported the training of a permanent underclass; Greenberg and Collins saw basic writing as a means to expand the vision of who belongs in the academy. The stakes are high in these conflicting stories—the representation of students is very different, and the survival of basic-writing programs themselves was at stake.

The issues addressed in the Shor/Greenberg/Collins debate—whether basic-writing courses and programs perpetuated social inequality or gave economically marginalized students access to the academy—were actually foreshadowed in David Bartholomae's "The Tidy House," originally published in 1993. In this essay, Bartholomae also raised questions about the purpose of basic-writing programs and courses, suggesting that they did not—or did not only—provide an access point for students who might not otherwise be admitted to higher education. Bartholomae argued against "the grand narrative of liberal sympathy and liberal reform" that had produced basic writing. He characterized the arguments emerging from the Shaughnessy era as frames of "outreach, of equal rights, of empowerment, of new alliances and new understandings, of the transformation of the social text, the American University, the English department." In this version of the story, Bartholomae intimated, basic writing played an easy role, a role that offered accommodation to students seeking to move from one class to another. But Bartholomae cautioned that instructors and institutions should not let basic writing rest too easily. Instead, he contended that "basic writing program have become expressions of our desire to produce basic writers, to maintain the course, the argument, and the slot in the university community; to maintain the distinction (basic/normal) we have learned to think through and by" (315).

"The Tidy House" captured the debate about basic-writing courses and programs that would play out four years later in the Shor/Greenberg/Collins discussion. Bartholomae focused on whether the term *basic writing* retained any strategic value in helping the university address the needs of students and the structure of the curriculum. He supported the long tradition of work within basic writing that has pushed deeper understandings of academic expectations while resisting oversimplified notions of remediation or negative labels for students and their writing. Even as he concluded that introductory composition might be a better environment, in courses where "professionals and students think through their differences in productive ways" (325), Bartholomae sought to protect spaces in which the needs of students labeled "basic writers" can be met. The article seems to support the abolition of basic-writing programs in places, as when Bartholomae wrote, "We have constructed a course to teach and enact a rhetoric of exclusion and made it the center of a curriculum designed to hide or erase cultural difference, all the while carving out and preserving an 'area' in English within which we can do our work" (323). But Bartholomae clearly asserted that he was not advocating the immediate elimination of basic-writing courses (325). At the same time, his insistence that basic writing can be read as simultaneously "an attempt to bridge AND preserve cultural difference, to enable students to enter the 'normal' curriculum but to insure, at the same time, that there are basic writers" (315) and his concerns about the ways that conversation about basic writing no longer seems to enable conversation about literacy standards (325) pointed to a major overhaul, if not outright abolition, of basic writing.

Looking back at this flash point almost fifteen years later, it is possible to see the opening for many of the structural changes that have taken place around basic-writing courses and programs since this time. Ultimately, the issues raised here led to questions about the economic implications of these courses and programs for students and for instructors teaching the courses. While there are certainly courses designated "basic writing" taught in many institutions across the U.S., various approaches to delivering writing instruction have created alternatives to basic writing in four-year schools (see Lalicker for a summary of alternative approaches to basic-writing programs). Greg Glau's "Stretch at 10: A Progress Report on Arizona State University's Stretch Program" indicates that the ASU stretch program, a model in the field for creating a year-long composition course that replaces the basic writing plus FYC model, has generally succeeded. (It is also a model of institutional evaluation, demonstrating the ways that a program can set up useful assessment questions over time.) Gerri McNenny and Sallyanne Fitzgerald's *Mainstreaming Basic Writers* characterizes the "post-remedial" university, noting that "the presence of a political climate unfriendly to the needs of nontraditional college students" also seems to be a new institutional reality (3). The studio model (Grego and Thompson, "Repositioning Remediation"), the CUNY mainstreaming model (Soliday, "From the Margins to the Mainstream"), and the stretch model (Glau, "Stretch at 10"), then, all represent different ways that writing program administrators have conceived curricula that will support and advocate for basic writers while moving away from the structure of basic writing. Each of these alternatives represents new versions of the story of basic writing and students in basic-writing courses.

THE ORIGINS OF BASIC WRITING

As this analysis demonstrates, basic writing is a highly politicized subfield of composition studies. CUNY's basic-writing program emerged as a result of the implementation of open admissions in the 1960s, and in the past forty years, basic-writing programs have been vulnerable to shifting politics and associated funding cuts. At virtually any point in these past decades, educational reform proposals have created the possibility of cuts to basic-writing programs or changes in admissions policies that would have the effect of shunting basic writers to other institutions. CUNY Trustees essentially eliminated open admissions; Florida, Georgia, and California all made changes that have had the effect of restricting basic-writing programs (McNenny and Fitzgerald 3). The connections to current politics emphasizes the very modern nature of basic writing. But as Shor's "Our Apartheid" suggested, the history of basic writing in America can be read as something that goes back far beyond the CUNY years. One of the most interesting developments in recent basic-writing scholarship is a line of research that challenges two notions: that basic writing is a relatively recent development, and that it flourished in open admissions institutions. This work stems from examination of historical evidence about the existence of basic writing programs in more elite institutions. While this development lacks the drama associated with the other two flash points we have identified here, we nonetheless see this scholarly evolution as an important moment in the continued development of basic writing's story because it leads to additional questions about the origins of the issues addressed through basic writing around student access.

New historical scholarship that places basic writing back beyond CUNY, then, creates an alternate narrative for basic writing with a different point of origin. Scholarship by Neal Lerner, studying writing at Dartmouth College, and Kelly Ritter, looking at work done at Yale and

Harvard universities, directs our attention to elite liberal arts colleges and the role that basic-writing programs play in framing students' experience. When basic writing emerges out of the Ivy League, it also turns stereotypes about basic writers and basic writing on end. Basic writing's links to CUNY have solidified the connection between basic writing and open admissions in the American higher educational context. Basic writers are easily assumed to be students whose economic or educational past did not prepare them for college. The notion of basic writers in the Ivy League challenges that, as Ivy League students by definition are well prepared for the experiences in their highly selective institutions. A basic-writing narrative that might begin in the Ivy League, then, is a narrative that will challenge assumptions about academic literacy.

Studying the Writing Clinic at Dartmouth College, which from 1930 to 1960 provided writing conferences for students who sought out additional help or were referred to a writing tutor, Lerner explored the practices of basic-writing instruction provided at an elite institution. The clinic—whose establishment was covered by the *New York Times*—was viewed by faculty as a place for "incorrigible" students. The *Times* described it as a service offered by the English department to undergraduates who have difficulty with their "writing assignments in other courses" ("Dartmouth" 57).

As the *Times* notes, all Dartmouth students were welcome to take advantage of the clinic, although Dartmouth's records indicate that the faculty viewed the students who would have need of the clinic in starkly negative terms. Over time, the *Dartmouth Bulletin* and committee reports characterized the students who might need the Writing Clinic in terms such as "flagrant offenders," "students whose English is defective," "students who through causes other than carelessness seem unable to meet [Dartmouth] standards," or "students prone through ignorance to write badly, illiterately" (Lerner, "Rejecting the Remedial Brand" 16–17). In this frame, basic writers are those who willfully flaunt faculty expectations ("flagrant offenders") or those who possess some vague personal failing ("defective" English or "ignorance").

Lerner chronicled the Dartmouth faculty's efforts in this period to improve student writing by the force of expectation. Faculty standards, it was asserted, could keep students from being careless, and the Writing Clinic would remedy students' ignorance about writing. Throughout the 1950s, a Dartmouth Committee on Student Excellence consistently urged faculty to simply insist on high-quality writing; faculty didn't need to actually teach students how to write, merely to announce their expectations for high standards of performance. Students here are framed as lazy, with great potential. The inherent selectivity of a college like Dartmouth builds an element of exclusivity into the frame; the notion of an Ivy League college rests on a reputation for academic excellence that is consistently threatened by "flagrant offenders" of the language. The Writing Clinic, then, framed basic writing as a diagnostic antidote to ignorance. The clinic presupposes that individual intervention can help a student cure his writing problems, and it takes the writing problems outside the regular curriculum. It inferred that writing instruction need not be the purview of the faculty; writing expectations simply need be clear, and the well-motivated student will rise to the occasion. Those students who were not well motivated could be dealt with in what seemed to be the academic equivalent of a woodshed, where writing problems— defined only as deficiencies in spelling or usage—could be addressed on an individual basis. Lerner noted that Dartmouth also took a lead in calling for secondary school reform to improve writing, setting up a narrative in which the secondary schools become the source of the deficiencies in Dartmouth's students.

Ultimately, the Writing Clinic model reflected a medical model for writing deficiencies. In the wake of the three-year study that Albert Kitzhaber and Vincent Gillespie conducted of the clinic in the late 1950s (Lerner, "Rejecting the Remedial Brand" 24), Dartmouth eventually dropped the service because of the dissonance between the language of the clinic and the image Dartmouth otherwise sought to convey. Kitzhaber himself seemed to encourage the idea that faculty expectations alone could raise student performance; his report noted, "The overwhelming majority of Dartmouth students can write decent prose if they are convinced that it is important for them to do so" (25).

Whereas Dartmouth developed the Writing Clinic as a means of addressing writing deficiencies, Yale College developed the "Awkward Squad," a program that pulled students from regular English courses to offer them remedial instruction to remedy writing deficits from the late 1910s to 1960. Ritter noted that this program coincided with efforts to expand the Yale student body in periods of financial crisis ("Before Mina Shaughnessy" 17). At Yale, the function of the basic-writing program was "to delineate acceptable literacy practices and to sift out and re-acculturate students who were determined to be out of line with the local standards for first-year intellectual work" (20–21). Like the Dartmouth

Writing Clinic, the Awkward Squad was designed to remedy deficiencies. The Awkward Squad was designed as a drill program, with "rote drilling of mechanics rather than a site for broader writing practice" (22). Ritter's examination of public discussions of writing suggests that throughout the Ivy League, a corrective model of writing dominated. Underprepared students were singled out for clinical treatment—an individualized response that cast students as outsiders, as patients who required intervention. Writing instruction, in fact, was placed outside the purview of the regular curriculum. Yale, like Dartmouth, assumed that the ability to write fluent academic prose was a prerequisite for full inclusion in the first-year class. Remedial writing instruction, then, pushed writing itself outside the bounds of the institution.

Ritter's study of Harvard's basic-writing program in the early part of the twentieth century illuminates a more progressive narrative about basic writing. Harvard defined its basic writing courses as first, remedial for students whose writing "is found to be unsatisfactory," and then supportive ("a more advanced course in writing" for students "who want further training/instruction") (*Before Shaughnessy* 102), and then more remedial (for students whose writing is deemed to be "unsatisfactory in any course") (103). Harvard additionally had a Committee on the Use of English by Students, created to address the Harvard Board of Overseers' concern that students "fail to write correct, coherent, and idiomatic English" (104). Like Yale's Awkward Squad program, the Harvard program provided opportunities for deficient writers to be assigned additional, extracurricular writing tasks to overcome their problems— although the committee also saw it as its responsibility to help students whose writing suffered because of difficulties with arrangement and expression (108). Thus Harvard's remedial model simultaneously supported a medicalized model of literacy crisis (in which individual deficiencies can be cured with targeted instruction) while opening up a more progressive narrative in which students' writing could be nurtured on a variety of features. The Committee on the Use of English's efforts to get faculty to refer students to its services assumed that the Harvard student body included a proportion of men—which Ritter noted was at once point quantified as about 10 percent of the student population— who would need additional help.

A basic-writing narrative rooted in the Ivy League still focuses on themes familiar to the CUNY narrative. As Ritter noted, much of the historical correspondence at Yale revolved around the question of whether members of the Awkward Squad really belonged at Yale. While Harvard seems to have assumed that a proportion of its students would need additional assistance as writers, the academic programs laid out to support those students were designed to ensure that basic writers' performance could be changed so that high Harvard standards would prevail in the end, a sentiment similar to that underlying the Dartmouth Writing Clinic's work. Comparing the Ivy League story with the CUNY story, we see one fundamental similarity: the creation of basic writers as a category set apart from the rest of the student body. The creation of basic writers isolates students from the norm.

Basic writers, as Lerner's examination of Dartmouth and Ritter's of Yale and Harvard illustrate so vividly, are always defined in a local context. A tenet of assessment theory, as well, is that the best assessments are local. Looking at basic writing through the lens of modern assessment theory, we see clearly that basic writers are defined not by any objective criteria but by relative criteria used, in contexts as disparate as Ivy League institutions and local community colleges, for well over a century to single out some students. Critiques of writing ability have frequently emerged in periods of social change; writing courses (or clinics) have been developed as a result of frames that identify student writers as outsiders in need of a cure. The power of basic writing as a field lies in its ability to push back against this frame and to recast the story of writing as one that includes all writers in college. Ritter notes that expanding our stories about basic writing can assist us to "uncover other silent or invisible student populations that are at risk of being forgotten through the convenience of standardized histories and limited labels." She joins basic writing with composition studies more generally, emphasizing our shared aim of "true inclusion of all writers in our first year curricula" ("Before Mina Shaughnessy" 39)—a point shared by Bartholomae in "Tidy House." Reframing basic writing as a practice with a longer history enables us to reframe students as those who are, already, ready for college.

MAKING USE OF STORIES

This flash point review illustrates the importance of narrative in establishing legitimacy and enacting relationships. The ever-present political tensions surrounding basic writing have prefigured tensions about writing that now affect composition studies more generally (current debates about writing assessment and accountability are, in many ways, extensions of debates about basic writing, although that point is itself beyond our mission in this chapter). One clear lesson that emerges is the need for those of us in basic writing to have a story to tell: if we don't tell our own stories, then others will tell stories about us and our students, and the messages in those stories may well be at odds with our own aspirations. Again and again, critics of basic writing have positioned basic writers as students who don't belong in college, and basic writing scholars and teachers have had to respond defensively. We've learned, however, that we can be assertive about our students' experiences, and the proliferation of alternative forms of basic writing has been accompanied by scholarship exploring the effectiveness and impact of arrangements such as Arizona State University's stretch program (Glau) or the studio approach to basic writing at the University of South Carolina (Grego and Thompson). Cathy Fleischer's study of teachers and community organizing argues that teachers can "change the way in which curricular issues are depicted—as they mix and phase their way through educating, mobilizing, planning, acting, advocating" (119). Basic-writing scholars and teachers need to think like organizers as we frame our courses and our scholarship. In the classroom, we need to be explicit with students in the messages we craft about writing, inviting students to see the ways in which their own writing is a political act. In our scholarship, we need to be clear about the ways we frame writing, taking care to use frames that serve our students well. And we need to explore ways to engage with our communities (on campus and beyond) to show that basic writing—and basic writers—is part of the collegiate writing experience.

2

TEACHING COMPOSITION IN THE MULTILINGUAL WORLD
Second Language Writing in Composition Studies

Paul Kei Matsuda

The student population in U.S. college composition programs is not what it used to be. This statement rings true regardless of which period in the history of composition we happen to choose as a reference point—in fact, composition studies evolved in response to a series of literacy crises (Lunsford, "Politics"). Yet, the implications of the demographic shifts are especially pertinent today. Over the last century and a half, U.S. higher education grew from a parochial institution for a select few from privileged socioeconomic, religious, ethnic, and linguistics backgrounds to a provider of mass education for people from a wider range of backgrounds. The growing diversity of student population has also made U.S. higher education highly heterogeneous in terms of the language backgrounds that students (as well as teachers and researchers) bring with them. Today, with the globalization of economy and information, teaching writing to college students is not just about preparing students for academic, professional, and civic writing within the national boundary; it is also about preparing students—both domestic and international—for the increasingly globalized world that has always been, and will continue to be, multilingual.

In comparison with other categories of diversity—especially race, class, and gender—issues concerning language have long been underrepresented in the mainstream discourse of composition studies. There are a number of possible reasons for the lack of attention to language issues. One possibility is the _disciplinary division of labor_ between composition studies and second language studies, which institutionalized the assumption that the student population can be divided neatly into first language and second language groups, and working with the latter is the sole responsibility of second language specialists (Matsuda,

"Composition" 700). Another possibility, which is more deeply rooted in the history of U.S. higher education in general, is the *myth of linguistic homogeneity*, in which the state of English monolingualism not only is considered an ideal goal but has already been taken for granted (Matsuda, "Myth" 637). As the linguistic diversity of the student population has become undeniably clear, and as the institutional urge for globalization continues to grow, second language writing is beginning to gain recognition as a concern for everyone involved in the field of composition studies (including *you*).

This chapter provides an overview of some of the historical developments related to the status of second language writing issues in composition studies while providing a sense of the state of the art. To this end, I survey—from historical and contemporary perspectives—the representation of second language issues in major journals and conferences in composition studies as well as the development of various administrative and pedagogical practices. For the purpose of this chapter, I focus on writing in English as a second language in the context of North American higher education—particularly in the disciplinary context of composition studies. Before discussing the place of second language writing in composition studies, let me provide a brief overview of some of the key terms and concepts.

DEFINING SECOND LANGUAGE WRITING AND WRITERS

Second Language writing emerged in the latter half of the twentieth century as an interdisciplinary field of inquiry situated simultaneously in several language- and writing-related fields, including applied linguistics, foreign language education, composition studies, and Teaching English to Speakers of Other Languages (TESOL), among others. The field addresses a wide range of issues situated in various disciplinary and institutional contexts by drawing on theoretical and methodological insights from these fields. It is a site of intellectual activities that draws from and contributes to these fields, all of which overlap with one another in various ways. The field as a whole focuses on a wide variety of second or foreign languages in various geographic and institutional contexts as well as educational levels. Second language writing can be characterized as a "symbiotic field" (Matsuda, "Situating" 111–12) because it does not have its own site of praxis; rather, second language writers are subject to the institutional practices of various related fields, including composition studies, which has jurisdiction over various writing courses and programs, including basic writing, first-year composition, advanced composition, technical writing, business writing, writing across the curriculum, and the writing center.

The term *second language writing* (usually without a hyphen), or "L2 writing" for short, is a technical term that refers to writing in any language that the writer did not grow up with, including the third, fourth, fifth language, and so on. There are many other terms that are used almost interchangeably, each with its own connotations and limitations. In U.S. higher education, where English is the dominant language, English as a second language (ESL) writers has been a popular term since the 1960s, whereas in K-12 contexts, the term has shifted to the somewhat awkward acronym ESOL (pronounced "ee-sol," ESOL stands for English for Speakers of Other Languages or English Speakers of Other Languages, neither of which seems to make sense) and then to the currently popular English Language Learners (or ELL). These and other alternative terms are constantly being coined to move away from the negative connotation that their predecessors have acquired over time. While those are well-meaning efforts, years of constant struggle for nonstigmatizing terms seems to suggest that any attempt to find a stigma-resistant alternative is ultimately futile—until people begin to challenge and dispel the very notion that being a nonnative English speaker is somehow a deficit (Matsuda, "Proud" 15; for a detailed discussion of the *difference-as-deficit* view, see Canagarajah, 11–14). In the context of higher education, the terms *second language writers, ESL writers,* and *multilingual writers* have been widely accepted.

In U.S. higher education, the term *ESL* has traditionally been used in reference to both international ESL students and resident ESL students, although the distinction has not always been clear. Teachers and researchers often used the term in referring to a particular group of students without detailed descriptions of the characteristics of the population, and the lack of clear definition has led to confusion and sometimes even conflicts among teachers and researchers. The term has also been problematic for some resident students who, associating ESL with being "foreign," resist the institutional label imposed upon them, as Christina Ortmeier-Hooper has documented in the context of a first-year writing course. More recently, with the growing recognition of the presence of resident students, the term *generation 1.5* has been coined as a way of describing college ESL students who are U.S.-educated learners of English and whose linguistic profile is distinct from that of prototypical international ESL students (Harklau, Losey, and Siegal; Roberge, Siegal, and Harklau).

This term *generation 1.5* has been helpful in that it has drawn attention to the traditionally neglected resident ESL student population; however, the term is not without its problems. Like the term *basic writing*, it has been used in referring to a wide variety of students, and many teachers and researchers do not seem to agree on its definition. Some define it as early-arrival resident ESL students (immigrant students who came to the United States before middle school); others use it exclusively in referring to late-arrival ESL students (those who came after middle school); yet others include all resident students. The term, because of its strong impact, also seems to have contributed to collective amnesia about the historical presence of resident ESL writers and efforts to address the presence and needs of those students (Matsuda and Matsuda, "Erasure"). To address these complications, some researchers are beginning to argue for the need to make a distinction between international and resident ESL students, and to make finer distinctions based on the specific context of research and instruction (Ferris, *Teaching*; Matsuda and Matsuda, "Erasure").

The boundary between first and second language gets further complicated in light of the wider range of linguistic backgrounds that students bring with them. For example, English may still be the second and perhaps less dominant language for students who began to acquire it at a young age, but they may have developed a relatively high level of proficiency compared to those who came in contact with English much later in life. In the debate over the status of different varieties of English, such as Indian English, Singaporean English, African American Vernacular English, and Hawai'ian Creole English (each of which is a rule-governed, systematic linguistic system), the question of the boundary between language and dialect is often more political and ideological than linguistic. In the United States, the difficulty of drawing a clear line became apparent in the public controversy over Ebonics (see "CCCC Statement on Ebonics"). These complexities notwithstanding, the general distinction between first- and second language writing still plays an important role in considering students who come from opposite ends of the spectrum.

Writing in a second language is not completely different from writing in the first language. Indeed, both first-language and second language writers face similar categories of challenges in developing rhetorical expertise and discursive repertoire in particular rhetorical situations. Yet, that is not to say that they are without important differences. While "no one is the native speaker of writing," it is important to keep in mind that second language writers are facing the demands of writing as a second language *in a second language* (Matsuda and Jablonski). Because second language writers often have had relatively limited exposure to the dominant variety of English in general and to formal English written discourse in particular, learning to develop writing proficiency in English can be more challenging than it is to lifelong users of dominant English varieties (Silva, "Toward"). For users of different varieties of English, such as users of African American Vernacular English or Singaporean English, the knowledge of English structure that they have stored in their heads may be different from that that is in the heads of students who grew up speaking a dominant variety of U.S. English. For native users of, say, Mandarin Chinese, who have learned English as an adult, it may take many years before they can fully acquire English-specific features such as articles, prepositions, and plural noun inflections, which do not exist in their native language.

Another possible difference is that second language writers may be highly literate in their native language, and may be able to apply literate strategies from their native language as they write in English. The use of translation is also a possible resource for second language writers; although the effectiveness of translation as a writing strategy can vary depending on the writer's second language proficiency level (Kobayashi and Rinnert), it can allow second language writers to tap into the knowledge base they have already developed in another language. Studies of multi-competent language users (i.e., individuals with advanced proficiency in multiple languages) by Ellen Bialystok, Vivian Cook, and others also suggest that second language writers may have expanded their intellectual capacity as a result of the constant demand of working with a broader range of linguistic and discursive resources. (For an accessible introduction to the advantages of bilingual research into multi-competence and cognitive advantages of multilingualism, see King and Mackey.)

A BRIEF HISTORY OF SECOND LANGUAGE WRITING IN COMPOSITION STUDIES

Second language writing issues became an important concern among teachers and administrators of first-year writing programs in the latter half of the 1940s, when the conclusion of the Second World War brought an influx of international students to U.S. higher education and, consequently, to first-year writing programs. In response to this situation, many writing programs developed separate sections of first-year writing programs for "foreign" students (as they were then called) who were yet to develop the level of proficiency in English deemed appropriate for college-level work. Although this population of students continued to enroll in mainstream first-year writing courses at many institutions, the discussion at CCCC came to a sudden halt after the 1966 meeting, when the creation of the TESOL organization institutionalized the disciplinary division of labor. (See Matsuda, "Composition" for a detailed account of this development.)

In the late 1970s, the rise of basic writing and the growth of resident ESL writers at open admissions institutions, most notably the City University of New York, brought second language writing issues back to composition studies. In the early years of basic writing, insights from second language studies were actively incorporated into basic-writing theory and pedagogy, although the goal was to help users of nondominant varieties of English whose difficulties were, at least on the surface, similar to those of second language writers. Meanwhile, second language writers were often placed in basic writing classes because not all institutions had separate ESL writing courses, and because features of texts written by basic writers and second language writers were not always distinguishable. This placement may have been productive, as Alice Roy argued ("Alliance"; "ESL"), when the decision was principled—rather than haphazard—and when the basic writing teacher had a background in second language instruction; in other cases, however, the placement was based on the lack of resources, and both groups of students may have suffered the consequences, as James Nattinger, Sandra McKay, and others pointed out. Even with theses interdisciplinary interactions, second language issues tended to play a marginal role in the professional discourse of basic-writing specialists until well into the 1990s because of the persistence of the binary oppositions between first and second language, and between native-born and foreign-born populations. (See Matsuda, "Basic" for more details.)

Influenced by the development of writing research in composition studies, second language writing began to grow as a research topic within the field of TESOL. In the 1980s, some second language specialists who had developed expertise in second language writing by happenstance (Blanton et al.; Kroll, "Composition") began to attend CCCC to import insights from second language studies to composition studies in general. With the support of Lynn Quitman Troyka, the CCCC authorized the creation of an ESL Special Interest Group (1980–81) and then the first ESL Committee (1981–87). Although the number of ESL-related sessions was relatively small in the early 1980s, it began to grow toward the end of the decade. Yet, partly because of the expansion of the scope of composition studies and the increasing tendency for specialization, sessions related to second language issues tended to attract a relatively small number of CCCC members, those who were developing a special interest in those issues. The experience was frustrating to many who attended CCCC as part of their effort to bring insights from second language studies to "mainstream" composition studies (see, for example, Johns, "Too Much"; Silva, Leki, and Carson). Although there already were second language writers in many mainstream composition programs, the numbers were still too small to instigate a "profession-wide response" (Valdés).

By 1990, the number of foreign-born people in U.S. higher education had reached the 2 million mark, about 65 percent of whom were U.S. citizens (Otuya). In the meantime, the number of second language writing specialists both at CCCC and TESOL reached a critical mass, and second language writing came to be recognized as an interdisciplinary field of inquiry. The rise of the field was marked by the publication in 1990 of *Second Language Writing: Research Insights for the Classroom*, edited by Barbara Kroll, and by the inauguration in 1992 of the *Journal of Second Language Writing*, edited by Ilona Leki and Tony Silva. In 1992, CCCC also created the second ESL Committee with Tony Silva as the chair. The committee was not allowed to continue beyond the first term, however; instead, Silva established a new Special Interest Group on Second Language Writing, which has been meeting since 1995. To continue the effort to integrate a second language perspective into all aspects of CCCC, I proposed the creation of the new Committee on Second Language Writing. Since the committee came into being in 1998, it has been coordinating various activities related to second language writing at CCCC, including workshops, SIG meetings, and open meetings on Saturday. The committee continues to be active under the new leadership of Susan Miller-Cochran, who joined me as a cochair in 2004, and Christina Ortmeier-Hooper, who replaced me in 2008.

As the field entered the twenty-first century, the status of second language issues at CCCC changed drastically. Over the last decade, an increasing number of journals, such as *College English, College Composition and Communication, Computers and Composition, Journal of Basic Writing, WPA: Writing Program Administration* and *Written Communication* have come to include articles focusing on second language writing, and at professional conferences, second language issues have become much more visible. Many established figures in composition studies have also begun to pay attention to language issues in their work, and a growing number of graduate students and emerging scholars are actively seeking cross-disciplinary training in both composition studies and second language studies through coursework and by attending relevant sessions, workshops, and conferences. In practice, however, second language issues are yet to be fully integrated into the intellectual work of every writing program administrator (Matsuda, "Embracing") and, more important, into the consciousness of every writing instructor who comes into contact with second language writers in the classroom.

THE "CCCC STATEMENT ON SECOND-LANGUAGE WRITING AND WRITERS"

One of the major turning points in the place of second language writing in composition studies was the publication of the "CCCC Statement on Second-Language Writing and Writers," a document developed by the CCCC Committee on Second Language Writing and adopted by the CCCC Executive Committee in November 2000. The statement was also endorsed by the Board of Directors of Teachers of English to Speakers of Other Languages (TESOL) in March 2001. The CCCC statement defines second language writers in North American higher education broadly, encompassing "international visa students, refugees, and permanent residents as well as naturalized and native-born citizens of the United States and Canada" (669).

The document states that issues related to second language writing permeate all aspects of composition studies—theory, research, instruction, assessment and program administration—because language is inextricably tied to all aspects of writing. Increasingly, second language writers are found in writing courses of all levels and types, including basic writing, mainstream first-year writing, advanced composition, business and technical communication, and writing centers. In addition, as the writing-across-the-curriculum movement continues to promote the importance of integrating writing into instruction and assessment in courses across the curriculum, second language writers are finding themselves in situations where they are being assessed not only for their knowledge and expertise in the disciplines but also for their writing and language proficiencies. For these reasons, second language writing cannot be considered a concern only for a handful of specialists; instead, it needs to be seen as an integral part of all areas of composition studies.

In fact, the CCCC statement calls all writing teachers, researchers, and administrators, regardless of their background or interest, "to recognize the regular presence of second-language writers in writing classes, to understand their characteristics, and to develop instructional and administrative practices that are sensitive to their linguistic and cultural needs." It also urges "graduate programs in writing-related fields to offer courses in second-language writing theory, research, and instruction in order to prepare writing teachers and scholars for working with a college student population that is increasingly diverse both linguistically and culturally" (670).[1]

SECOND LANGUAGE WRITERS AT VARIOUS SITES OF INSTITUTIONAL PRACTICES

As I mentioned earlier, issues related to second language writing permeate all aspects of composition studies as an increasing number of second language writers find themselves in various sites of institutional practice influenced by composition teachers and researchers. Traditionally, critical masses of second language writers—i.e., populations that were large enough for faculty members and administrators to make significant and sustained programmatic and pedagogical changes—were likely to be found at internationally recognized research institutions and at urban, open admissions institutions. Over the last two decades, however, the demographics of U.S. higher education have changed drastically—especially in terms of students' ethnic, national, and linguistic backgrounds. Reflecting the rise of the multilingual student population educated in U.S. high schools, many institutions—regardless of type—are beginning to enroll highly qualified resident students whose language proficiency and literacy backgrounds do not fit the profile of traditional college students.

---

1.   At the time of writing this chapter, the statement was being revised and updated with a broader scope to include issues in the writing center, writing across the curriculum/writing in the disciplines, and writing for graduate students.

At the same time, the growing interest among college and university administrators in globalizing their institutions as well as the desire to attract academically successful international students who also bring foreign capital (at an out-of-state rate) means that the number of international students has continued to increase even in the aftermath of 9/11 and during an economic crisis on a global scale. As a result of these demographic shifts, writing programs at all levels are now facing the challenge of making the curriculum appropriate for all as students bring a broader range of linguistic and cultural differences to the classroom. I will conclude this chapter by discussing some of the key issues facing various types of writing programs that are influenced by the disciplinary perspective of composition studies.

First-Year Writing

The first-year writing program has long been the primary site of discussion related to second language writers because of the ubiquitous nature of the requirement. With the unsurpassed level of linguistic diversity in the college student population, an increasing number of first-year writing programs are witnessing the presence of multilingual writers in mainstream writing courses taught by teachers who may be experienced at teaching writing in general but not at working with second language writers of various kinds. In response to the demographic shifts, many institutions are creating—or increasing the number of—separate sections of first-year writing courses for second language writers. This practice is appropriate and necessary for those students who benefit from additional language instruction and who feel more comfortable in the presence of others who share the same experience (Braine); yet, requiring students to take the separate section may be problematic for students who resist the implications of separate placement on their identity positioning (Ortmeier-Hooper). For these reasons, it is important to keep the placement optional (Silva, "Examination" 41) and to make all sections of first-year writing courses ESL friendly. It is also important to provide opportunities for professional development; all writing teachers are already second language writing teachers. Institutions might also consider designing writing courses to capitalize on the linguistic and cultural diversity that the new population of students brings as a way of enhancing the globalization efforts for all students involved (see Matsuda and Silva for an example of such curricular innovation).

Basic Writing

At institutions where the number of second language writers has been relatively small, those students are sometimes placed in basic-writing courses. This placement is appropriate if the teachers understand the needs of second language writers and are ready to address those needs. This is not always the case, however, because basic writing and second language writing developed largely in parallel disciplinary worlds (Matsuda, "Basic"). As I have mentioned in the context of first-year writing programs, it is important to create second language sections of basic-writing courses while helping all basic-writing teachers develop the ability to work with a broader range of basic writers. Another consideration is the issue of stigma. While the notion of taking five or more years to complete a bachelor's degree is becoming more common in the United States, many other countries follow cohort systems where students move through the curriculum year by year; in this context, not being able to graduate in four years may carry a social stigma. Having to take extra courses that do not count toward graduation is not only a source of embarrassment but also a financial burden for students who come from different educational and economic systems. (While U.S. students may also experience a similar sense of stigma, the implications are often different in a different cultural context.) Since second language writers are taking English writing courses at an advanced level of second language proficiency, it would make sense for these courses to provide credits that count toward foreign language requirements (Martino).

Professional Writing

Professional writing is another important site of institutional practice where second language writers meet composition studies. At many institutions, students in business, engineering, and other applied sciences are required to take business or technical writing courses as part of their major requirements. Since these majors are popular among international students, many professional writing programs enroll a large number of second language writers. Professional writing has also been one of the subfields of composition studies that has long focused on global communication. Yet, second language issues have not been widely understood or discussed in the professional literature or in textbooks. Although professional communication textbooks often focus on international issues, they tend to conceptualize would-be technical writers—the primary audience of those textbooks—as native users of dominant varieties of English, while positioning second language writers as the linguistic and cultural Others (Matsuda and Matsuda, "Globalizing"). Although it is important to continue to consider issues in global communication, language issues as well as the role of users of different languages also need to become an integral part of the intellectual conversation.

Writing across the Curriculum/Writing in the Discipline

The efforts to integrate writing into courses across the curriculum as well as to involve faculty in various disciplines in teaching discipline-specific writing conventions have resulted in an increased use of writing as a means of instruction and assessment. While these efforts may have enhanced student learning in many ways, they may also have created additional challenges to some second language writers who are successful in learning the materials but who may struggle with writing (Johns, "Interpreting"), especially in contexts where faculty members are not able to provide appropriate feedback and guidance to help them develop their discipline-specific language and writing proficiency. The intellectual and institutional work of WAC/WID specialists, then, also needs to include a consideration of language issues in teaching and assessing writing in courses across the curriculum. Furthermore, a greater cooperation with specialists in English for Academic Purposes/ English for Specific Purposes would be important, as there are many areas of overlaps.

Writing Centers

Second language writing is also important to writing centers because, at many institutions, second language writers often constitute a majority of writing center clients. In response to the unique issues second language writers bring to the writing centers, it may be necessary to reexamine some of the fundamental assumptions of the writing center, which were developed with monolingual English users in mind. For example, the common practice of focusing on global issues (e.g., content, organization, idea development) before local issues (e.g., grammar, style, and mechanics) may not work as well for students with lower proficiency. A study of Japanese students by Tim Ashwell has shown that, depending on students' writing proficiency, focusing on global issues first does not affect students' ability to revise successfully any more than providing local feedback first or mixing global and local feedback. Another example is the use of peer tutors as opposed to expert teachers who are not only proficient writers and readers but also people who have expertise in second language writing instruction. Peer tutors, who are by definition sympathetic readers but not experts in the teaching of writing or language, may not be able to meet the needs of clients who have an advanced knowledge of the subject and discipline-specific genres yet are struggling to express their ideas in the second language.

Graduate Writing Courses

With the dominance of English as the lingua franca of international scholarly communication, and with the growing presence of international graduate students in master's and doctoral programs, many institutions are beginning to realize the need to develop writing courses for graduate students. While scholars and researchers in composition studies have been relatively quiet on this topic, applied linguists specializing in English for Academic Purposes have been examining issues in scholarly publications (e.g., Casanave; Casanave, Pearson, and Vandrick; Flowerdew; Flowerdew and Li; Li and Flowerdew; Tardy) as well as textbooks and reference materials focusing on writing for graduate students in various disciplinary contexts (e.g., Swales; Swales and Feak). This is one of the areas in which composition studies can learn a great deal from applied linguistics in terms of research insights as well as curriculum design and instructional practices.

INTELLECTUAL ISSUES AND CONTROVERSIES

As the need for addressing second language issues becomes increasingly obvious in these various sites of institutional practices, the interest in second language writing also seems to be growing not only among second language specialists but also among composition specialists who work in various subfields. Yet, there still is a dearth of research and scholarship on second language writing situated in the disciplinary and instructional context of composition studies. While some contexts, such as the first-year composition programs and writing centers, are relatively well represented, these and other contexts require even more thorough reexamination of assumptions and institutional practices. The following are some of the issues that are currently being explored or need to be explored in the near future.

Multilingualism as the Norm

Writing programs in U.S. higher education—as well as the intellectual field of composition studies, which has grown out of that particular historical and institutional context—have been based on the assumption of English monolingualism as the norm. This assumption has become increasingly inaccurate as the linguistic diversity of the student population has intensified over the last few decades (Matsuda, "Myth"). It is important for composition scholars, regardless of specialization, to reexamine how and to what extent the monolingual assumption pervades the field and its intellectual practices, and to consider ways of moving beyond those unexamined assumptions.

Writing Assessment

Given its serious implications for students' academic progress and success, writing assessment is a topic that is not to be taken lightly for any students. It is particularly important for second language writers who may encounter additional challenges in courses and programs that may not be adequately designed to address their language and literacy development needs. Some topics of interest in this regard are the use of standardized test scores for placement (Crusan), directed self-placement, classroom writing assessment, and exit exam requirements (Johns, "Interpreting").

For those who are involved in the administration of writing programs at various levels, the shift in student demographics points to the need for a reconsideration of placement options that are currently available (Matsuda and Silva; Silva, "Examination") and that can be developed in the future. The issue of students' sociolinguistic identity also needs to be taken into account (Costino and Hyon). Since students often choose placement options without a clear idea of the costs and benefits of all available options, what is also important is to review the larger questions of placement procedures—the process by which students are informed about their options, assessed for their current proficiency and needs, and placed into various courses and sections.

The Role of Language

While there are many similarities between instructional practices for first-language and second language writers, one important difference is that most second language writers who take writing courses are in the process of developing their second language proficiency. Their mental representation of second language "grammar" (defined in the technical sense as the knowledge of phonology, morphology, syntax, and lexicon) may differ from that of first-language users. Addressing language issues in the writing classroom is not easy because it requires the teacher to have some knowledge of the structure of the English language and the nature of second language acquisition as well as ways of providing feedback on language issues. The last point is challenging even for second language writing specialist because research on the long-term effects of error feedback is still inconclusive (Ferris, "Grammar," *Treatment,* Truscott and Hsu).

Global Literacy

In recent years, institutions have begun to emphasize the importance of global literacy for all college-educated students. NCTE's definition of 21st Century Literacies also includes two items that are relevant to global literacy: "Twenty-first century readers and writers need to . . . [b]uild relationships with others to pose and solve problems collaboratively and *cross-culturally*" and "[d]esign and share information for *global communities* to meet a variety of purposes" (emphasis added). It is important to keep in mind that communicating cross-culturally often involves multiple languages, and that global communities are multilingual by default. Composition specialists need to embrace the multilingual reality of the global community and today's classroom by exploring ways to engage all students in the development of global literacy. In that context, the multilingual and multicultural resources that second language writers bring to writing programs can be seen as an important asset (Matsuda and Silva). In other words, the question is no longer limited to how to prepare students from around the world to write like traditional students from North America; it is time to start thinking more seriously about how to prepare monolingual students to write like the rest of the world.

The Internationalization of Composition Studies

Partly as a result of the institutional urge for internationalization and global engagement, composition scholars are becoming increasingly interested in internationalizing the field. In many cases, internationalization efforts take the form of traveling to other countries to share insights from U.S.-based research and forging alliances with writing researchers from around the world through conferences and

publications. While these developments are encouraging, it is important to keep in mind that in international contexts, writing in English often means second language writing, and insights from the United States, where the monolingual myth has long prevailed, may not be directly applicable. Even in contexts where English is the dominant language, the variety of English may not be the same as the dominant U.S. variety, and the politics of language differences in those contexts may not be the same as those encountered in North America. To internationalize the field effectively and ethically, U.S. composition specialists need to learn more about the sociolinguistic and institutional contexts of other countries. Before trying to reach out to others, however, U.S. composition studies many need to come to terms with the issues of globalization and multilingualism within its own institutional contexts.

3

REMAPPING PROFESSIONAL WRITING
Articulating the State of the Art and Composition Studies

Tim Peeples and Bill Hart-Davidson

In 1993, Patricia A. Sullivan and James E. Porter published "Remapping Curricular Geography: Professional Writing in/and English" in the *Journal of Business and Technical Communication*. In 2007, when Thomas Kent was asked by Dorothy Winsor, then the editor of *JBTC*, to identify the most significant article published during his tenure as editor of that same journal, he selected "Remapping." Kent argues that the Sullivan and Porter article "remains timely in disciplinary and institutional terms," and "the thrust of their argument clearly continues to resonate with us" (12). Primary among these resonating arguments, Kent singles out two. First is the clear and persuasive evidence that in 1993 professional writing constituted an "emerging" independent field of study and research; by 2007, Kent asserts confidently that professional writing had moved from the status of "emerging" to become a fully "established" field of its own. Second is the persuasive argument that we think about and understand disciplines in general and professional writing specifically in terms of the spaces or geography they occupy and their associated spatial or geographical relationships:

> Sullivan and Porter invited us to think differently about the nature of curricular space within our academic disciplines. By providing an alternative vocabulary—saturated and infused with the metaphor of curricular geography—to describe the allocation of disciplinary space, Sullivan and Porter asked us to reconceptualize the formation of our academic disciplines. Instead of understanding a discipline as a subdivided formation of relatively autonomous fields within fields . . . they suggested that we might be better served by understanding a discipline as being a confederation of epistemological paradigms that shift, float, and even intermingle relative to one another. (13)

In addition to reframing ways we think about and understand disciplines, and professional writing in particular, "Remapping" makes clear that disciplinary spaces/geographies are constructs, created over time and dynamically readjusted through contestations about the nature and function of spaces and relations. (14) In their article, Sullivan and Porter recontest the space of professional writing by exploring various geographical rearticulations of that space relative to English.

This chapter participates in the ongoing (re)construction of professional writing, recontesting the space of the field, with a focus on its relation to and with composition studies.[1] Rather than pretend to comprehensively frame the state of the art in professional writing, we (1) return to some of the arguments made in "Remapping" to rearticulate Sullivan and Porter's set of competing spatial constructions of professional writing in relation to related fields, primarily composition studies; (2) examine a few locations within the field that suggest some of the primary geographies and spatial relations demarcating the field; (3) identify spaces of inquiry that most closely connect professional writing and composition studies; and (4) identify other spaces of inquiry that are more exclusively associated with professional writing and more significantly articulated with other fields but are key to any mapping of the state of the art in professional writing. As a result of this work, we aim to achieve the goals set out for each of the chapters within this collection: to define a specific area of scholarship (e.g., professional writing) as it relates to composition studies and in terms of its current state of the art, and to do so in ways that highlight key characteristics of the specific field of focus.

MAPPING PROFESSIONAL WRITING AND COMPOSITION STUDIES

In "Remapping," Sullivan and Porter begin with a definition of professional writing that asserts multiple identities. At once, professional writing is understood (1) as a research field, focused primarily on investigating writing in workplaces; (2) as a workplace activity, as in writing

---

1.   Though Sullivan and Porter use "rhetoric/composition" in their own mappings, we are using the phrase "composition studies," in great measure because that term resonates with this collection. This exchange of terms, however, is not without its dangers. "Rhetoric and composition," "composition studies," "writing studies," and "rhetoric and writing studies" are some of the terms used to define a field of related interests. However, these various terms reflect a range of divergent disciplinary geographies and have, in some instances, been vigorously debated and rearticulated (e.g., Crowley, "Composition Is Not Rhetoric"). Though we will use the term *composition studies* interchangeably with *rhetoric and composition*, we encourage readers to understand our purposes within this context rather than as a simplification or erasure of articulations that are, indeed, contested within the field.

done by anyone in the workplace (i.e., professionals-who-write) and/ or as in writing done by designated writing experts (i.e., professional writers); and (3) as a curricular entity, most commonly in the form of service courses (e.g., business writing and technical writing) but also in the forms of majors, concentrations, minors, certificates, and graduate programs (392). Though many may agree that these multiple identities do indeed define professional writing, and may agree that they even adequately describe the field as it is today, the meaning of professional writing and the meanings of the three separate identities that they identify as making up the whole of the field change in significant ways when mapped differently: though the elements of our mental maps might be shared, divergent mappings lead to divergent meanings.

In their 1993 article, Sullivan and Porter argue there is one emerging view of "English" challenging the traditional one that equates English with literary studies: that emerging view defines the focus of English on the activities of reading and writing or, even more generally, written language. Within such a map of English, writing studies, including professional writing and composition, assume more prominent roles or visible and valued spaces within the geography of English. Within that view, though, there are divergent mappings of professional writing vis-à-vis composition studies. In one view, composition studies occupies a space at a level equivalent to English education, literature, linguistics, and creative writing, wherein professional writing is subordinated to composition studies, placing it among the equivalents of advanced composition and first-year writing, for instance (see figure 1).[2]

In another view, professional writing is mapped as a separate but equal field in relation to composition studies, situating the two at equivalent levels with English education, literature, linguistics, creative writing, and technical communication (see figure 2). Of these two mappings, we would argue that figure 2 more accurately reflects the current relationships between professional writing and composition studies. Though clearly related fields, the two are separate, rather than one subordinated to and within the other.

---

2.   We use only the portion of the maps constructed by Sullivan and Porter that focus on the relationships between professional writing and composition studies. Their aim was to remap the space of professional writing within English, leading to maps that included other areas of study within the geography of English. Our aim is to examine and rearticulate the spatial relations between professional writing and composition studies more narrowly.

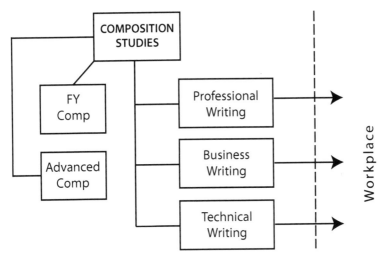

Figure 1

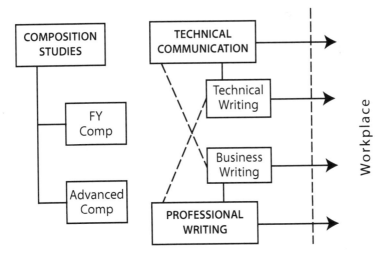

Figure 2

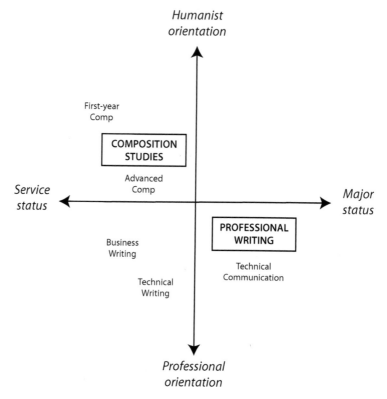

Figure 3

We propose a third map that locates professional writing and composition studies, along with some related areas, on two continua, one extending from service status to major status and another extending from humanist orientation to professional orientation (see figure 3).

This third map rearticulates professional writing and composition studies in relation to geographies other than those demarcated by English departmental spaces. Mapped within and under English, professional writing and composition studies assume close relations, either subordinated or separate but equal. Mapped along the continua of service status/major status and humanistic orientation/professional orientation, the two fields assume less closely related relations.

The practice of multiple mapping here is more than an academic exercise. The shifting geographies of professional writing from a subdivision of composition studies (figure 1) to a separate but equal space within and under English (figure 2) to a distinct ideological formation and academically positioned entity also shift the meanings, futures, and interests of professional writing in terms of research, pedagogy, and otherwise. To understand and participate as a teacher-scholar within the state of the art of professional writing today requires a remapping (figure 3) of still present and competing mappings of the field (figures 1 and 2) as well as an understanding of all three at once. Within the material-social practices both within and outside of academia, all three mappings coexist and exert power on what professional writing is and can be.

For example, in much the way figure 1 suggests that professional writing is the learning and practice of a subset of composition studies then applied in the workplace, many within and outside of the academy still carry such a mental map and set of meanings with them, exerting power on expectations of what professional writing can and should be; they see professional writing as the application of knowledge and skills learned as part of composition studies and, more generally, English. In figure 2, professional writing loses its direct connections to and with composition studies, a mapping that can lead some to disconnect the powers of what composition studies offers—such as a keen awareness of recursive, iterative, individual composing processes, and the gendered and raced elements within language practices. Additionally, the mapping of figure 2 suggests an endless yoking of professional writing to the service-oriented entities of business and technical writing. To understand and participate effectively as part of professional writing, one must understand the ongoing impacts of meaning that result from the mappings of both figures 1 and 2. All mappings lead to a range of particular (mis)understandings; the previously illustrated (mis)understandings of professional writing stemming from figures 1 and 2 still lead, positively though, to significant lines of research, including questions like "To what extent do continuing linkages to English and composition studies limit curricular, pedagogical, and/or professional possibilities for professional writing/professional writers?" and "In what ways can practices within and knowledges from composition studies empower writers within professional writing contexts?" We explore some of these shared and divergent spaces of inquiry in later sections of this chapter.

As we look at the third map of professional writing and composition studies (figure 3), we see the potential for a possible future of writing studies that flips the relationships in figure 1. As professional writing continues to develop toward major-status, and as we see composition studies continue to develop a more extensive network of relations largely located in the space of service (e.g., basic writing, first-year writing, writing centers, writing across the curriculum and in the disciplines, and advanced composition), might the future of composition studies be located within and under departments of professional writing or in departments with names like Writing and Rhetoric that include flagship majors in professional writing? Programs at Michigan State, Stanford, and Central Florida, just to name a few major and nationally recognizable ones, seem to suggest that such a spatial reorganization might be of and in our futures. At the same time, shifts in what first-year writing courses can and should be, and can and should include, might reflect this rearticulation of composition studies and professional writing. In particular, we are thinking of Downs and Wardle's work on first-year writing as writing about writing, also discussed later in this collection, David Fleming's work on re-creating rhetoric as a course of study, increased numbers of first-year writing programs designed as introductions to writing in the disciplines, new first-year writing textbooks like Dominic Delli Carpini's (*Composing a Life's Work*), and the number of first-year writing textbooks that now include sections that were previously located within professional writing (e.g., sections on document design). These remappings (e.g., local and material) and rearticulations (e.g., theoretical, historical, pedagogical, and curricular) are themselves key aspects of and lines of research within the state of the art of professional writing today, and the effects of these remappings and rearticulations lead to significant lines of professional writing research.

INTRASPATIAL GEOGRAPHIES OF THE FIELD

One way to understand a space is to see it in relation to other locations and spaces. Up to this point, we have been exploring the geography of professional writing in relation to composition studies. Another way to understand a space is to stand in it and look around to see what forms the place one inhabits, and where the space is demarcated from other spaces, its "intraspatial geography." In researching this chapter, we informally asked a variety of colleagues within the field—those who self-identify with and are active within the professoriate of professional writing and, at the same time, composition studies—what they would suggest as best ways to orient others to the field. There was a striking commonality both in terms of how most of these scholars had entered the field and in terms of what they would advise as an effective entrée or orientation to the field. The majority were oriented to the field in ways reflective of figures 1 and 2: they came (in)to it as instructors for service courses related to professional writing (e.g., business and technical writing). And yet almost unanimously, they suggested the best entrée or orientation to the field would not be via the route they entered but, instead, through study of and immersion in the intraspatial geography of the field.

What marks and demarcates this intraspatial geography of professional writing? All we surveyed mentioned a similar set of academic journals and a number of book-length sources. Mapping the field via landmarks of these sorts not only carries forward the spatial/geographical approach we are borrowing, but it reflects, also, what Geoffrey Sauer, David Dayton, and Carolyn Rude argue in "Bodies of Knowledge for Technical Communication," wherein they point to two key "libraries" that they see as establishing—dynamically—the landmarks that define the field.

Technical Communication Quarterly, Technical Communication, the *Journal of Business and Technical Communication,* and *IEEE Transactions on Professional Communication* form, through article-length and special-edition oriented discourses, some of the most central geographies of the field. Inscribed in the titles of these journals are historical traces that continue to mark the space of professional writing. These ongoing relations are reflected in still-powerful terms like *technical, business,* and *communication.* And yet, as the mappings in figures 1, 2, and 3 might indicate, professional writing animates a disciplinary space with clear connections, also and simultaneously, to a number of other fields. These relationships lead to an additional set of journals that point one toward other key spaces demarcating the intraspatial geography of professional writing, spaces crucial to an understanding of the field's identity as a dynamically reconstructed geography. These other journals include *College Composition and Communication, Written Communication, JAC: Journal of Advanced Composition, Computers and Composition, Kairos,* and *Technostyle.*

In the titles of these journals, we see a clear and ongoing connection to and with composition, writing, and technology. Beyond these lies an important set of journals more associated with and to the space of rhetorical studies, perhaps professional writing's chief theoretical source (Sullivan and Porter, 408). These include the likes of *Rhetoric Review* and *Rhetoric Society Quarterly.* Along with these additional discursive landmarks stand a number of journals that reinforce the geography of professional writing that is associated with figures 1 and 2, such as *Intercom*, the *Journal of Business Communication*, the *Journal of Technical Writing and Communication*, and *Business Communication Quarterly*. There is also a very large set of journals beyond those listed here that taps into related disciplinary fields animating the space of professional writing. These others reach into fields like ethics, management, organizational theory, human-computer interaction, design, linguistics, translation, cultural studies, computing sciences, anthropology, and qualitative research design, just to name a few. Though the spatial relations suggested by such interdisciplinary journals reflect important characteristics of and research areas in/for professional writing, they map what is more akin to the *inter*spatial geography of the field than its *intra*spatial geography. The *intra*spatial geography of the field is marked by the central terms—composition, communication, writing, rhetoric, technology, business, and technical—located in the titles of these journals, as well as the contents and histories read within and across their pages. Professional writing is located "here."

A number of book-length, edited collections combine with these journals to demarcate the most commonly pinpointed intraspatial geography of professional writing. A few of the early collections marking this space include *Writing in Nonacademic Settings* (Odell and Goswami), *Worlds of Writing: Teaching and Learning in Discourse Communities of Work* (Matalene), and *Textual Dynamics of the Professions* (Bazerman and Paradis). Following these early examples are two key theory and research collections, *Professional Communication: The Social Perspective* (Blyler and Thralls) and *Writing in the Workplace: New Research Perspectives* (Spilka), and another collection—*The Practice of Technical and Scientific Communication: Writing in Professional Contexts* (Lutz and Storms)—that helped map the varied professional/workplace contexts that were being drawn within the boundaries of professional writing. Later collections doing similar work but more consciously directed toward new, advanced students to the field include *Central Works in Technical Communication* (Johnson-Eilola and Selber), *Professional Writing and Rhetoric: Readings from the Field* (Peeples), and *Writing a Professional Life: Stories of Technical Communicators On and Off the Job* (Savage and Sullivan).

Inscribed in the titles and tables of contents of these sources are central features of professional writing's landscape. Unlike journal titles, which are restricted by past powerful articulations, book titles have the historical independence to reflect current and changing geographies of the field. As a whole, these titles reinforce connections to and with "technical communication," for instance, but they—individually and as a whole—point toward a geography heavily marked by "writing" in "nonacademic," "professional," and "workplace" "contexts." Inscribed, simultaneously, by both "writing" and "communication," the landscape of professional writing is marked by a broad rhetorical orientation, one that expands the notion of what we mean by "writing" beyond the textual. And covering a terrain that expands, broadly, into a space marked by "nonacademic," "professional," and "workplace" contexts, professional writing reflects a space not bounded by or within the scope of the "technical." Similarly, inscribed in the tables of contents from these sources are central features of professional writing's landscape. Section headings like "Assessing the Influence of New Technologies" (Odell and Goswami), "Online Environments" (Johnson-Eilola and Selber), and "Professional Writing as Technologically Situated Action" (Peeples) individually and collectively mark the significance of changing technologies to the field of professional writing. These collections share additional foci marking a collective sense of the field's geography, including a focus on rhetoric/discourse, context/community, ethics/power, audience/user, pedagogy, and the relationships and differences between school/work or academics/nonacademics. Professional writing is, therefore, also located "here."

The expansiveness of professional writing drawn within and by these sources is also reflected in the development of other books that focus on more narrowly inscribed places within the field's intraspatial geography. These more focused sources are often editions within a specialized series, including the following:

- Allyn & Bacon Series in Technical Communication (Rude, *Technical Editing*; Dombrowski, *Ethics in Technical Communication*; Kostelnick and Roberts, *Designing Visual Language: Strategies for Professional Communicators*; and Barnum, *Usability Testing and Research*);

- ATTW Contemporary Studies in Technical Communication (e.g., Dautermann, *Writing at Good Hope: A Study of Negotiated Composition in a Community of Nurses*; and Katz, *The Dynamics of Writing Review: Opportunities for Growth and Change in the Workplace*);

- Wiley Technical Communication Library (e.g., Hackos, *Managing Your Documentation Projects*; and Schriver, *Dynamics in Document Design*); and

- Baywood's Technical Communication Series (e.g., Lay and Karis, *Collaborative Writing in Industry: Investigations in Theory and Practice*; Dragga and Gong, *Editing: The Design of Rhetoric*; and Allen and Deming, *Publications Management: Essays for Professional Technical Communicators*).

Series titles, like journal titles, are restricted by their historical articulations with and to "technical communication," but the names of the individual books within these series mark key locations that collectively, and more dynamically, define the space of the field. Editing, ethics, visual and document design, usability, composition, writing review, management, and rhetoric: each and all point to key places that mark the geography of the field and that point to the ongoing scholarship that reconstructs and reflects the state of the art of professional writing as a field. This set of landmarks can be traced in the similarly functioning discursive space of journal special editions, a form of edited collection, if you will. All of the above can be found, for instance, within special editions of *TCQ* dating back to 1993, with additional foci including computers/digital technologies, law, program administration, science, health/ medicine, pedagogy, cultural studies, government/public policy, and research. Many of these special issues reflect the interdisciplinary links and pathways mapping the space of professional writing that includes but also extends beyond its intraspatial geography.

These locations demarcating the intraspatial geography of the field not only orient the field, and the people and discourses that reconstruct it, but they point to what has been and is the state of the art of the field or, more generally speaking, the geography within which the state of the art resides and participates in rearticulating the field. Taken together with the rearticulated relationship with composition studies explored in the previous section of this chapter, the intraspatial geography mapped here constructs professional writing as more than a practical or applied subset of composition studies. It also constructs a field distinct from, though articulated with and to, technical communication and business and technical writing. Professional writing is marked by interests in the rhetorics that are needed to perform well in nonacademic and, particularly, workplace contexts. These interests may and do overlap with composition studies and technical communication, as these fields, too, are at least partly interested in rhetorics. But the geographies of each field's interests are distinct, marking distinct spaces for composition studies and professional writing.

PRIMARY ARTICULATIONS BETWEEN PROFESSIONAL WRITING AND COMPOSITION STUDIES

Though professional writing and composition studies inhabit distinct spaces, some key articulations connect the two fields, nevertheless. Without such articulations, the mappings of figures 1, 2, and 3 would all lack any sense of validity. To mark these fields as distinct is, therefore, not to mark them as antithetical or opposite. In this section, we explore some of the primary connections between the two fields.

A number of articulations between composition studies and professional writing are actually traced through the chapters within this collection. The issue of "transfer," for instance, has long stood as a curricular and pedagogical issue of importance within both professional writing and composition studies. Within professional writing, in particular, the school/work and academia/industry divides have led to a number of studies related to the transfer of writing/rhetorical expertise across contexts (e.g., Anson and Forsberg; Beaufort, *College Writing and Beyond*; Dias et al.; Dias and Paré), and they continue to animate the state of the art in professional writing. The ways we do, can, and should study professional writing, as is the case in composition studies, have included strong focus on ethnographic and other qualitative research methodologies. Writing across languages, internationalization, globalization, translation studies, etc.—all areas of inquiry and interest within professional writing—also create articulations with composition studies' now-emergent attention to second language writing. And digital rhetorics and new media, while long one aspect of composition studies (e.g., Selber; Selfe, *Technology and Literacy*) and a growing area of awareness and centrality (e.g., Yancey, "Made Not Only in Words"), are in fact so central to professional writing that "writing" seemingly always carries with it a digitized, multimediated element.

Perhaps the most significant articulation between professional writing and composition studies resides in shared connections to rhetoric.[3] Even when direct references are absent, as is the case in headings

---

3.   Examining the nature of each discipline's connections to rhetoric, as well as what constitutes the shared connections composition studies and professional writing

and chapter titles throughout most of this collection, rhetoric plays a significant role in the shaping of and discussions about composition studies. *Cross-Talk in Comp Theory: A Reader* (Villanueva) is perhaps one of the leading anthologies in composition studies, and throughout its contents, rhetoric is a recurring piece. *On Writing Research: The Braddock Essays, 1975–1998* (Ede) celebrates award-winning composition research works spanning more than two decades that are, according to Lisa Ede, of particular value for "what they can reveal about the development of composition studies as a scholarly discipline" and that make ongoing connections to rhetoric, especially from the late 1980s on. Though "composition studies," "rhetoric and composition," and "composition" do not necessarily reflect the same meanings and geographies, and are even strongly contended among some, they are for others interchangeable units, articulating rhetoric quite clearly to composition studies.

Indeed, Richard Graves's *Rhetoric and Composition: A Sourcebook for Teachers and Writers*, clearly utilizing "rhetoric and composition" as its identity, shares numerous cross-indexed pieces and/or scholars with both *Cross-Talk* and *On Writing Research*. Connections between professional writing and rhetoric are equally as crucial to the geography of professional writing as the connections between composition and rhetoric are to the geography of composition studies. As noted in our discussion of the intraspatial geography of professional writing, rhetoric is one of the common links across edited collections that are key to defining the space of the field. In their 2004 study, "TPC Program Snapshots: Developing Curricula and Addressing Challenges," Nancy Allen and Steven Benninghoff found through surveys of professional writing programs that the top two principles and topics across all programs include audience and rhetorical analysis, and they found that the "strongest single category [of core concepts] was rhetorical analysis" (162, 170).

The ways this articulation with rhetoric manifests in each field, however, diverge. Each field reflects, studies, and extends understanding of a rhetorical emphasis on the connectedness between writer, text, reader, and context. The predominant focus in composition studies has been and continues to be on the writer within this rhetorical network. This focus has led to powerful understandings of and strategies for enhancing the composing processes of individual writers. Rather objectified processes of invention, for instance, within the rhetorical tradition are

---

have with rhetoric, exceeds the scope of what we intend here, and indeed would lead to a set of valuable studies in and of itself.

brought within composition studies into the embodied and affective worlds of individual writers in the act of writing; invention and writers in the acts of inventing are studied, theorized, and retheorized in forms of pedagogical practices that enhance this crucial work of writing and writers. Also rather objectified categories of audiences and writers within the rhetorical tradition are examined and understood more thoroughly through composition studies as embodied individuals of difference, raced, gendered, and classed. Composition studies' focus on the writer has also led to valuable studies, theories, and strategies about and for writerly agency and difference.

In contrast, the articulation between rhetoric and professional writing has manifest with greater focus and emphasis on contexts, rather than individual writers. Indeed, histories of professional writing, told both as growth out of composition studies as a subfield (e.g., represented in figure 1) and as an independent field preceding and then developing in some parallel forms with composition studies (e.g., Connors, "The Rise of Technical Writing Instruction in America"), situate the exigency for an independent field in the need to address writing done within specific, nonacademic and/or workplace *contexts.* Like composition studies, professional writing has brought attention to studies, theories, and strategies related to composing processes, but within the field of professional writing, these studies (e.g., Broadhead and Freed; Faigley; Katz; Spilka, "Orality and Literacy") tend to focus on the social situatedness of these processes. The writer and her/his agency are also of interest within professional writing, but here, focus is more on authorship and authoring within specific contexts (Slack et al.; Winsor), and agency is often merged with discussions of ethics and organizational change (Amidon and Blythe; Doheny-Farina, "Creating a Text"; Faber; Herndl and Licona). In his tracing of the term *rhetor* through the early centuries of Greek rhetorical history, Jeffrey Arthurs describes in the rhetor what is very closely aligned with conceptions and practices of professional writers. Arthurs argues that "the term rhetor had the technical denotation of a professional orator/politician/advocate, one who actively participated in the affairs of state and court" (2). Arthurs's study defines the rhetor, therefore, as one who practices and theorizes authorship-*within-context.* The rhetor is also, for Arthurs, an advocate and civic leader. These context-, practice-, and action-oriented features attributed to the ancient Greek rhetors reflect professional writing's sense of writer/agency and writing/authorship, with the professional writer as a contextually situated and active advocate for users/readers/audiences.

As a result of a shared articulation to rhetoric, composition studies and professional writing also share attention to audience. In *Cross-Talk*, Victor Villanueva includes Lisa Ede and Andrea Lunsford's "Audience Addressed/Audience Invoked: The Role of Audience in Composition Theory and Pedagogy" within a category of "givens" within the field of composition studies: attention to audience is a given within composition. Similarly, audience is cited by Allen and Benninghoff in their survey of professional writing programs as the highest-ranked principle taught in most or all professional writing courses: attention to audience is a given and, indeed, a defining principle in professional writing. The Ede and Lunsford piece situates well the differences, though, between the ways composition studies and professional writing tend to practice and understand audience. In their article, Ede and Lunsford associate "audience addressed" with a reader-heavy emphasis, locating perhaps excessive authority for meaning and effectiveness in the reader or audience. At the same time, they associate "audience invoked" with a writerly focus, less willingly attributing that concept to placing excessive authority for meaning and effectiveness on the writer but, nevertheless, acknowledging the need for a balance between the addressed and the invoked audience. They also associate audience invoked more squarely within composition studies, and associate audience addressed with speech communications and other approaches to writing and rhetoric. Diverging from composition studies, professional writing leans significantly toward audience addressed, acknowledging full well that in the final analysis all audiences are invoked and that writers throughout the processes of their work are constantly invoking an audience or audiences.

Professional writing often reframes reader/audience in the form of user and/or a specified organizational or contextual role embodied by (if possible to know) a specific individual or set of individuals. In this reformulation, professional writing generates and advocates practices that close the distance as much as possible between writer and reader/user/audience. Professional writing engenders practices that move writers from positions of "writing to" audiences, beyond even "writing for" users, to "writing with" (when/if possible) others. Audience becomes an active, productive role often from the start of writing through assessment of its effectiveness and into the ongoing, iterative process of

writing/revising. Audiences within professional writing become participants in the most concrete ways possible.

An additional distinction between approaches to, understandings
of, and practices related to audience in composition studies and professional writing is the emphasis in professional writing on writing to
multiple audiences. Within the sorts of material contexts that engender
professional writing, writing rarely attends to the needs, biases, assumptions and warrants, histories, etc. of a single audience. Writing in such
contexts quite normally is for multiple audiences with different needs,
expectations, relations, etc. Even when addressing a single person, that
individual is often multiply and complexly situated within an organizational context, and even in such instances, professional writing attends
actively and rhetorically to possible secondary, tertiary, and other distant
audiences who can always-already have access to and might have need
for something that has been written (e.g., a lawyer or policy maker).

Therefore, both composition studies and professional writing share
strong articulations with rhetoric, yet the specific articulations they
each form with rhetoric reflect key differences between the two fields.
These differences should not be seen, though, as absolute or ultimately
judgmental of the other. Looking to the other can strengthen each,
and many productive lines of research can be generated through this
activity of looking across. For instance, understanding the specific writing processes of individual writers and their differences in effectiveness
within specific organizational contexts, or studying the role of invoking
audiences otherwise not expressed as needed or expected of readers
within specific organizational contexts, would lead to valuable studies of
writerly agency within professional writing. The aim is not to pull apart
the fields of composition studies and professional writing but to understand each to better understand the other, and to better understand the
nature and practice of rhetorical action more generally.

GEOGRAPHIES OF THE STATE OF THE ART BEYOND
COMPOSITION STUDIES

Though composition studies and professional writing share spaces
within and as part of their field-specific geographies, they each extend
beyond the other into spaces crucial to their identity and any discussions of their state of the art. To close, we offer two additional maps
that we hope will start a new round of conversations about where the
intersections among the two fields are and will be in the years ahead.

The first view is one that we hope is relevant for considering the kinds of career options for students with two- or four-year undergraduate, as well as master's, degrees in writing, understood here to be something other than but not always entirely separate from programs in creative writing. Both composition studies and professional writing have grown more distinct from English in the geographical space of higher education in the U.S.—both in terms of curricula, as major and minor degree programs are formed, and in terms of the institution, as departments of writing gain independent status from departments of English (see CCCC Committee on the Writing Major; Giberson and Moriarty; O'Neill). And of course, students, parents, faculty, and staff affiliated with these programs want to know where those with degrees in writing will work.

We can turn to the U.S. Bureau of Labor Statistics database tool called the National Employment Matrix to see projections for change by occupation and industry through 2018. The table below highlights trends that we believe are representative of the broader economy as a whole, and of shifts in the demand for skills and dispositions that align well with rhetoric and writing.

Table 1: Projected Job Growth for Writing & Editing Careers 2008–18

Occupation	Industry	2008–2018
Writers & Editors	All	Up 14.8 percent
Writers & Editors	Management, scientific, and technical consulting services	Up 88.8 percent
Technical Writers	All	Up 18.2 percent
Technical Writers	Management, scientific, and technical consulting services	Up 47 percent

Source: U.S. Bureau of Labor Statistics National Employment Matrix, <http://data.bls.gov/oep/nioem?Action=empios&Type=Occupation>.

The national trends for workers whose primary expertise is in writing and editing is favorable through 2018, with overall growth above the national average for all occupations. Across all industries, the demand for writers and editors is expected to rise, fueled by growth in the professional services areas of the economy and largely in spite of significant downward trends across all manufacturing areas, including manufacturing of high-tech electronics. This trend holds true for technical writers as well, incidentally, indicating that we should expect to see less demand for people to write "documentation" to accompany products and more demand for people whose written work, research, etc. is the primary product.

Dramatic growth for writers and editors, and for technical writers, is expected in areas such as scientific and technical consulting and management consulting. These are areas where writing goes hand in hand with conducting primary research and data analysis, and where we might expect to see employers favor job candidates with expertise in social scientific research methodologies, for instance, as well as the ability to communicate the results of data analysis to a diverse set of audiences. This is a different picture of an editor who studies in an English department and becomes steeped in the great works of literature in order to go off to Manhattan to work for a literary publisher. Increasingly, our field's expertise, embodied in our students, will be tied to and expressed in occupational areas that lie outside the traditional humanities: business, science, and technology.

Our second map also presents a projection, this time in the form of what we hypothesize views of our colleagues in composition studies and professional writing would be when asked two questions related to the focus of each.

On a scale of 1–5, where 5 is "Strongly agree" and 1 is " Strongly disagree," how would you respond to the following:

1a. Composition studies researchers and scholars are likely to pursue the study of rhetoric with an emphasis on:

a. Writer(s)	1	2	3	4	5
b. Reader(s)	1	2	3	4	5
c. Technology	1	2	3	4	5
d. Organizations	1	2	3	4	5
e. Process	1	2	3	4	5

1b. Professional writing researchers and scholars are likely to pursue the study of rhetoric with an emphasis on:

a. Writer(s)	1	2	3	4	5
b. Reader(s)	1	2	3	4	5
c. Technology	1	2	3	4	5
d. Organizations	1	2	3	4	5
e. Process	1	2	3	4	5

2a. Composition studies knowledge and expertise has institutional visibility in:

a. First-year courses   1   2   3   4   5

b. Service courses   1   2   3   4   5

c. An academic major   1   2   3   4   5

d. A graduate concentration   1   2   3   4   5

e. A graduate degree program   1   2   3   4   5

2b. Professional writing knowledge and expertise has institutional visibility in:

a. First-year courses   1   2   3   4   5

b. Service courses   1   2   3   4   5

c. An academic major   1   2   3   4   5

d. A graduate concentration   1   2   3   4   5

e. A graduate degree program   1   2   3   4   5

This is a very preliminary attempt to put what amount to our intellectual values—what each field perceives itself spending the most time and attention on—in relationship to how those examining institutions of higher education might see those values manifest in curricular structures. We would hypothesize that the results of such research might look something akin to figure 4.

If we read this image like a clock, the right side, or the hours from 12 to 6 o'clock, represent the intellectual values categories, and the hours from 6 to 12 o'clock represent the institutional visibility categories as represented by curricular structures. By assigning a value from 1–5 to each of the categories, we create an irregular polygon that represents each field. The blue, solid polygon represents professional writing, and the red, slightly transparent polygon represents composition studies. Recall that the values here are hypotheses, representing what we would expect to see if we polled appropriate groups of our colleagues.

What we project in this mapping is, first and foremost, a significant amount of overlap between the two regions as a whole and in a few key categories. For instance, both fields have strong visibility in service courses, reflecting the legacy of writing instruction in U.S. higher education. Both fields have strong intellectual commitments to the study of process as well. Where there are nonoverlapping regions, we see some valuable complimentary trends that signal ways the fields have worked and perhaps should continue to work together. For instance, the depth and breadth of scholarly work on writers in composition studies is nicely

Figure 4

complimented by a similar depth and breadth of work in professional writing on readers and/or users.

Other nonoverlapping areas raise questions. The high visibility of composition studies expertise in first-year courses, for instance, does not carry over into four-year degree programs and majors in composition studies. Conversely, while many four-year writing degrees strongly reflect the expertise of professional writing, that field has little to no visibility in the first-year curriculum in U.S. higher education, broadly speaking. Should we work to bring about more of one or the other?

Professional writing has a consistently strong intellectual focus on technology, and we have seen (and noted here) a moderate focus on technology in composition studies as well. Is this the amount of overlap we can expect to see in the future? Or would we expect the trend to consider technology as an object of inquiry to continue to grow in composition studies? As it does, might we see it become less of a focus for professional writing?

These and other questions are perhaps the most valuable outcome of this and similar mapping exercises. Regardless of where the values for each criterion sit after data are compiled at any one time, we would expect to see these values change over time. And so a static snapshot like this one—even when supported by reliable and valid data from a large sample population—is at its best when it performs as a resource for raising questions and formulating plans to actively pursue those curricular and/or research projects that represent the values of both fields. This remapping of professional writing with a specific focus on the field's articulation with and to composition studies acts, at once, as a means for illustrating the state of the art of professional writing, unsettling our definitions of both composition studies and professional writing, and raising the sorts of questions that iteratively re-create the dynamics of our discipline.

4

WRITING CENTER SCHOLARSHIP
A "Big Cross-Disciplinary Tent"

Lauren Fitzgerald

Writing centers are complex places, and, as such, bring forth a wide variety of questions for us to explore. And those questions, in turn, give rise to a wide variety of research methods, a sort of big cross-disciplinary tent, equally comfortable for the linguist, the historian, the anthropologist, and the compositionist, as well as others.

Neal Lerner

In his keynote address at the 2004 Thomas R. Watson Conference, Neal Lerner captured an essential quality of research and scholarship on writing centers. Because writing centers are "complex places," offering both sites of and methods for writing instruction to writers from a range of discourse communities within and beyond educational settings, writing center scholarship calls for an array of research methods. If smaller in scale, writing center studies' "big cross-disciplinary tent" bears a striking resemblance to the heterogeneity of composition studies ("Seeking" 55). Recent writing center scholars have addressed, for example, history (Boquet, "'Our'"; Lerner, *Idea*), basic writing (Bawarshi and Pelkowski), second language writers (Williams and Severino, *Second*), WAC (Mullin), writing program administration (Ianetta et al.), assessment (Lerner, "Writing"), technology (Neaderhiser and Wolfe), new media (McKinney), and mentoring graduate assistants (Rowan). As a result, this chapter intersects with a number of other chapters in this volume.

Unlike composition studies, however, writing center scholarship gained prominence only recently, around the turn of the twenty-first century. But this is not to say that there was an absence of scholarship beforehand. The late 1970s and early 1980s saw the founding of the field's two major periodicals—the *Writing Lab Newsletter* and the

Writing Center Journal—soon followed by national (now international) organizations, conferences, and a scholarly press, and paralleled by a steadily increasing stream of dissertations and master's theses (Lerner, "Introduction"). Yet when writing center scholars cast their gaze across the field in the late 1990s, many seemed disappointed. In a 1997 National Writing Centers Association conference keynote, Christina Murphy infamously derided the "absolute bankruptcy of writing center scholarship" (qtd. in Gillam, "Call" 3). Three years later, writing for the twentieth-anniversary issue of the *Writing Center Journal*, Joyce Kinkead and Jeannette Harris were at best guardedly optimistic: "At this point in their history, writing centers have not realized their potential as sites of research" (23).

Just a year later, the scene changed dramatically. In a 2001 *College English* review of several writing center titles, Jeannette Harris seemed to breathe a sigh of relief when she declared that "for a while it looked as if the term *writing center scholarship* might be an oxymoron" (662). The most tangible indication that scholarship in this field was no longer a contradiction in terms was the publication, in 1999, 2000, and 2002, of three single-authored books on or closely related to writing centers: Nancy Maloney Grimm's *Good Intentions: Writing Center Work for Postmodern Times* (which emerged as the most influential of the books Harris reviewed), Cindy Johanek's *Composing Research: A Contextualist Paradigm for Rhetoric and Composition* (which, like Grimm's *Good Intentions*, won the National Writing Center Association's Outstanding Scholarship Award), and Elizabeth Boquet's important contribution *Noise from the Writing Center*. Like composition studies, the writing center field is not one that overprivileges books, but as a coin of the academic realm, books can go a long way toward legitimizing a marginalized field, not least because they are expansive enough to provide an overview and critique of previous research and scholarship—and therefore to establish that there *is* a field to view and critique. Following quickly on the heels of these publications were two edited collections that made similar claims for the field's legitimacy: *Writing Center Research: Extending the Conversation* (Gillespie et al.) and *The Center Will Hold: Critical Perspectives on Writing Center Scholarship* (Pemberton and Kinkead). Likewise, the number of theses and dissertations produced after 2000 showed "remarkable growth," exceeding the number of those from all previous decades combined (Lerner, "Introduction" 6). Summing up the current state of the field, Melissa Nicolas finds that "writing center scholarship is on the cusp of a new generation." What is needed, as a result, is reflection on "our lore and scholarship" since the direction of this "second generation will be in response to the foundation that has been laid during the past two-and-a-half decades" ("Why" 4).

As part of such reflection, this chapter examines examples of the three methodological approaches that undergird most writing center scholarship and, indeed, most scholarship in composition studies: historical, theoretical, and empirical inquiry. One way to consider the differences between such divergent modes of inquiry is in terms of the kinds of questions they ask (see Johanek 27). As Robert Connors suggests, historical inquiry asks about what happened, where we come from, and how we got where we are now ("Octalog" 17, 31). Theoretical inquiry, by contrast, asks about the position from which we view such data: What enables us to see what we see? Empirical inquiry, both qualitative and quantitative, asks, What do we know, and why does what we know matter? Though posing different questions, these methods are each usually used in writing center studies to test assumptions—whether to prove them right or to challenge them. Moreover, in practice, there is a great deal of overlap and dialogue between these forms of inquiry and between the scholars who engage in them. These categories make up, therefore, not binding distinctions but a provisional heuristic for mapping out the emerging contours of writing center scholarship. (For a more detailed categorization, see Sarah Liggett, Kerri Jordan, and Steve Price's useful "Mapping Knowledge-Making in Writing Center Research: A Taxonomy of Methodologies.")

I begin with historical inquiry primarily because doing so will introduce writing centers to readers who are just learning about them; for the same reason, my approach throughout the chapter is historical. Next, I turn to theory, which has been crucial to the field because it helped writing center studies to engage in conversation with the diverse enterprises of composition studies. Then I move on to the use of empirical methods. Though quantitative methods in particular fell out of favor in the 1980s and '90s, recent years have shown a renewed interest in numerically and statistically based writing center research. Using these methods, scholars have tested the assumption that writing centers themselves have a relatively brief history, especially when compared to that of composition instruction; that they emerged and remain distinct from classroom writing instruction but are nonetheless supplemental to it; that they uniformly deliver "remedial" instruction in order to assimilate marginal or marginalized students into the mainstream of institutional literacy practices; that the usually undergraduate and therefore apparently unskilled staff must be equally regulated, their relationship with student writers hands off and "nondirective" in order to maintain the writers' autonomy and responsibility, regardless of the students' preference or linguistic, cultural, or educational background. As scholarship in the field continues to show, writing centers are much more long-lived, dynamic, and intellectually rigorous and creative sites than such assumptions suggest and as such make excellent sites for research. Finally, I address three prominent areas of conflict in the field: between the assumption that, on the one hand, writing centers are primarily localized phenomena or, on the other, that they are generalizable; around assessment methods and the values they express; and between writing centers and composition as sites of instruction and scholarship. Such conflicts, in fact, signify the health of writing center studies and point out directions that new twenty-first-century scholars might pursue.

HISTORICAL INQUIRY

At the turn of the twenty-first century, historical research on writing centers rose to national attention with the publication of Elizabeth Boquet's "'Our Little Secret': A History of Writing Centers, Pre- to Post-Open Admissions." Along with winning an NWCA Outstanding Scholarship Award, this article "signal[ed] a wider recognition of the importance of writing centers (and the study of writing center work)," as Rebecca Jackson, Carrie Leverenz, and Joe Law point out, because, unlike earlier writing center histories, it appeared in the commemorative issue of *College Composition and Communication* that marked the CCCC's fiftieth anniversary (131–32). Representing some of the newest research on writing centers, this historical turn is indicative of the particular moment in the field—"the cusp of a new generation"—that Nicolas gestures to, when the scholarship is in a position to reflect on its past and to formulate the research agendas of the future.

An outcome of such reflection is that the history of writing centers has been, as Alice Gillam asserts in her introduction to *Writing Center Research*, "revised and challenged" (xxiv). Before this revision, a commonplace view of the contemporary writing center was that it was born of the unrest and democratic spirit of the late 1960s and early 1970s, and particularly the open admissions movement on college campuses across the U.S. (Carino, "Open" 31–35). In this view, prior developments were seen as either not relevant to writing center origins or as "a dark past in contrast to an enlightened present" (Lerner, *Idea* 16). In the mid-1990s, one of the first historians in the field, Peter Carino, investigated the early history of writing centers and found not only that they took root well before open admissions ("Open" 33) but also that "this history is not a neat march of progress from current-traditional gradgrindianism to theoretically sophisticated nurture. Early centers . . . were a much more variegated and complex phenomenon than has been represented in writing center discourse" ("Early" 104).

Boquet's study of twentieth-century writing center literature builds on Carino's view of this history as "variegated and complex." In one noteworthy instance of the intersection of theory and historiography, she writes, "The history of the writing center is . . . best told as a history whose intentions are cross-cut by Foucauldian accidents, by unanticipated outcomes" ("'Our'" 479). Her key example focuses on the way writing centers moved from "method" to "site," which, rather than "a neat march of progress," resulted in both advantages and disadvantages. The writing center as "site," for instance, is "sacrosanct, as distinct from the classroom," and a place of "counter-hegemonic work" *as well as* a position in the academic hierarchy, a space where students and their problems can be "sent" (470, 467, 469).

Lerner's extensive archival research also builds on Carino's work, but takes a different tack from Boquet's, attending less to the development of writing centers than to their beginnings. His *The Idea of a Writing Laboratory*, 2011 recipient of NCTE's David H. Russell Research Award, follows up on Carino's speculation "that centers evolved from a classroom format known as the laboratory method" ("Early" 105) and traces these beginnings further back than does Carino, as simultaneous with the emergence of first-year composition in the late nineteenth century. There are at least two important implications of Lerner's findings: first, that the method of instruction that would develop into what we now know as writing center tutoring emerged within and alongside classroom-based writing instruction; and second, that these origins deserve to be recuperated because they have much to teach us still. In his words, "[T]he loss of the writing laboratory is a loss of possibility, a loss of the very heart of the writing center's past" (*Idea* 2).

If the 1970s did not mark the origins of writing centers themselves, they nonetheless laid the groundwork for much writing center scholarship and professionalization. Indeed, so dramatic was this growth that

Lerner suggests that it might have caused the field's "historical amnesia" about writing center origins (*Idea* 16). The most influential writing center scholarship to result from this early professional activity was Kenneth A. Bruffee's work on collaborative learning and peer tutoring (most notably in his two "'Conversation of Mankind'" articles) and Stephen M. North's "The Idea of a Writing Center." Bruffee's contributions have proved foundational to much current thinking about peer tutoring (Kail), but it is North's article that has continued to have the greatest impact on how writing center studies understands itself. According to Boquet and Lerner's coauthored reception study, North's "Idea" in fact "limited" the development of the field largely because it became "lore-ified,"—used repeatedly as "a handy collection of statements about writing center identity and ethos, always at the ready to support writing center workers but with little explanatory power" (172, 183). Boquet and Lerner's critique of North, a project unthinkable just a decade ago, is only one sign that the field has gained perspective on its own project through analysis of its history. Another is the Writing Centers Research Project's Materials Archive and Oral History Archive, currently housed at the University of Arkansas at Little Rock. This archive includes collections "of spoken memories and written records—to preserve writing center history and facilitate scholars' research" as well as "oral interviews with historically significant writing center professionals" ("Materials Archive"; "Oral History Archive").

THEORETICAL INQUIRY

Theory seeks to answer a different set of questions from historical studies of writing centers, questions concerned primarily with how we see or understand what it is we are examining. Where historical method cannot, as Connors noted, tell us what to do next ("Octalog" 23), theory, especially as it is linked to practice, can and often does. Nonetheless, theory and history are not mutually exclusive in writing center studies. Both are used to challenge assumptions, and theory often draws on history and vice versa—as evidenced, for example, by Boquet's use of the historically focused theories of Michel Foucault. Following the foundational work of early '80s scholars such as Bruffee and North, theory was also the crucial next phase in writing center scholarship. By the mid-1990s, Carino found that "theory beckon[ed] as a means of establishing disciplinary and institutional respectability" for a field that was, at that point, "not recognized as a discipline" ("Theorizing" 125). While the vast majority of these theoretical applications took place in articles, I am focusing here on the common concerns of three books—Grimm's *Good Intentions*, Boquet's *Noise*, and *The Everyday Writing Center* by Anne Ellen Geller, Michele Eodice, Frankie Condon, Meg Carroll, and Boquet. Each has proven deeply influential to this area of writing center studies, in part because *as* books they are expansive enough to explore the territory fully as well as sum up and critique previous thinking. (For a more recent theoretically informed monograph, see Harry C. Denny's *Facing the Center: Toward an Identity Politics of One-to-One Mentoring*, published too recently for consideration here.)

One of the most important of the common concerns of these books is the use of theory to enrich practice. Such a view is hardly unique. Carino, for instance, called for

> the writing center community . . . to see theory and practice in a multivocal dialogue, with theory providing a means of investigating practice, practice serving as a check against theoretical reification, and both proceeding with an awareness of the political context in which writing centers function collectively as a professional community and individually in institutional contexts. ("Theorizing" 136)

Subsequent scholars answered this call, often through the use of personal narrative "intertwined with theory" (Briggs and Woolbright xii). Though collectively distancing themselves from individualized personal stories, Geller et al. nonetheless describe their method of writing *The Everyday Writing Center* (subtitled *A Community of Practice*) as "theoretical explorations woven into descriptions of life on the ground in the writing center" (9) and advocate "an almost invisible weaving of practice and theory" as "a way of looking at learning and leadership" (48).

Yet Grimm's, Boquet's, and Geller et al.'s books share the more specific concerns of challenging assumptions about writing centers. Rather than relatively straightforward, administratively efficient, and institutionally complacent entities, writing centers for these scholars represent a myriad of richly interconnected complexities, gaps, and conflicts. Specifically, Grimm, Boquet, and Geller et al. reconceptualize writing centers' relations to their institutional settings, reconsider the identities of the writers they serve, and reformulate the roles and educations of tutors—all of which, they believe, should ultimately aim toward changing institutions.

Though employing different postmodernist theories, Grimm and Boquet, for example, offer institutional critiques that hold writing centers and writing center workers accountable. Drawing on the work of, among others, Brian Street and the New London Group, Grimm points to the complicity of writing centers in unfair educational literacy practices, particularly when these centers do the institution's dirty work of regulating nonstandard student populations. Rather than helping individual writers, our well-intentioned attempts instead manage to pin the blame on them. Using the metaphor of noise as a means of orchestrating a range of postmodern theories, Boquet echoes many of Grimm's concerns, "refusing an identity construction that merely positions the center as a reduplication of the sound of the academy" (*Noise* 141–42). Such refusal in turn requires a deeper understanding of not only the institutional setting but also everything involved with being a writer in a writing center. Grimm picks up on a key issue for a number of writing center theorists when she critiques the ideals of "nondirective" tutoring, which hold writers solely responsible for their literacy practices, directs tutors to be strictly hands off, and makes any breach of this boundary an ethical issue. Such ideals enact what Grimm, borrowing from Street, refers to as the autonomous model of literacy (*Good* 30) and link to a rich vein of writing center scholarship that similarly calls into question the feasibility of such hygienic interactions (Clark and Healy; Clark; Shamoon and Burns, "Critique" and "Plagiarism").

For most of these theorists, the best, most powerful, and, indeed, only way to execute this reimagined vision of institutional relationships, writing centers, and writers is through the preparation of what Geller et al. call "the heart of the writing center"—"the tutors as learners and writers" who staff these centers (13). Such preparation is decidedly *not* "training" (59), nor even "education" in any normative or familiarly curricular sense (Grimm *Good* 120, Boquet *Noise* 78). It is rather what Boquet has famously called "a higher-risk/higher-yield model for writing center work" (*Noise* 80). Geller et al. suggest that such risks might include the apparent ethical breach of "consciously decid[ing] to go too far" in a tutoring session (27); other theorist-practitioners seem to embrace this model when they explore moments of coauthoring between tutors and writers (Carrick) or tutor subversions of such institutional regulators as Turnitin.com (Brown et al.). The high yield of such moves includes tutor learning, research, and knowledge production, as evidenced, for instance, by the fact that Brown et al. were peer tutors (and most of them undergraduates) when they wrote their response to Turnitin.com, which was subsequently published in the *Writing Center*

Journal and won the International (formerly National) Writing Centers Association Outstanding Scholarship Award.

Most important of all, these scholars suggest, is that by transforming our views about and practices regarding writing centers, writers, and tutors, we might in turn be able to transform our institutions. Such transformation might occur through peaceable means, with directors positioning themselves as "change-agents" (Geller et al. 90) or by "theoretically integrat[ing] their work into the teaching and research mission of higher education" (Grimm, *Good* 83). Or such change might occur as what Boquet calls the "monstrous" consequence of the necessarily radical work of writing centers: by "*bastardizing* the work of the institution," posing "a threat from within," and "amplify[ing]" rather than "contain[ing]" student demand, writing centers might well become places "powerful enough to allow for the mutation and potential reorganization of our system of education" (*Noise* 32, 67, 51).

EMPIRICAL RESEARCH

As in composition studies, empirical research in writing center studies describes a wide range of methodologies, serving as it does as an umbrella term for both the qualitative and quantitative. Qualitative approaches to writing center studies have often proved to mesh the best with other forms of scholarship in the field, for instance in theoretically informed case studies and ethnographies (Gillam, introduction xxii). Though writing center historians have drawn on quantitative methods (Lerner, "Seeking"; Boquet and Lerner), such methods have also provided the starkest contrast with these other forms of writing center scholarship, primarily because they are not easily aligned with the humanities perspectives that deeply inform this work. Yet like historical and theoretical studies on writing center work, both qualitative and quantitative methods are similarly used to test assumptions—about, for example, the function of talk in writing center sessions, about nondirective ideals for all writers, and about the preconception that writing center scholarship is primarily humanities centered.

A qualitative method that has steadily gained ground over the last fifteen years is discourse analysis, which often draws upon sociocultural and sociolinguistic theories (including by Goffman, among others) (Robert Brown; Susan Murphy; Bell and Youmans). Discourse analysis has proven to be a useful means of testing the assumptions of the foundational scholarship of Bruffee and North regarding the central importance of "conversation" and "talk" in writing center tutorials (Blau, Hall, and Strauss 20–21; Thonus 228; see Susan Murphy 64; and Robert Brown 73). Because of the insights it can offer into language and culture, discourse analysis is also an especially productive method for examining how writing centers can best serve second language writers, helping to fill out otherwise slim offerings of research in this area. In their special issue on *Second Language Writers in the Writing Center* for the *Journal of Second Language Writing*, Jessica Williams and Carol Severino report that much of this research concerns the ways in which "the interactional structure of sessions with L2 writers" contrasts with those of native speakers and indicates "the need to strike a balance between providing L2 writers with the information and guidance they sorely need and the broadly accepted WC philosophy that writers should take and maintain ownership of their own texts" (167; see Blau, Hall, and Sparks; Bell and Youmans; Cogie). Williams and Severino suggest that future empirical research in this area might include "case studies as well as survey research of L2 writers' perceptions of and level of satisfaction with their tutors' strategies" (170; for an example of such a case study, see Severino and Deifell).

There is a twenty-year tradition of quantitative research in writing center scholarship (Thompson et al. 79). Yet, as Gillam points out, this tradition took a backseat to other research methods when "the research paradigm in composition studies shifted in the mid-1980s from one that favored social science research to one that favored critical, theoretical scholarship" ("Call," 18). By the turn of the century, however, as Gillam notes, empiricism was "finding new advocates," notably with the publication of Johanek's *Composing Research* (introduction xxvi). Johanek's book was important to this renewed interest not only because she clearly explained quantitative methods and often applied them to writing center examples, but also because she delved into the very question of methodological choice: rather than choosing methods first—especially when this choice is based on the apparent, and often unfounded, conflicts between the sciences and the humanities—the problem, the question we wish to answer about it, and the context of both should come first and they should determine the method (or methods) we use (1–2).

In part because of Johanek's work, Linda Bergmann suggests that the writing center field is in a "state of transition" from humanities- to social science–based research models. Unlike twentieth-century writing center directors, who "tended to be untrained in and suspicious of quantitative research and used case studies and anecdotal evidence to support the things we learned," graduate students in twenty-first-century rhetoric and composition programs

> are asking how accepted ideas and practices can be tested by empirical research, both qualitative and quantitative, with clear and repeatable methodologies and falsifiable hypotheses. Inspired by works like . . . *Composing Research*, they are questioning received lore and "what everyone has always believed." (Ianetta et al. 31, 33)

Further evidence of this transition is the 2009 publication of the *Writing Center Journal*'s first all-empirical issue (29.1). As coeditor of *WCJ* at the time, I can attest that these articles appeared together as a result of the authors' timing rather than editorial solicitations. They also stand as strong examples of trends in writing center empirical research. For example, to determine the state of online writing center operations, Stephen Neaderhiser and Joanna Wolfe draw on the most comprehensive "resource for researchers working on projects related to writing center administration" (59) and an important quantitative development in its own right, the Writing Centers Research Project biennial survey (initiated around 2000 with so much else), which gathers benchmark data from hundreds of participants about how writing centers operate and are administered. And like most writing center scholarship, these articles test assumptions. Karen Rowen, for instance, challenges beliefs about mentorship in the writing center community by analyzing surveys of and interviews with writing center graduate student administrators and directors. (This article, "All the Best Intentions," is especially useful as a model because Rowan reflects on her methodological choices, including her decision to mix research methods.) Likewise, by analyzing three years of data collected through online tutoring requests, Carol Severino, Jeffrey Swenson, and Jia Zhu correct the misperception that nonnative speakers of English tend to focus their feedback requests on grammar. Interestingly, the article in this issue that most forcefully takes up Johanek's (and Bergmann's students') call for the quantitative over the anecdotal—Isabelle Thompson et al.'s analysis of tutor and writer satisfaction surveys about more than four thousand conferences—also points out how interrelated the concerns of both empiricists and theoreticians can be. Reflecting Grimm's challenge to the nondirective ideal, these authors conclude, based on their research, that the usual prohibitions against tutor directiveness and expertise are unsupported.

CONFLICTS AND CONTROVERSIES

All fields have their points of disagreement and dissent. Such debates are a sign of healthy intellectual engagement and, as a result, can be potentially rich sites of research. Three prominent areas of conflict emerge from the scholarship I've described and therefore concern the nature of research and methods in writing center studies. The first focuses on the conflict between valuing the local or the general and has multiple implications, including the second conflict, which concerns the nature of such local research as it is conducted through writing center assessment. The third, and most important for the position of writing center studies as a whole, is the apparent conflict between writing centers and composition, both as sites/methods and as fields.

Two poles that the writing center field is often pulled between are, on the one hand, what Carino has called "the contextual ideology," valuing the individual characteristics and local contexts that make each writing center unique, and, on the other, "the communal ideology," valuing larger claims based on generalizations that hold true across multiple writing centers. The former has a long tradition in writing center studies and is one Carino himself favors, "for it respects the diverse obstacles individual centers face" ("Writing Centers" 10–11). The latter is supported both by the theorists I cite above and quantitative researchers seeking large-scale, reproducible results. Geller et al., for instance, declare that they "actively worked against the meme of the highly contextualized, 'localized' writing center" as they looked "for common projects that offered some potential for generalizability across writing centers" (1). In a study based on data from the Writing Centers Research Project Survey, Griffin et al. similarly argue, "Although writing center literature valorizes centers' local identities, we also need to recognize the value inherent in being part of a national body" (5). This conflict plays out across the field in a number of ways, including through the pervasive divide between theory and practice—Grimm, for example, applies theory "in order to extend decisions about practice beyond consideration of the local context" (*Good* xv). But perhaps more relevant for our purposes, it speaks to conflicting definitions writing center research. Muriel Harris compellingly argues for the value of "local, institutional knowledge," or

> that type of research being done year after year, semester after semester, as part of a writing center administrator's work. It is the localized, contextualized

inquiry in which a director studies aspects of his or her own center and institution as part of the process of shaping the writing center. To a degree even greater than is the case with composition programs, writing centers are—and must be—shaped to fit their particularized surroundings. ("Writing" 76)

Echoing Griffin et al.'s appeal to "the benefits of the national perspective" (6), Melissa Ianetta, by contrast, argues that such a focus has serious implications for the growth of the field *as* a field: "[I]f each center is uniquely shaped by its context, as the common argument goes, what kinds of research can speak across these myriad locations, moving beyond . . . the 'this-is-what-we-do-at-my-writing-center' genre?" (37).

This tension between local and national (or, increasingly, international) research in writing center studies is one that is not easily resolved. As Harris points out, a fact on the ground for writing center directors is that in order to justify continued funding, they must conduct such local research—that is, assessment—because there are usually no institutional mechanisms in place to gather information about writing center students and services in the ways that there typically are for other forms of campus writing instruction. But the nature of this assessment research—including not only how we gather data but what we choose to study in the first place, how we understand that choice, the questions we ask to guide our study, and the rhetorical effects of our findings— is also a source of controversy. Summing up a tradition that holds that the audiences of such research demand certain kinds of methods and results, Harris writes, "Quantitative data are simply more convincing to most administrators than qualitative results, and so, writing center directors . . . seek methodologies that produce quantitative data" ("Diverse" 8, see Johanek 59). The theorists I discuss above, however, disagree. For Grimm, "statistical evidence . . . doesn't take me into discussions that convey the intellectual work of the writing center" (*Good* 7). As she explains in a later essay, such quantifiable results as "grade analysis, retention data, counts of student visits, and surveys of student satisfaction do not shift writing centers from narrowly defined service units to a more broadly defined research mission" ("In" 46). Boquet worries about "what happens when we fetishize the numbers": "I fear, sometimes, that we are too willing to give our institutions *what we think they want*, whether or not it is what *we want* or, ultimately, even what *they want*" (*Noise* 43, 41). Geller et al. are similarly "troubled by the assimilationist idea of this approach" (116); annual reports should focus on "the things we want our institutions and our professions to value" (121).

This question of the aims and audience of writing center research is also apparent beyond local situations, in the most vexing conflict in writing center studies, the field's relationship to composition studies. Writing center scholars have long felt—and have the evidence to show—that composition studies has not valued their research. Lil Brannon and Stephen North, founding editors of the *Writing Center Journal*, and Boquet and Lerner, former *WCJ* editors who markedly strengthened the journal's scholarly standing at the beginning of the twenty-first century, have been probably best situated to see that the relationship of writing center studies to composition studies was (and is) less than reciprocal. As they point out, whereas *WCJ* articles typically cite publications in composition and rhetoric, articles in composition journals seldom draw on writing center research (Brannon and North 9; Boquet and Lerner 180–81). However, as Gillam suggests, such imbalance might well be at least partly the result of writing center scholars' own "inflated claims of difference" between writing centers and writing classrooms (Gillam, "Call" 18; see Boquet and Lerner 171, 174–75). Gillam goes on to suggest that the situation has been further complicated by the "mixed message" that writing center scholars have "sent . . . about the aims and audience for writing center research" by, "on the one hand, declaring independence from the composition community through research that would prove the distinctiveness of our work and, on the other hand, claiming full membership through research that the composition community would recognize as worthy" ("Call" 18).

DIRECTIONS FOR TWENTY-FIRST-CENTURY WRITING CENTER STUDIES

This is an exciting time to contribute research to writing center studies. Under this "big cross-disciplinary tent," there is a great variety of assumptions to test and conflicts to explore with an ever-wider array of methods. Questions that arise from the (as of this writing) current controversies of the field suggest some possible directions for future research. For instance, How "inflated" are the "claims of difference" between writing centers, composition, and other writing programs? Lerner suggests a qualitative study that addresses the ways that any "session is nested within layers of participants' actions, intentions, and understandings" by recording the session, interviewing all participants—writer, tutor, teacher, and director—and analyzing the student's text ("Seeking" 74–75), but this question might easily be answered through a historical analysis or through a theoretical lens (or both), not to mention other kinds of empirical studies. Another pressing question that emerges from current writing center controversies is, How we can develop methods of assessment that enact and convey writing center values? Lerner urges us to look for a greater variety of research methods, goals, and audiences, for example, by exploring "the benefits that tutors . . . draw from their work" ("Writing" 61, 71). Additionally, can there be cross-institutional research that attends to local concerns as well as produces knowledge relevant on a national scale? Answering both of these questions is the IWCA Outstanding Scholarship Award–winning Peer Tutor Alumni Research Project, which surveys former tutors from universities across the U.S. about the benefits of their work (Hughes, Gillespie, and Kail) and models what a new mode of assessment through cross-institutional research might look like.

But since writing center studies is a field constantly—and increasingly—on the move, you will find that most of the new directions for research are ones I don't, and couldn't, address here. (Indeed, by the time you read this, writing center studies will already be different, perhaps dramatically so, from what it was when I wrote this chapter!) To find your own direction, look for the current assumptions and controversies in your center, among your colleagues, and in professional conversations, and also look for the gaps in the knowledge circulating in these contexts. Once you have found your exigence, read widely in the scholarship about your topic with an aim of entering the conversation and moving this conversation forward. What questions have yet to be asked, much less answered? What are the best methods for answering them? Who would benefit from these answers? Why?

And look to the profession itself. The writing center community does a remarkably—and at the risk of resegregating the field, I would say uniquely—good job of providing students with pathways into the profession. First of all, writing centers are oriented toward students not only by serving them but, as the Peer Tutor Alumni Research Project makes clear, also by employing and educating them. It is true that many of these students are undergraduates, and at least since Bruffee, the field has enthusiastically supported this peer-to-peer emphasis. Recently, however, attention has been devoted to the special place of graduate student tutors and administrators in writing centers, for instance, with the International Writing Centers Association "Graduate Student Position Statement" (Eckerle, Rowan, and Watson), Rowan's study of graduate student administrators, and a recent collection on graduate students in the writing center, *(E)Merging Identities* (Nicolas). And there has been long-standing support of graduate student writing center research, evidenced both by Lerner's list of master's theses and dissertations ("Introduction") and by the IWCA Graduate Research Grant (information about which is available on the IWCA website or in the back pages of the *Writing Center Journal*). Because of the nature of writing center work, scholars and practitioners alike in this field are deeply committed to demystifying academic literacy practices, including those in writing center studies. (See, for example, Boquet's ["Disciplinary"] and Lerner's ["Situated"] reflections on researching their writing center–focused dissertations and DeCiccio et al.'s discussion of publishing in the field.) Such demystification can make a new researcher's entrance into the field both easier and even more exciting.

5
WAC'S DISAPPEARING ACT

Rita Malenczyk

In their contribution to this volume, "Creation Myths and Flash Points," Linda Adler-Kassner and Susanmarie Harrington invite us to view the field of basic writing through the conflicting narratives of its history. In this chapter, I similarly recount the narrative of writing across the curriculum (WAC). I argue that instead of conflicting stories, however, what WAC presents us with is essentially one master narrative, one of revelation, community building, and continued conversion. In a perfect storm–like convergence of forces spanning the last three decades (the emergence of composition as a field, the National Writing Project, the federal government), English teachers interested in writing met each other, spread the gospel of WAC to their faculty, and started programs that, taken together, became a curricular movement—one that was successful largely because it appealed to the interests of faculty and the concerns of administrators alike. These shared interests, and the willingness of WPAs to build on them, transformed the way writing programs are institutionalized on campuses. Many colleges and universities now have some version of a writing-in-the disciplines program, with writing not confined solely to the first-year composition course but seen, rather, as the shared responsibility of faculty in all departments, at all levels.[1]

I argue here, however, that we may be reaching the end of that story as WAC begins to look in various ways at its disappearance, a disappearance actually predicted by one of WAC's founders, Barbara Walvoord, in 1996 and by another WAC pioneer, Susan McLeod, shortly thereafter. On the twenty-fifth anniversary of WAC,[2] Walvoord speculated in the

---

1.   It could be argued that the WPA Outcomes Statement for First-Year Composition takes the presence of WAC on most campuses for granted: see <http://wpacouncil.org/positions/outcomes.html>.

2.   It is a truth universally acknowledged that what we think of today as WAC began at Central College in Pella, Iowa, when Walvoord faced a scheduling conundrum. See McLeod, "The Future."

pages of *College English* on what the future of the movement might be; she suggested—in an argument that seems eerily prescient sixteen years later—that, without careful and consistent attention to the changing landscapes of academia, WAC was in danger of dying. WAC, she said, had to find ways of surviving within new realities, as colleges and universities (as they are wont to do) shifted their priorities:

> WAC must decide how to relate to other movement organizations. It cannot ignore them, and on most campuses, I believe, WAC cannot survive as Switzerland; it simply does not have the funding base, the powerful national engines, the "new" look that will attract funding, or the ability to retain followers to itself alone. . . .Those followers themselves often want to, and must, combine WAC with assessment, critical thinking, and other movements. WAC, I believe, must dive in or die. ("The Future of WAC" 69–70)

A year after Walvoord's essay appeared, McLeod reiterated some of her points, but with more trepidation, referring pointedly to an incontrovertible fact of academic life—the need for departmental identification:

> [T]here are two clouds I see on the horizon with regard to the future of WAC programs, both of which are danger signs in terms of program survival. The first has to do with the way many WAC programs are structured. Because they are by definition cross-curricular, such programs do not fit into a recognizable academic compartment . . . they are often located, administratively and physically, outside the usual departmental structures. . . . Any program that lies outside the hierarchical structure of the academy or that goes against the usual way of doing business is always in danger of being absorbed into a more recognizable structure. ("WAC" 68)

I propose that what Walvoord and McLeod predicted is, in fact, coming true, but with a twist: that despite WAC's "followers" having done what Walvoord suggested they do, i.e., "combine WAC . . . with other movements," nevertheless WAC, if not dying, is gradually being subsumed or dispersed into other disciplines or programmatic structures, and therefore being transformed into something other than what it was before, something perhaps less obviously about writing alone (what that "something" is remains to be seen). I submit, however, that this transformation does not equal death, and that far from being a sign of the movement's failure—as McLeod, in her essay, seems to fear—it is rather a logical outgrowth of WAC's success, more like a reincarnation than a final ending. Like reincarnation, I argue, it is something to be celebrated, as former WAC leaders gain greater—if perhaps different—institutional power; as WAC principles become something faculty take for granted as part and parcel of good practice; as students come to see writing as something that will and should be done anywhere, in any class.

In this chapter, after briefly summarizing the early part of the WAC narrative, which shows how at one time WAC had the status of Hot Educational Trend now enjoyed by, for example, first-year experience programs, I fast-forward into the present. Using three areas studied by WAC scholars—programmatic structure, curriculum, and faculty development—I demonstrate how WAC has been, or is in the process of being, dispersed into other structures and disciplines, many of them covered in this volume. Over time, it appears that the work of WAC administrators, faculty, and scholars has come to overlap with, or has moved into, other areas, calling into question not only the status of WAC as a separate entity but also the definitions of other concepts. This is not necessarily a bad thing, but rather the kind of healthy questioning that should go on in any discipline, particularly one concerned primarily with program development. If, for example, we argue that it is possible to write "beyond" the curriculum, then what is the curriculum, anyway? What is the college (or university)? What is a WPA? What is writing?

BEGINNINGS

When contemporary composition scholars speak of WAC, or writing across the curriculum, they refer to the educational trend that took hold in the late 1970s as an outgrowth of two seemingly opposing forces: first, the writing process movement, and second, administrative pressures on WPAs (often English department faculty trained in literature) to respond to the so-called literacy crisis depicted in the 1975 *Newsweek* article "Why Johnny Can't Write" (Maimon 19). The importance of the latter is, perhaps ironically, difficult to overstate. Just as funding is now—or has recently been—channeled into first-year experience programs and retention initiatives, in the mid- to late 1970s funding was directed at WAC, to solve a "literacy problem" created by the media. Though few college administrators, legislators, or political leaders appreciated the complexities of what it actually means to learn to write (hence the cries of "Back to basics!" that followed Johnny down the halls), the pseudo-crisis spawned in part by this article enabled any number of WAC leaders to develop their programs and do research, as federal grant money for writing initiatives suddenly became available.

And with this money came revelation. Elaine Maimon, a pioneer in the WAC movement, has described her experience as the new director of composition at Beaver College:

> The new dean (whose tenure lasted only one year) summoned me to his office and threw the magazine [i.e., *Newsweek*] at me. "What are you going to do about this?" he demanded. At the end of that month, at the MLA (Modern Language Association) meeting in San Francisco, I found the answer. (19)

Thrown back on her own intellectual resources for "the answer," Maimon proposed (and had accepted) an MLA paper on the teaching of writing; found, at a conference dominated by literary scholars, a few like-minded colleagues who were looking for the same kinds of answers about how to handle the new administrative demands; and, with some of them, attended Mina Shaughnessy's now-well-known talk "Diving In," which called for interested parties to contribute to a new field: composition.[3] A fortuitous encounter on a cable car with Harriet Sheridan, then dean of Carleton College, turned into a working lunch during which ideas for curriculum development in writing were shared. As a result of this meeting, Maimon, her faculty colleagues, and college administrators went on to start a WAC program at Beaver, applying for and receiving an NEH grant to help fund the program (20–25).

Similar stories of making alliances and getting funding for new WAC initiatives are related in what might be the best treatment to date of the early part of WAC's history, Susan McLeod and Margot Soven's 2006 collection *Composing a Community*. In this book, authors (including Maimon) who built WAC programs at a range of institutions, from small liberal arts colleges to Ivy League universities to state university systems, discuss their work in generating those programs. Toby Fulwiler and Art Young, for example, describe how they led faculty workshops

---

3.   Though Shaughnessy's name is associated primarily with basic writing, Maimon makes it quite clear that she and her soon-to-be-colleagues experienced "Diving In" as transformative for the field of English studies in general, especially given its venue. Maimon: "It was highly unusual for the MLA to devote a ballroom to a forum on the teaching of writing. Never before or since, at least in my MLA experience, was there a greater buzz in a ballroom. Shaughnessy . . . challenged the standing-room-only crowd to react against conservative academics who saw the teaching of writing as a matter of 'guarding the gates' or 'converting the natives'. Shaughnessy urged us to dive into a new scholarly field—a field that we could help create" (20).

and negotiated departmental politics at Michigan Tech; Christopher Thaiss of George Mason University discusses building a partnership with the nascent Northern Virginia Writing Project, including middle and high school teachers in GMU's WAC faculty development program; and Charles Bazerman, in an article coauthored with Anne Herrington, describes his growing interest in disciplinary genres while teaching at CUNY and attending WAC events throughout the country.

In responding to the "literacy crisis," why did these faculty choose to develop WAC programs and not, say, instead give increased attention to first-year composition? Why did they view the "crisis," in other words, as diffused across the curriculum and not concentrated solely at the first-year level, where it had historically resided (at least in the public's view)? The answer is that as composition began to develop a body of knowledge about how writers learn, the first-year course alone came to be seen as insufficient. As David Russell points out, "WAC's growth coincided with—and in many ways helped create and shape—the professionalization of composition as a field." WAC programs addressed the newly discovered fact that the choices writers make depend on rhetorical (and disciplinary) context, something not genuinely available within the confines of a first-year writing course. Furthermore, as Russell notes, "research began on what writing in the disciplines is really like, how, for example, the humble and ubiquitous 'research paper' takes many forms and has many functions across the curriculum, reflecting the methods, values, and epistemology of the discipline" ("Introduction" 8). In addition to discovering the complexities of audience and rhetorical situation, compositionists also acknowledged that the teaching strategies developed in National Writing Project workshops could be used in any number of situations, including content-based courses.[4]

Whatever their impetus, the early curriculum development efforts

---

4.   See, in particular, Watson. For more information on the National Writing Project, see its website, www.nwp.org. As the website explains, the NWP began with the Bay Area Writing Project in 1974, brainchild of James Gray at the University of California, Berkeley. Today it consists of over two hundred local and regional writing project sites nationwide, all hosted by colleges and universities. Their purpose is to train and deploy "teacher-consultants" who conduct summer institutes and other faculty development efforts for teachers in elementary, secondary, and postsecondary institutions. As the NWP Core Principles state, "Writing can and should be taught, not just assigned, at every grade level. Professional development programs should provide opportunities for teachers to work together to understand the full spectrum of writing development across grades and across subject areas" (www.nwp.org).

described above eventually became full-fledged programs that have largely been sustained over the last thirty or so years. Due to individual scholarly interests as well as local circumstances, however, not all of these programs have evolved the same way or have developed the same emphasis in their design. Some have focused on helping faculty use writing as a tool for learning, others on helping students understand the disciplinary genres they need to learn in their majors and careers; some are structured around a series of requirements, while others run on the goodwill and camaraderie of the faculty. For example, at the University of Vermont, WAC pioneer Toby Fulwiler sustained—until his fairly recent retirement—a program that was largely based on a core of faculty who participated in WAC workshops several times a year and incorporated writing, in various ways, into their courses; there was no recognizable curriculum and no formal WAC or WID requirement for students (Harrington). In contrast, the University of Missouri's nationally known Campus Writing Program still has a highly formalized structure: students are required to complete a specially designated upper-level writing-intensive course before graduation. Said courses are approved by a Campus Writing Board consisting of faculty from different disciplines and schools across campus. The approval takes place according to a series of guidelines developed by the board: these guidelines specify numbers of pages students should write, requirements for drafting and revision, preferred number of assignments, and class size (*Campus*). These are the two basic models usually replicated—though certainly with some variation, depending on local circumstances—at colleges and universities around the country.[5]

PROGRAMMATIC AND CURRICULAR STRUCTURE; OR, THE FADING "W"

I recount this history, and point up the two prevailing models of WAC still in existence, to make two points. The first is that WAC, though part of composition studies, is yet outside it. While WAC directors are usually (though not always) at least English if not composition faculty, writing-across-the-curriculum programs depend for their existence—as McLeod

---

5.   Writing centers have also helped sustain WAC requirements and faculty development to a greater or lesser degree at a wide range of institutions. At Purdue University, for example, which does not have a centralized series of WAC requirements, the writing center nevertheless supports faculty and departmental efforts to incorporate writing into their courses and curricula (Bergmann). See also Fitzgerald and Stephenson 122–23; and Barnett and Blumner 401–72.

points out—on faculty and departments in other disciplines who deliver the courses in which the writing is taught. WAC programs rely, too, on funding and support from larger administrative entities as well as on the consensus of the academic departments whose faculty are teaching in the program.

The second, and perhaps more significant, point for my argument is that the relative value of these two models has been debated by WAC directors and scholars since the WAC movement began to gain a foothold on campuses; this is in large part because one model retains the "W" while the other does not. Some argue that the establishment of specifically designated writing-intensive courses absolves faculty from the responsibility of incorporating writing into as many of their classes as possible—a responsibility that should in fact be encouraged, since one of the premises of WAC is that more writing is better (see, for example, White, "Re" Writing-Intensive Course Criteria"). Others, however, believe that a writing-intensive course requirement helps maintain faculty investment in writing, assures that writing will in fact be assigned in certain courses, and—most important for the current discussion—helps sustain the visibility of the program. A course that is flagged writing intensive—or "W" or "WI"—retains, obviously, the "W," and thus emphasizes the existence of the WAC program on campus.

However, due to WAC's existence both outside of and within departmental structures, there is a trend toward elimination of the "W," if not of the writing it stands for.[6] Given the fact that any one university

---

6.   It may be stating the obvious to note that the meaning of "writing" itself is continually being questioned within composition studies; such questioning has had even further consequences for WAC. Both writing tutors and teachers have had to take account of two additional developments in the field of writing instruction: the need to compose in digital environments—something one heard relatively little about in the 1970s and 1980s—and the related (and continually growing) scholarly interest in visual rhetoric. On many campuses, such as Clemson University and the University of North Carolina–Greensboro, WAC has therefore become CAC—communication across the curriculum—to account for the role oral and visual, as well as written, communication plays in scholarly writing, and to accommodate new and emerging technologies as well. Donna Reiss, Dickie Selfe, and Art Young addressed this shift in their 1998 collection *Electronic Communication across the Curriculum,* inviting a range of scholars to address the impact of new technologies (and describe their practical response to that impact) on tutoring, writing in the disciplines, peer review. Scholarly investigation into the topic of technology and writing continues, with a special 2009 issue of *Across the Disciplines, Writing Technologies and Writing across the Curriculum: Current Lessons and Future Trends;* this journal issue addresses the concerns that have both arisen and remained since 1998 (and since Reiss et al.'s 2001 addendum to their book; see their "WAC Wired"). As guest editor Karen

can fit only so many requirements into its curriculum, other curricular movements—notably, a widespread national effort toward general education reform—have of necessity bumped up against existing WAC programs and are beginning to change the way WAC is conceptualized, identified, and delivered. A fall 2010 thread on the WPA-L listserv provides evidence of this change. In the thread, entitled "Writing Intensive Course Criteria," one WPA posed a question pertaining to program design, requesting models of writing-intensive course requirements to help her develop a new writing-in-the-disciplines curriculum (Tuten). While some WPAs responded to her request by sharing their criteria, one notable exception was Martha Townsend, for fifteen years director of the highly regarded Missouri program. Townsend shared what she saw to be significant shifts in how WAC is not only delivered but also, for lack of a better word, marked:

> [S]ince general education is constantly being revised everywhere all the time, I simply want to point out that some of the most exciting work going on with WAC/WID now involves *moving away from labeled or flagged courses* and moving toward the [planned] infusion of writing within a whole curriculum (or a large part of one) across a student's entire degree program. It's a tremendous shift that's taking place, and it will be years before this new model becomes dominant, if ever. Lots of practice and experimentation and publication of results need to go on yet. ("Re: Writing," 3 October; emphasis added)

Townsend was joined in this opinion by other WPAs, notably Barbara Bird of Taylor University in Indiana, who in the same thread described a new collaboration between her writing program and Taylor's general education director. Following assessment and student feedback, Taylor University will soon require departments to take more responsibility for judging their students' writing by embedding it within major, not university, requirements:

> Our new program . . . is requiring each department to 1) articulate writing outcomes for their majors; 2) create a curriculum map that indicates where they teach toward those outcomes. This map includes which courses have which types of writing assignments, where they will teach the appropriate

---

Lunsford points out in her introduction, such issues as how online environments impact the composing process (and the definition of "writing") will always be with us, while new concerns—e.g., intellectual property in online environments, computer archiving of materials—have begun to draw scholarly attention.

information literacy for their majors, [at] what level each course deals with writing . . . and a few other elements. ("Re: Writing")

Two elements stand out as common in both the Missouri and the Taylor initiatives. First, as I have already noted, the model of designated writing-intensive courses (which still holds sway at many institutions) has run up against general education reform; instead of trying to sustain the differences between WAC and general education, however, WAC directors are deciding that it is in the best interests of both their students and their programs to acknowledge the places where the two intersect, even if that means making writing less obviously visible than it had once been. This decision is perhaps being made because the directors have only a limited say in the matter. While English or Writing departments might be able to structure first-year composition programs more or less to their liking (and even that is circumscribed to an extent by such things as articulation agreements), WAC programs need the approval of deans, faculty senates, and other entities involved in campus-wide curricular reform at any given institution.

Second, and possibly more interesting, is the trust more WPAs now seem to place (if the Taylor University model is any indication) in departments and faculty to articulate their own writing outcomes. Though WAC has always involved faculty from all disciplines in such efforts, the last several years have seen a subtle shift in the ways those faculty contribute to WAC curricula. For many of WAC's thirty-plus years, the WPA responsible for WAC on any campus was typically responsible for introducing faculty to WAC and inculcating them with principles of good practice, which principles the faculty then employed in their teaching; the WPA remained the *locus* of expertise. Now, however, as Townsend ("Re: Writing," 10 October) has noted, more faculty than ever before are arriving on more campuses with prior experience of WAC teaching. (I will discuss this situation as it pertains to faculty development in more detail later in this chapter.) While the Taylor University model—or at least Bird's description of it—still retains the word "writing," it is highly possible that in such programs, what will disappear will be not the word "writing," or even the "W" in "writing," but the WPA. At the very least, the function of the WPA in WAC programs will likely change: where once the WPA was the One with Expertise, now the WPA may be the One Who Acknowledges (or, perhaps, Shares) the Expertise of Others. Such a change in function seems a logical extension of principles that earlier

WAC scholarship such as Walvoord et al.'s *In the Long Run* saw as part of good administrative practice.[7]

EXPERTISE WITHOUT WALLS

If the definition of WAC expertise, and who possesses it, has been called into question by recent curricular trends, so, too, has the idea that students can really learn writing in the disciplines—in other words, become experts in the writing in their fields—in the traditional classroom. As a result, the last several years have seen an increase in collaboration with the external audiences for whom those students will eventually write. A glance at recent issues of *Across the Disciplines*—one of two journals devoted to WAC scholarship—as well as other journals sees WAC administrators and teachers looking increasingly to nonacademic locales for ways to provide more authentic writing preparation for students. For example, in the December 2008 issue of *ATD*, Kate Kiefer and Aaron Leff describe their experience teaming students in a science writing class with community agencies that needed help producing a variety of texts for a range of real audiences—e.g., webtexts for teenagers on the effects of smoking, books for children on anatomy and physiology, and brochures on various topics for adults. While, as Kiefer and Leff acknowledge, such partnering efforts are hardly new—some date back to the 1980s—the service-learning movement of the 1990s seems to have rejuvenated them, with its stress on civic engagement having had the added effect of showing students and teachers the benefits of writing for readers outside the classroom.

Anne Beaufort's 2007 *College Writing and Beyond* foregrounds the pedagogical reason for this more outward-looking approach. Beaufort's book-length study traces the progress of a student who switched majors from history to engineering and, not surprisingly, was struck by the differences in writing between the two majors. He

---

7.   Walvoord and her colleagues note, in this study of how faculty in WAC programs developed as teachers through time, that historically WAC efforts (and studies) have tended to follow "the Pilgrim's Progress model of faculty change"—in which one person with expertise incites a gradual conversion in the minds and practices of faculty outside of composition. However, such change is in reality more complicated and, to be effective, must take into account the other disciplinary constructs, curricular movements, and time commitments that require teachers' attention (6–7). I read Walvoord et al.'s work as suggesting that, ultimately, any WAC director cannot, and should not, hope to turn out clones of him- or herself when doing faculty development—and, if such hope is indeed vain, then WAC curricula may ultimately look nothing like what early WAC pioneers envisioned.

was even more struck, however, by what happened once he got out of school. Working as an engineer brought him into contact with rhetorical exigencies for which his writing-intensive classes had failed to prepare him. In a lengthy letter to Beaufort written two years after graduation, he describes these exigencies:

> There's many more drafts than I've ever done before, much more exhaustive peer review and the peers are not very stable so you have to show the thing to them once and they'll have their comments, if you show the same thing to them the next day they'd have different comments. So when you incorporate the comments and send it back to them it's still not done. . . . The peer review seemed kind of artificial in class, you know . . . in what I'm doing now . . . you wanna make sure you're understood. You're too involved in it to read it the way someone else would. Legal and also if you're trying to convince people this is the direction we should go, you wanna make sure . . . you answered the questions. Often if you make one change in one document it might affect all the other documents for the entire product, which would be six documents possibly so it's a lot of work initiating an engineering change notice, . . . something we've come to groan at. (117)

Experiences such as the ones Beaufort's student describes—in which reviewers not given response guidelines by a teacher can be unpredictable, if not arbitrary; in which the number of drafts (aka "the thing") one writes is dictated not by the number of weeks in a semester but by the demands of a variety of readers; and in which the legal repercussions of written documents take center stage—are difficult if not impossible to replicate in the traditional classroom, where students know that, in the end, nobody except the teacher is reading their work. WAC scholars such as Beaufort and teachers such as Kiefer and Leff are, then, looking to redefine sites of learning, asking implicitly if we should expand our ideas of what, actually, a classroom is.

Such a notion is certainly not alien to scholars who have, for at least the last ten years, been exploring the relationship between community literacy and WAC. While high school–college connections have been a concern of WAC scholars since the beginnings of the movement, more recent work has called for WPAs involved in WAC to spend more time reaching out to their surrounding communities. In a landmark essay, "Writing Beyond the Curriculum: Fostering New Collaborations in Literacy," published in 2000 in *College English*, Steve Parks and Eli Goldblatt proposed a revisioning of WAC, suggesting that its "uncritical alliance with disciplines" may not, in fact, be the best thing for faculty whose teaching, research, and service takes them into the community (those "who collect folklore or oral history, sponsor community writing projects, or facilitate school-based publications") (585). Nor may such an "uncritical alliance" necessarily serve the best interest of students. Parks and Goldblatt suggest an "expanded conception" of WAC:

> [W]e should imagine our project as one that combines discipline-based instruction with a range of other literacy experiences that will help students and faculty see writing and reading in a wider social and intellectual context than the college curriculum. Reconceptualization of WAC requires increased collaborations among university, school, and community partners as well as a greater sense of commitment by writing program administrators to literacy *in the regions where our institutions are located.* (585–86; emphasis added)

Parks and Goldblatt then go on to describe and critique such collaborations between their writing program at Temple University in Philadelphia and the surrounding community. In his 2007 book *Because We Live Here*, Goldblatt describes his and his colleagues' community work in more detail, giving a rich ethnographic picture of what such a commitment might look like. Similar efforts have also been described in recent issues of *Across the Disciplines* (see, for instance, Lettner-Rust et al.) and as ongoing research projects in the WAC Clearinghouse's Research Exchange (see, for instance, Halbritter and Lindquist). WAC has found its way out of school and into the neighborhood, problematizing the notion of "discipline" and asking WPAs to revise their idea of "community"—as well as of "curriculum" and "classroom"—to include "the regions where our institutions are located."[8]

FACULTY DEVELOPMENT: COMMUNITY BUILDING, CONVERSION, AND AUTHORSHIP

If WAC's movement from the traditional classroom and into the community has called into question the legitimacy of programs' emphasis on writing in the disciplines, so, too, has the recent scholarship in faculty development. Where said scholarship once focused on one of two areas—how to teach students what they need to know in order to write in their majors, and how faculty develop as teachers in WAC

---

8.   WAC has also ventured into the area of extra-academic *topics.* See the special issue of *Across the Disciplines* on writing about, and after, 9/11: <http://wac.colostate.edu/atd/911/index.cfm>.

programs—more recent work has begun to take a more complicated view of what it means to write in a discipline in the first place and, therefore, what it means to teach discipline-specific writing.

Whatever the differences in WAC program design, one thing all programs have in common is a training component for those who teach in them. Typically, such training—or faculty development—consists at least in part of attendance at a workshop, or series of workshops, which covers a fairly standard set of areas: teaching the rhetoric of disciplines, responding to student writing, using writing-to-learn strategies in classes, and incorporating peer review into classes, to name a few. Such workshops have historically functioned to introduce faculty to WAC's first principles and convert them (if you will) to the efficacy of WAC as a way of teaching that can, fortuitously, help students understand the subject matter of academic fields as well. The published scholarship on faculty development has for the most part reflected the content of these training programs (and some book-length works are often used, in fact, as texts for the programs). Books such as John Bean's *Engaging Ideas* and Katherine Gottschalk and Keith Hjortshoj's *The Elements of Teaching Writing* are two such works, while Walvoord et al.'s *In the Long Run* falls into another category: the study of how faculty develop as writing teachers over time. In addition, books such as Segall and Smart's *Direct from the Disciplines* and Monroe's *Local Knowledges, Local Practices* provide experiential essays on WAC teaching from faculty in a range of academic departments on the editors' campuses.[9]

The latter two texts point, however, to an issue I alluded to earlier in this chapter: a shift in the amount and quality of knowledge faculty outside English now bring to WAC programs. In the 2010 WPA-L thread on writing-intensive course criteria mentioned earlier, Martha Townsend of the University of Missouri commented on changes she has seen in faculty with the success of WAC over the last twenty years. Where once WAC directors needed to show resistant faculty the efficacy of WAC principles, the presence of WAC on many campuses has greatly reduced that need:

> Over the years, the assumptions of new faculty have, I believe, shifted substantially. . . . Often times, new faculty arrived having been part of WAC initiatives

---

9.   In another type of faculty development—one that encourages instructors outside of English to acknowledge and share their own expertise—some WPAs bring faculty from their own campuses together to create collections of essays on teaching in the disciplines. These are typically intended for local use; see, for example, Hesse, "Re: Writing."

at their previous institutions. And, of course, they encountered faculty in our institution who had been working with WAC/WID principles for quite some time—faculty who, for the most part, had positive experiences to relate, making the new folks eager to join in. Increasingly, faculty both here and elsewhere, know enough—now, finally—that they don't expect the English Departments to do it all. Case in point: I facilitated a WAC faculty workshop in Georgia a couple of weeks ago for 20 or so faculty from many disciplines—and not one of them questioned to any degree the ideas being presented. . . . I see that happening more and more often. ("Re: Writing," 10 October)

Greater knowledge on the part of faculty now means less need for conversion; this has changed the scholarship on faculty development and enabled it to move forward in productive ways, albeit ways that may not be directly applicable to WAC on many campuses. What Townsend describes above—the taking for granted by disciplinary faculty of the efficacy of WAC principles—has resulted in scholarship that is, one might say, post-faculty development, with the most cutting-edge research looking at faculty's own writing and writing processes in addition to their teaching. In *Engaged Writers and Dynamic Disciplines: Research on the Academic Writing Life*, Chris Thaiss and Terry Myers Zawacki explore how faculty perceive the concepts of "academic writing" and "alternative writing" and how those perceptions, in turn, affect their response to the writing of students. Arguing that developments in composition studies—scholarship on ESL learners, feminist theory, genre theory, basic writing—have necessarily problematized the teaching of one dominant disciplinary discourse, Thaiss and Zawacki's study finds some WAC faculty, at least, resisting stable disciplinary conventions and genres in their own writing, and explores the extent to which those faculty allow their students to experience the same resistance or experiment with other generic forms. Their study, in the end, asks how teachers might be able to move beyond the traditional stable category of "academic discourse" to provide students with a truer, if messier and more complex, picture of how scholars actually write.[10]

---

10.   Though faculty expertise in WAC seems to be growing and shifting, large-scale assessment of WAC still lies in the hands of composition faculty and administrators. Though WAC assessment has always reflected the rich contexts within which students learn to write—longitudinal studies of student development such as Haswell's *Gaining Ground in College Writing* and Sternglass's *Time to Know Them* being cases in point—"rich context" is coming to mean that those responsible for assessment are engaging with at least some of the issues discussed in previous sections of this chapter. See, for example, Rutz and Grawe.

CONCLUSION: HOW WAC IS LIKE A SHARK

In her plenary address to the 2008 International Writing Across the Curriculum Conference in Austin ("Future"), Susan McLeod was apparently more sanguine about WAC's prospects than she had been in 1997. While still warning the conference attendees about issues they needed to be watchful for—the intrusion of government into assessment, for example—her tone is overall positive and optimistic about WAC's survival. Citing research that shows WAC programs are not only alive and well but proliferating (having increased in number considerably between 2008 and 1989), she ends with the following:

> I remain optimistic about [WAC] as a force for educational change. Writing Across the Curriculum has survived and is thriving 35 years after it began. I look forward with intense interest to following future developments; many of you here will be helping to create that future, and I wish you well.

And, in fact, much evidence suggests that McLeod was, and remains, correct. Colleges and universities all over the world, let alone in the U.S., continue to run well-attended and well-funded WAC faculty workshops. Mike Palmquist's WAC Clearinghouse (wac.colostate.edu), *the* central location for WAC teaching resources, scholarship, and program descriptions, just celebrated its twenty-eighth anniversary. The programs described on the WAC Clearinghouse, as well as many others, are alive and kicking. WPAs, including this author, continue to receive reassigned time for directing those programs, and our job descriptions continue to include assessment, faculty training, and curriculum development. And a new book, Richard Arum and Josipa Roksa's *Academically Adrift*, has just called to the public's attention the need for writing in all disciplines. It is possible that *Academically Adrift* may be another "Why Johnny Can't Write" and restore WAC's 1970s status as That Which the Government Is Funding Today.

So, how on earth can I claim that WAC is "disappearing"?

It is possible, of course, that I am entirely overstating the case. One can certainly take another view and say that, given the evidence above, WAC is in fact healthier and more visible than it has ever been—in some ways, the very presence of this chapter in this book also supports that view. One must remember, too, that the changes I have described here have not occurred on all campuses, and some schools will be slower to implement those changes than others. While the University of Missouri, for example, with its long history of a strong WAC program, may be ready to move into a more integrated with general education model, my own campus—Eastern Connecticut State University—has historically had fewer resources for WAC and is, therefore, somewhat less fully evolved. If I tried, for example, to get the faculty at ECSU to forgo writing-intensive designations for courses, I would be accused of "not caring about writing"—and since I want to be seen as caring about writing, and want the faculty to care about writing, I will continue to embrace the writing-intensive designation. For now.

I would, however, like to return to the concept of "transformation" I introduced early in this chapter. What I am arguing here is that WAC is not so much dying as it is changing, and that if we resist necessary changes—if, in other words, we refuse to allow WAC to run its course, even if that course is into a kind of oblivion in which "W" or "WI" designations, WAC directors, and faculty in need of conversion no longer exist—we risk not allowing it to shape the academy in important ways, ways its pioneers may not have envisioned. It's not clear, for example, that such early WAC adopters as Elaine Maimon and Susan McLeod saw the greater leadership roles that were in store for them—Maimon as a college president and McLeod as a dean. There are undoubtedly others whose leadership skills not only helped them develop WAC programs but also pushed them farther into positions of greater authority within the academy, thereby placing into power people who care about writing and have the ability to influence curriculum so that writing is taken for granted as something each curriculum, everywhere, needs, in every department. Early WAC adopters may also not have seen the extent to which faculty would embrace the movement so that it became simply part of the scene, with writing something they taught in each class (and something they could write and publish about); nor would they have seen students taking for granted that they would have to write in every class.

To have them doing this: now this is success, whatever we call it in the end.

6

SCHOLARLY POSITIONS IN WRITING PROGRAM ADMINISTRATION

Jeanne Gunner

This chapter is a sketch of writing program administration as an intellectual field. The approach I take is grounded in WPA history and theoretical orientations, as well as in the tensions, arguments, and epistemological orientations that give the field its intellectual vitality. Coming out of textual studies and with a materialist orientation, I favor examination not only of major authors and their publications but also of self-defining and revealing, if marginal, professional documents, including editorial policy statements, the ancillary contents of edited collections, and "flash point" texts—those that have created an angry "buzz" or righteous endorsement. Within composition studies, the social nature of language is a given, but I see writing program scholarship as especially social, as active and embodied, and thus this sketch of the field's internal and external struggles, how they arose, and what turns they have taken in recent years. Rather than a comprehensive review, this is a conceptual framework, one those interested in WPA scholarship may find useful in situating their reading in the field, and one that, hopefully, will encourage an integration of WPA issues with the critical inquiry of composition studies overall.

Reviewing the article titles in the field's specialized journal, *WPA: Writing Program Administration*, the chapter titles in the edited collections that were the first WPA scholarly books, and now the titles of individual books of WPA scholarship can provide a quick sense of the major concerns of WPA scholarship. Skimming through the bibliographies and works cited lists in all of the above provides a sense of how this body of work connects with composition studies. And picking up a copy of any of the field's main journals—*CCC*, say—and searching through for citations of WPA books, chapters, and articles enables one to assess the impact of WPA scholarship on the larger field. If prospective WPAs were actually to follow all these steps, they would end up with a fairly strong knowledge not only of what the intellectual issues and controversies are, but perhaps also of what they ought and need to be. That second point—regarding *need*—will be a particular concern throughout this chapter.

Deducing the nature of WPA scholarship from the above exempla, a newcomer to the field would likely end with an impression of the field's most traditional and conservative parameters. Knowledge of what's been done is clearly necessary, but because WPA work is still a relatively new enterprise, because it has such an interesting range of ideological views, institutional natures, cultural challenges, and continuing identity conflicts, it is an area that has special need for researchers and theorists who work against the grain as well. This discussion therefore will be double-voiced: it moves between the historical practices of mainstream scholarship and critical reflection on them.

WPA SCHOLARSHIP: SOME OFFICIAL DEFINITIONS AND THEIR SOCIAL HISTORY

Editorial guidelines, calls for papers, and authorial rationales are useful in helping to define the traditional, in-field sense of what WPA scholarship is. Looking at past and current examples from these genres, we can see a consistent official stance and strong consensus emerge as to what reasonably constitutes scholarly work in the field. Consider the "Author's Guide" published in each issue of *WPA: Writing Program Administration*, the journal sponsored by the field's primary professional organization, the Council of Writing Program Administrators. The editorial policy that in effect both shapes and limits the scholarly field suggests the highlighted topics as the main scholarly interests of WPA work:

> *WPA: Writing Program Administration* publishes articles and essays concerning the organization, administration, practices, and aims of college and university writing programs. Possible topics include the education and support of writing teachers; the intellectual and administrative work of WPAs; the situation of writing programs within both academic institutions and broader contexts; the programmatic implications of current theories, technologies, and research; relationships between WPAs and other administrators and between writing and other academic programs; placement; assessment; and the professional status of WPAs. (2008, 5)

In this policy statement, WPA scholarship can be construed as inquiry into specific internal administrative tasks of the sort practiced in most programs ("placement; assessment"). The often pragmatic nature of WPA research is evident in the categories of "education and support of writing teachers" and "programmatic implications of current theories, technologies, and research": constructed in this way, the scholarly interest consists of professional training and resource issues and translating the broader work of composition studies into critique and innovation or renovation of program practices; here, the WPA's scholarly agenda is to serve as conduit and translator, mining mainstream scholarship as almost the manufacturing arm of a research industry. The writing program, as the editorial policy represents it, is a systemic entity, one that inhabits an institutional context and interacts with other entities and individuals within that context; here, the notion of WPA scholarship becomes less instrumentalist and more social, opening up inquiry into the nature of the program as it is locally situated (a service unit, a research/teaching program or department) and in open-ended "broader contexts" (public discourse on writing and writing instruction, professional writing). The editorial policy goes on to note in a second, and secondary, paragraph that the "editors welcome empirical research (quantitative as well as qualitative), historical research, and theoretical, essayistic, or reflective pieces," expanding the methodologies and genres deemed characteristic of WPA scholarship.

The specificity of these scholarly field markers has increased over time, even as the concept of scholarship has shifted from almost exclusively pragmatic to what might be called more rhetorically self-conscious and less nationalistically defined (the earliest versions of the editorial guidelines specifically include U.S. and Canadian institutions, but no national references appear in the post-1994 version; a U.S. innovation, the writing program seems to have become so transnational an institutional structure that overt inclusiveness is no longer necessary). Compare the current journal focus to its first iteration in 1979 (an editorial template that remained in place for ten years) when the shift from newsletter to peer-reviewed journal was made:

> The Editors of *WPA* invite contributions that are appropriate to the interests and concerns of those who administer writing programs in American and Canadian colleges and universities. Articles on teaching writing or research in composition are acceptable only if they deal with the relationship of these activities to program administration. (*WPA* 3.1 1979)

In 1990, the following sentence was appended to the original statement, revealing the shift from a professional community-building focus
to a clearly instrumentalist scholarly orientation:

> WPA is especially interested in articles on topics such as *establishing and main-
> taining a cohesive writing program, training composition staff, testing and evaluating
> students and programs, working with department chairs and deans, collaborating with
> high school or community college teachers,* and so on. ("Author's Guide," 1990;
> emphasis added)

In retrospect, the wording suggests an authoritarian, even patriarchal, turn, emphasizing standardization and normativity, an uncomfortable unilateralism allied to an agenda of WPA control and efficiency.
As a result, scholarship and administration in this period threatened to
become one and the same, with administrative purpose subsuming theoretical inquiry into its specific categorical interests.

The current "Author's Guide" replaced the above in the fall of 1994,
with then-editor Douglas Hesse noting in his inaugural issue that with
this editorial policy change he intended "to signal not some fussy purity
of genre distinction but [my] belief that contributions to knowledge and
practices in writing programs come in many forms" (7). Those many
forms were indeed proliferating. Consider some of the groundbreaking WPA works published in 1995 and 1996 alone: Joseph Janangelo
and Kristine Hansen's *Resituating Writing: Constructing and Administering
Writing Programs*, whose title lifts the social over the reified nature of writing programs and whose opening line in Charles Schuster's foreword
announces, "With this volume of scholarly essays, the concept of writing
program administration as a significant expression of academic scholarship comes of age" (ix); the WPA Executive Committee's "Evaluating the
Intellectual Work or Writing Program Administrators: A Draft," the first
organizational response to the pressure for WPA professionalization;
Catherine Latterell's "Training the Workforce" and Mark Long, Jennifer
Holberg, and Marcy Taylor's "Beyond Apprenticeship," among the first
articles to call attention to the shortcomings of a skills-based graduate
practicum tradition and to identify collaborative administration as one
means of materializing the WPA's intellectual work. The titles of some
works in this brief but paradigm-shifting period themselves tell the social
history: Christine Hult's "The Scholarship of Administration"; Sally Barr
Ebest's "Gender Differences in Writing Program Administration"; Hildy
Miller's "Postmasculinist Direction in Writing Program Administration";

even Greg Glau's "The 'Stretch Program': Arizona State University's New Model of University-level Basic Writing Instruction," a pragmatically focused discussion of a socially responsive innovation in program form. From this point WPA scholarship gained complexity, if not mission clarity—which, given the earlier bias toward program standardization, was nonetheless an important and productive shift. Over the next several years, many WPA scholars continued to work in a generally instrumentalist mode, but many also explored the theoretical and critical paths laid out in the mid-1990s (and of course these are not pure and distinct categories). As edited collections of WPA scholarship began appearing regularly (and as they still flourish today), the coexistence of differing scholarly formations of WPA work became more apparent. I'll address the issue of taxonomizing WPA scholarship at a later point, but for now I'll use the following terms to illustrate the different orientations of WPA scholarship in the last ten years:

Efficiency	*Hybrid*	*Resistant*
Administrative Problem-Solving for Writing Programs and Writing Centers: Scenarios in Effective Program Management (Myers-Breslin)	*The Writing Program Administrator as Researcher: Inquiry in Action and Reflection* (Rose and Weiser)	*Kitchen Cooks, Plate Twirlers and Troubadours: Writing Program Administrators Tell Their Stories* (George)
The Writing Program Administrator's Resource: A Guide to Reflective Institutional Practice (Brown and Enos)	*The Writing Program Administrator as Theorist: Inquiry in Action and Reflection* (Rose and Weiser)	*Tenured Bosses and Disposable Teachers: Writing Instruction in the Managed University* (Bousquet, Scott, and Parascondola)
The Allyn & Bacon Sourcebook for Writing Program Administrators (Ward and Carpenter)	*The Promises and Perils of Writing Program Administration* (Enos and Borrowman)	*Historical Studies of Writing Program Administration: Individuals, Communities, and the Formation of a Discipline* (L'Eplattenier and Mastrangelo)
		Discord and Direction: The Postmodern Writing Program Administrator (McGee and Handa)

In the "Efficiency" category, the collections' contents reflect for the most part a range of ideological stances on what the writing program and the WPA's role in it is, but, as with the *WPA* editorial stance through 1994, the collective purpose is what we'd now call managerial: the WPA is the administrative center of an administrative unit whose charge is problem solving, meeting institutional needs, and mediating cultural issues (such as labor conditions) in the context of the first two tasks. "Efficiency"

scholarship, progressive or conservative, has an ultimately managerial agenda and is directed to a program-stabilizing end. In the Myers-
Breslin collection, the subsections define the areas of efficiency interest:
"Selection and Training"; "Program Development"; "Professional Issues
of Departmental Authority and Professional Development." Similarly,
the subsections in Ward and Carpenter's collection are "Who Are You
as Administrator?"; "Administering, Managing, Leading"; "Teaching
Assistant Training and Staff Development"; "Curriculum Design and
Assessment"; and "Promotion and Professional Issues for WPAs."
Rhetorically, the WPA scholar in this efficiency model typically speaks
to a closed community; he or she does not invoke an audience outside
WPA work.

The Rose and Weiser collections have played a key role in claiming a
research- and theory-informed identity for WPA scholarship. In a kind
of disciplinary uplift, they argue for the logic of WPAs' multimethod-
ological practices, including "historical/archival, theoretical, empirical,
and hermeneutic inquiry processes" (*The Writing Program Administrator
as Researcher*, vii), and for recognizing WPA research as "not categori-
cally different from other research in rhetoric and writing studies"
(ix). Naming the traits that characterize good WPA research (vii–viii),
their introduction to the first collection establishes an important professional bulwark: WPA inquiry can claim demonstrable, reviewable,
mainstream scholarly credentials. The "hybrid" status can be seen in
the editors' articulation of the WPA scholarly means and scholarly end,
however: "[R]esearch in writing program administration is theoretically-
informed, systematic, principled inquiry *for the purpose of developing, sustaining, and leading a sound, yet dynamic, writing program*" (ix; emphasis
added). The text intermingles a professionalizing agenda of researched,
critical, self-reflective work that is then coupled with pragmatic, pro-
gram-focused applications—a model of WPA scholarship as essentially
praxis and, again, bounded by a specific institutional site and audience.

The second collection, *The Writing Program Administrator as Theorist*,
published in 2002, shows a newly ascendant strand of critical work, which
I've called "resistant" because it typically provides an examination of the
traditional instrumentalist approach; problematizes the WPA figure;
transgresses conventional WPA boundaries (in terms of WPA identity as
well as of an insular WPA space of the kind implied by the 1999 Rose and
Weiser purpose statement); and frequently includes what I would call
WPA alternative discourse, or at least personal discourses put to the end

of institutional and cultural critique (see the essays by Richard Miller, Mara Holt, and Doug Hesse in particular in the George collection). The editors offer a pragmatic rationale for the collection—the enabling of WPAs to "develop greater understanding of the programs they direct" (3) and to "theorize their work in order to understand it, improve its quality, and develop its professional knowledge base" (4)—in asserting "the importance of clarifying, for both our academic colleagues and the broader public, the ways in which WPAs' theoretical work is like the theoretical work in other academic and disciplinary contexts." But they also construct WPA scholarship as the professional equivalent of scholarship across the curriculum and articulate explicitly a new, outward focus with the recognition of a "broader public" whose perception of the field helps define it. WPAs must not only apply theoretical insights in this paradigm, but also "develop new theories of their own about their work" (2).

The Enos and Borrowman collection embodies a shift in WPA scholarly discursive practices in that it is not organized into individual essays on WPA work areas. Instead, its nine divisions consist of narrative and reflective essays and dialogic responses to them, and some of the individual titles show a quasi–cultural studies influence: Ann E. Green's "Diversity Work and the WPA," for example, and Cynthia Nearman's "One White Girl's Failed Attempt to Unsilence the Dialogue." For the most part the text is organized according to junior WPAs' professional conflicts doing WPA work and senior WPAs' responses; the problem-solution format remains, though the range of issues considered relevant to WPA work is expanded well beyond an efficiency agenda. All of these works move us toward pluralized WPA voices, a recognition that the monolithic notion of "the writing program" is a social, reactive, and potentially active form.

The Rose and Weiser and Enos and Borrowman collections point to a phenomenon that the "resistant" critical strand embodies: the writing program as a self-consuming artifact. From the origin days, when establishing a writing program was an "eyes on the prize" goal, to the conservative era, when the program was treated as a perfectible object, the WPA gaze was assumed to be unmediated, and the program could be studied as an icon, complete in itself. In time, and influenced by the social turn and the critical wave of various post-structural theories, the scholarly gaze shifted away from the isolated program and the technician's stewardship role. This shift over time connects with social history, to be sure.

Generationally, early WPAs typically came out of literary studies, often bringing with them a New Critical frame, a lens applied to the writing program. As New Criticism taught, the object of study has its own proper form, outside of historical and ideological forces, reflecting an internal cohesiveness, not the author's (WPA's) personal views or other temporal influences. The writing program, like the literary work of art, might well have been conceived as having a universal, describable, prescribable form—an odd mixture of the aesthetic and scientific. Predating the influence of French critical theory, cultural studies, and postcolonial thought, the functions and practices of originary writing programs were perhaps inevitably unequipped to address issues of difference—except to serve as a standardizing force. Economically, the mandate of basic skills and standardization worked well to subsidize the proliferation of programs and positions for writing program administrators. This the period I have termed "conservative," a period, not coincidentally, coeval with the Reagan years. But by the 1980s a kind of deregulation was happening, as can be seen in watershed articles such as Maxine Hairston's "The Winds of Change," which appeared in 1982. The writing program had accrued enough economic and perhaps disciplinary power to become an active institutional agent, evidenced in the rise of varied program innovations—WAC, writing centers, and stand-alone writing programs.

It is only after Rose and Weiser's works, however, that we became our own object/subject of study, and from this study some of the most provocative critical work in our field has emerged (with the Bousquet, Scott, and Parascondola collection the most piquant example—and it continues to inflame and disrupt). Quantitative, qualitative, or otherwise in nature, WPA scholarship seemed finally to point self-consciously to the constructed nature of programs and their practices and so to our own assumptions and ideologies. After all, programs may have often been described mechanistically, but none seemed ever to function that way. And thus much of WPA scholarship is data that become metadata, data about data's own production. As Stanley Fish conceptualized it, a "self-consuming" artifact signifies most successfully when it fails, when it points *away* from itself to something its forms cannot capture" (4): the resistant strand of WPA scholarship takes up the program, and the WPA, too, not as a conventional institutional genre but as a social force; critiques both as politically and ideologically fraught; and seeks to construct a history of itself, a revalorization of scholarship as critical genealogy rather than managerial problem solving.

Parlor Press recently announced the new Writing Program Administration book series, and the officially sponsored scholarly topics still skew to the hybrid model. The managerial framework remains but has become more fluid: historical research, interdisciplinary theories, and social and political issues are included in the encouraged submissions. The list includes "[s]tudies evaluating the relevance of theories developed in other fields (e.g., management, sustainability, organizational theory)" along with "[s]tudies of particular personnel issues (e.g., unionization, use of adjunct faculty)"; "developing and articulating curricula"; and "assessment and accountability ("Announcements")." In all likelihood, twenty-first-century WPA scholarship will continue, on the one hand, to study the writing program and its conventions, but this work will be based in theory and research, not instrumentalist practice, and, on the other, it will broaden its audience and its critical sense of what a writing program is and can do. *The Activist WPA: Changing Stories about Writing and Writers*, published in 2008 by fellow contributor to this collection Linda Adler-Kassner, is of this new scholarly breed: Adler-Kassner's work proceeds from the critical idea of the writing program as a social force or genre rather than a static administrative unit. Her argument, stemming in part from her other scholarly work as an advocate for basic-writing programs and at-risk first-year writers, is that WPAs can reframe the public perceptions, or "stories," of writing and writers, the most dominant of which tell a tale of correctness and deficits, skills and remediation, and she draws on "strategies developed by community organizers and media strategists to shift those frames" (5). The individual text (whether individually or collaboratively authored) that is traditionally seen as the highest form of scholarly attainment will increasingly become a common form of resistant WPA scholarship.

WPA INTELLECTUAL ISSUES AND CONTROVERSIES

If we accept the fundamental premise of language as a social activity, then a discussion of WPA intellectual issues and controversies must necessarily be interested, biased, ideological, and any one organizational scheme will call out responses that change it. Again, my bias is to organize scholarly WPA work in political terms of conservative/progressive, which in turn privileges certain issues and conflicts as the defining ones of the field (and I invite those who find WPA scholarship engaging to imagine taxonomies of WPA issues and controversies different from that which I've constructed). In any case, a reader would find her way into the major controversies by asking: "What is a writing program?" and "What is a WPA?" From these two questions flow most of the issues and conflicts of the field.

Under the first question come all the arguments about writing curricula. Almost any active WPA is likely to champion some variation of process theory over prescriptive mimetic notions. The field arose by defining itself against the composing concepts allied to literature departments: belletristic essays intended to inculcate appreciation of the canon, for example, or imitation exercises premised, data-free, on a belief in writing as a set of best-practices writing skills, usually discrete in nature. With the study of rhetoric largely the business of speech departments, the English department had few available theories of composing and little cultural incentive to devote time to the study of writing, much less writing instruction. Writing was, through the mid-1960s, pretty much a middle-class enterprise, as the university itself had become. But the singular historical shift in access to higher education in the post-1960s made the study and teaching of writing suddenly critical (and suddenly a rich revenue source). Composition theories began to emerge, many times after writing programs and WPAs had (an argument I make in "Doomed to Repeat It?"). And hence the struggle over defining what a program is and what a program is supposed to do (to students). We see this struggle going on in less controversy-ridden terms today, with the rise of new media writing. For an interesting treatment of the history of major composing theories as they have shaped writing programs and curricula, see Tate, Rupiper, and Schick's *A Guide to Composition Pedagogies* (but see also Jeff Rice's critique of this compartmentalizing approach, "Conservative Writing Program Administrators").

Still, empirically and theoretically informed notions of composing don't necessarily resolve program-level curricular questions about subject matter, the role of research, visual rhetoric, technical and professional writing, rhetorical theory, new media writing, WAC, ESL, advanced composition, WID, literature. Curricular controversies tie to pedagogical methods, class size, instructor training, placement, evaluation, preparatory issues/remediation, requirements, plagiarism, and assessment. All of these, and many other material issues treated by scholars in the broader rhetoric-composition field, become intellectual challenges in terms of how they take on (or don't enter into) program form. Daniel J. Royer and Roger Gilles's work, "Directed Self-Placement: An Attitude of Orientation," is a good example of a common program practice treated as a topic of inquiry, to very productive and practice-changing results, and later taken up in a more political and theoretical vein by David Blakesley in "Directed Self-Placement in the University." The issue is an interesting one of power and authority: directed self-placement is a system that allows students themselves to assess their academic writing abilities, and then place themselves into the course level they believe is the most appropriate for them. For some, DSP subverts the expertise and professional responsibility that formal placement policies represent; for others, for others, it is a progressive and pedagogically valuable policy; and for most, DSP is a pragmatic way to reduce placement testing costs.

In 2000, the Council of Writing Program Administrators adopted the "WPA Outcomes Statement," which outlines learning goals for writing instruction and suggests how faculty can approach teaching and developing students' rhetorical and composing abilities. The reception of the "Outcomes Statement" reflects many current intellectual concerns in the WPA field. Should there be any document that attempts to capture the means and purposes of writing instruction? Won't such a document inevitably be used as a tool of standardization, applied regardless of institutional and social contexts? Can it speak to the range of theoretical orientations in rhetoric-composition? Or should we can the whole endeavor, course along with outcomes: the "abolitionist" argument, which has periodic revivals, calls for elimination of the universal freshman writing course requirement. WPAs and writing programs continue to be mistakenly placed in metonymic relation to the first-year course, discouraging recognition of the field as a scholarly site, tying it to a service model, and reducing its cultural capital. One might reasonably claim, therefore, that reorganizing the composition curriculum could help displace the diminished sense of composition in the university (which is the title of Sharon Crowley's well-known book on the topic—another flash point text). Crowley has been an advocate for abolition of the universal writing requirement and the development instead of a "vertical" composition curriculum, with students taking writing courses throughout their undergraduate studies at the point of need and interest, as they decide. WPA response to the abolitionist argument is usually interested but guarded, and very few institutions have eliminated required first-year writing courses.

The question of what a WPA is also brings a litany of intellectual issues and controversies. Some of the earliest centered on WPA authority and power (or lack thereof), usually seen in relation to the English department–writing program relationship and other conflicts of an institutional/cultural capital nature. For the minority report, Richard E. Miller, a prominent scholar and WPA, has published several essays that challenge the usual scholarly view of the professional WPA model. In "'Let's Do the Numbers': Comp Droids and the Prophets of Doom," for example, he defends the employment of nonspecialized writing instructors and argues for the institutional reality of writing program work as necessarily administrative in nature.

Much feminist WPA work examines the patriarchal structure of the field, the typically unequal status of female writing instructors and WPAs, and the presumed collaborative administrative style of the female WPA. The managerial critique is an important contemporary argument, with Marc Bousquet's call for the abolition of the WPA position/ function, "Composition as Management Science: Toward a University without a WPA" and Donna Strickland's theorizing of "The Managerial Unconscious of Composition Studies" the source of some of the more heated of recent controversies. Once again we see a historical trend in scholarly WPA work to move from a professionalizing struggle to claim space for the field and to establish WPA authority, to a self-critical recognition of a reproduction within of traditional, constricting values, to a radical critique of the enterprise/position as the institutionalization of a conservative agenda.

The affective realm of WPA work is another object of materialist critique, and Laura Micciche's *College English* essay, "More Than a Feeling: Disappointment and WPA Work," created a backlash of sorts among WPAs who resisted her analysis of how working conditions breed acceptance of limitations and diminished expectations; in earlier form, such analyses were tagged "victim narratives," with Wendy Bishop and Gay Lynn Crossley's "How to Tell a Story of Stopping: The Complexities of Narrating a WPA's Experience" often cited as such a work. These all connect to the problem of exploited full-time and contingent labor, a topic that draws very significant scholarly attention (more on this below). Critiques of the WPA position offered by Bousquet and Micciche have as one important antecedent another flash point piece, James Sledd's "Why the Wyoming Resolution Had to Be Emasculated: A History and a Quixotism," one of the first, and bitterest, critiques of the field's (ab)use of contingent faculty. The phrase "boss compositionists" is Sledd's, and its use as a reference to high-level tenured faculty and administrators in the rhetoric-composition field persists—as does the exploitation of contingent faculty.

SUB- OR SUBALTERN FIELD? WRITING PROGRAM SCHOLARSHIP AND COMPOSITION STUDIES

In a 1999 *WPA* article, "Identity and Location: A Study of WPA Models, Memberships, and Agendas," I argued that WPA as a field is insular and that we often end up talking to ourselves. In large part that may be an inevitable result of being so specialized (narrowly located) a field, exacerbated further by the presumed practical nature of WPA work. Because we have sought to build a community, and because we are in so specialized a field, most WPA journal scholarship has appeared in *WPA*, and few WPA topics appear in the mainstream journals. Perhaps an entwined editorial/authorial bias explains this phenomenon—editors can't cover areas in which they get no or few submissions, and authors may avoid journals that seem never or rarely to welcome their topics. I say this as a cautionary preamble to a harsh observation: WPA scholarship to date may have mainly influenced itself, not the field of composition studies at large.

This insularity is lessened if we consider as part of WPA scholarship the work published by WPAs that is clearly an outgrowth of and accompaniment to the scholarship areas outlined above. This work forms a liminal connection to composition studies, and it is the source of some of the most commonly cited work in the more narrowly defined field of WPA work. Again, contingent labor is one of the field-wide concerns that has major WPA scholars at the forefront. Eileen Schell and Patricia Stock's *Moving a Mountain: Transforming the Role of Contingent Faculty in Composition Studies and Higher Education*; Bruce Horner's *Terms of Work in Composition: A Materialist Critique*; and Tony Scott's *Dangerous Writing: Understanding the Political Economy of Composition* are examples of important scholarship on material conditions written by current or former WPAs and deeply informed by their WPA experience. Writing and program assessment is another area of prolific work built on writing program–based issues and practices, and again some of the major scholarship comes from former and current WPAs (Kathleen Blake Yancey, Brian Huot, and Edward M. White, to name just a few). Many critiques of writing as a cultural practice have had WPA authors (Rebecca Moore Howard, Anne Ruggles Gere, Sidney Dobrin, Tom Fox, Kurt Spellmeyer, John Trimbur, Lynn Z. Bloom, Paul Kei Matsuda). Andrea Lunsford and Kathleen Blake Yancey are perhaps the shining examples of WPA connectivity, working as they do in almost all WPA areas, plus, collectively, assessment, intellectual property, pedagogy, rhetorical theory, and new media writing, among other topics. Writing pedagogy also has its WPA authors: Joseph Harris, David Bartholomae, Nancy Sommers, and many others. Former and current WPAs Theresa Enos and Krista Ratcliffe write on gender issues and feminist theory, respectively. Louise Phelps, Stephen North, Thomas P. Miller: all are scholars recognized in the larger field, and all have been WPAs whose composition studies work emerges from/merges with their WPA knowledge.

When it comes to composition studies scholars who have not been involved in WPA work citing WPA scholarship, then we see the connectivity flow mainly one way. And yet a more dialogic engagement of WPA work with their scholarship would be valuable. What might Native American rhetorical theory scholar Malea Powell say about writing program formation, history, and practice in relation to her areas of scholarly interest? How might Deborah Brandt extend her studies of literacy practices and histories to writing program issues and archival work? Right now many extra–composition studies scholars who speak to composition do so out of a misguided "return" motif, as seen recently in Stanley Fish's call for a grammar-based writing curriculum and Cathy Birkenstein and Gerald Graff's composition textbook and ensuing *Chronicle of Higher Education* essay extolling the use of formulaic models of invention, which erupted as a controversy on the WPA listserv. When Birkenstein and Graff wrote back to a negative posting, the tenor of the conversation became conciliatory, and the controversy ended with a tentative agreement for the textbook authors to enter into professional conversation with WPAs.

As WPA work becomes more engaged with historical studies and cultural theories, we might begin to see WPA scholarship stimulate response and engagement beyond the current borders. Imagine a third-wave WPA journal that actively sought such scholarly interaction. Just as the *Journal of Advanced Composition* shifted to *JAC: A Journal of Composition Theory*, WPA might become *wpa3: Sponsoring Literacies*, or some other title indicating a third-generational shift of scholarly interest beyond important but WPA-limited issues in problem solving, small college programs, and the graduate practicum. And yet as the Research Grants Committee of the Council of Writing Program Administrators posted its 2009 invitation for proposals, the guidelines direct WPA researchers to "explain the problem . . . the methodology you plan to use to approach the problem . . . how the project will address the problem ("CWPA Call for Research Proposals")." At a time when subdisciplinary boundaries are reforming or dissolving in the larger English studies profession, the result of recent scholarly and curricular forces (such as digital humanities initiatives and cultural studies/transnational orientations), those in WPA work (and those most affected by it—our students) are best served by open-minded, boundary-pushing, and actively resistant forms of scholarly inquiry.

The limits of WPA scholarship are historical, not fated, not inherent. Those readers who are new scholars in composition studies can find valuable knowledge and research interests in what's been done by WPA scholars without having to commit to a WPA career. Those who do seek the WPA path can alter the scholarly conversation to bridge disciplinary communities in composition studies. In the line from Stanley Fish that I do find useful for WPA scholarly purposes, the writing program "points *away* from itself to something its forms cannot capture," and beyond the formal conventions of writing program work, much remains to be explored.

II

Innovations, Advancements, and Methodologies

7

REIMAGINING THE NATURE OF FYC
Trends in Writing-about-Writing Pedagogies

Doug Downs and Elizabeth Wardle

[Composition courses] shouldn't have some gratuitous or incidental content that serve[s] as a kind of alibi "occasion" for writing.
Michael Murphy

As far as I'm concerned, there's no looking back; it seems that our discipline has crossed a threshold at which composition as an introduction to writing studies now offers the most compelling pathway.
Andrew Moss

As the introduction to this volume notes, the advent of the field of composition studies was marked by the emergence of specialized theory- and research-based knowledge about writers, writing, discourse, and textual production. But while that knowledge quickly began to shape first-year composition (FYC) processes and pedagogies, only recently has that knowledge about writing become *an explicit focus of study* or the subject of students' own writing in FYC. In this chapter, we describe rationales and goals for making the knowledge of the field the studied content of FYC, and explore this "writing-about-writing" (WAW) pedagogy as an area of cutting-edge pedagogical research in composition studies. We begin our review with an overview of rationales for and theory underlying writing-about-writing pedagogy and its goals, and then describe a range of representative curricula. We conclude by summarizing early research regarding the efficacy of the approach, and suggest directions for further research on writing-about-writing curricula and their impact on composition studies.

THE SUBJECT AND ETHOS OF COMPOSITION STUDIES
Hang around the discipline of composition studies long enough, and eventually (whether in two weeks or two years), you'll find yourself asking,

"Why does it always seem to come back to teaching? Why do we seem unable to unhook the study of writing from the study of writing pedagogy?" We want to begin our chapter, which is on a kind of writing pedagogy that *is* the study of writing, by posing this question: Why does composition studies seem to be so inevitably, in Joseph Harris's terms, "a teaching subject"? Doing so allows us to offer an argument about the nature of this field you are beginning to investigate, and it lets us explain how we see "writing-about-writing" pedagogy as an embodiment of the field's ethos.

Composition studies as a field is at this point nearly fifty years old. Like other academic fields, it has a loosely defined (and continually redefined) set of central questions that create an area of research- and theory-based study. These questions include: How does writing work? How did a text get to be the way it is? How do writers get writing done? How is writing a rhetorical activity, and how are texts rhetorical discourse? How is writing technological? How is writing learned, and what are better and worse ways of teaching it? Like other academic fields, composition studies (which also goes by writing studies, rhetoric and composition, rhet/comp, and comp/rhet) is characterized by paradigmatic waves of thought shifting one to the next, each a strong reaction to (and usually against) the preceding paradigm. Always, these paradigms of thought about writing are expressed foremost in the pedagogies that accompany them. *Current-traditional* rhetoric, with its modernist emphasis on forms of, and form in, writing, was accompanied by writing instruction that focused on formal correctness and theme-based writing. The *process* paradigm, beginning in the early 1970s, focused on writing as an activity of recursive invention of ideas through prewriting, drafting, and revising, and saw writing instruction turn to emphasize "process over product" and strong expression of writers' own points of view. With the advent of *the social turn* in the late 1980s and early 1990s, researchers and theorists brought greater emphasis to the contexts in which writing takes place, reunderstanding writing not as simply emerging from a writer's thoughts, but as a response to particular writing situations and audience needs and expectations. Writing instruction in the social turn has been characterized by a focus on textuality, the social nature of language, and the analysis of how texts are culturally constructed and thus constrain writers and readers.

Today we see this emphasis evolving in a number of directions, particularly toward a focus on *technologies of writing*, which is making us rethink our understanding of the nature of writing and how it works, and another focus on the *politics of writing and literacy*, which explores the nature of writing and texts as social and cultural empowerment. The question that drives much of this book is, "What writing pedagogies and supporting pedagogical structures reflect current turns in our theorizing and research?" Our chapter discusses what has come to be known as "writing about writing" as a response to, in particular, a long-standing dichotomy between teaching form and content.

But before we directly take up the form and content concerns and the writing-about-writing pedagogy, we want to pause briefly to consider the ethos of the field that, we would argue, has remained unchanged through every paradigm shift so far. This ethos, as we understand it, helps to explain why composition scholars continue to dedicate themselves to resolving theoretical and ideological disputes as classroom questions with real material consequences for students. The formation of composition studies was predicated on, and continues to be most often defined by, the attitude that the professionals within it take toward writing instruction, writing students, and the role of writing instruction in higher education. We believe this attitude can be summarized (though far from exhaustively) in the following points:

1. A concern for the success of students as individuals bettering themselves through higher education, including writing instruction (the very formation of the field grew out of an interest in students who were not succeeding; see, for example, the work of Sondra Perl and that of Mina Shaughnessy);

2. A belief in the abilities of students, a centering sense that students are *already* writers with things to say (Bartholomae; Elbow; Murray);

3. A critique of educational structures, systems, and myths that impede students as writers, thinkers, and participants in civic life (Berlin); and

4. A conviction that if teachers think more carefully about their work, taking these other starting points into account, we can improve writing instruction *and* the institutions in which we teach (note the extensive amount of scholarly energy devoted to issues of writing instruction and writing program administration—such as the Council of Writing Program Administrators as well as its journal and "Outcomes Statement," for example).

Simply put, we understand the ethos of the field as largely resisting *deficit* models of writing instruction, which assume students know little, have poor writing abilities, and need "saving" from "bad writing." Instead, composition studies favors models of writing instruction that give *voice* to students, seeing them as able, engaged, and full of potential as knowledgeable individuals and able learners. These convictions seem to partially arise from our developing understanding, as theorists and researchers, of the nature of writing itself: that writing is not a set of universal, basic, fundamental *skills* that should be easily learned once and for all by the end of high school or the first year of college; but rather that writing is a *rhetorical activity* that is contingent upon the writer's situation; is imperfectible; and is learned over time and multiple situations (see, for example, the developmental perspectives on writing offered by Beaufort; Carroll; Haswell; McCarthy; Sommers; and Sternglass, among many others).

Composition studies' continuing concern with the nature of writing and the success of student writers has led to an argument in some circles that composition courses can serve as a place where students learn not only "how to" write but also how writing works. This writing-about-writing approach stems from decades of debate over what writing is and particularly how or whether the content of writing can be separated from its forms and procedures.

THE PROBLEM OF CONTENT AND FORM IN COMPOSITION COURSES

Since 1979, Richard Fulkerson has written three separate overviews of the state of FYC pedagogy for the journal *College Composition and Communication*. While there are certainly other useful analyses of composition pedagogy, we find Fulkerson's particularly helpful due to the frame he provides: an outline of what he sees as the necessary components of a theory of teaching writing and a discussion of the various theories currently at play. In a field that so highly values pedagogy, Fulkerson's attention to a theory of teaching writing seems understandable. He is not alone in arguing that all writing teachers have theories of teaching writing, whether they are aware of them or not. If teachers do not consciously understand and enact their theories, however, students can become confused and resistant to future writing instruction. These consequences of such teacher unconsciousness are important enough that Fulkerson has been willing to return to this discussion three times in thirty years.

Fulkerson argues that a full theory of writing must include:

- An axiology ("a commitment about what constitutes good writing") ("Composition Theory" 410);

- A procedure ("a conception of how writers go about creating texts, and perhaps a conception of how they should go about it") (411);

- A pedagogy ("some perspective about classroom procedures and curricular designs suitable for enabling students to achieve the sort of writing one values") (411); and

- An epistemology (our assumptions about "what counts for knowledge") (411).

Fulkerson originally outlined, in 1979, four axiologies ("Four Philosophies" 344–5):

- Formalist (writing that values form, including both correctness and style);

- Expressionist (expressivist) (writing that values self-discovery or expression);

- Mimetic (writing that demonstrates or conveys knowledge); and

- Rhetorical (writing that persuades an audience).

In his final (2005) overview, Fulkerson details what he understands as a variety of emerging rhetorical approaches: procedural rhetoric, composition as argumentation, genre-based composition, and composition as introduction to an academic discourse ("Composition at the Turn" 671). Here, Fulkerson adds a fifth axiology, critical/cultural studies (CCS), which focuses on helping students analyze and explore issues of culture and power (659).

Three of Fulkerson's axiologies—formalist, expressivist, and rhetorical—do not address the content of student writing but instead focus on what could be described as procedural knowledge or craft: how a writer goes about writing correctly or persuasively or creatively. These approaches seem to view the composition course as a content-less skills course, in that they assume a given set of procedural skills and knowledge can be taught equally well no matter what students write about. The two approaches that do address content (mimetic and CCS) hint at our field's inability to resolve the difficult question regarding the relationship of form and style to content. The mimetic approach, which highly values clear reasoning and accurate content, has, according to Fulkerson, "never been common in writing courses. It more usually exists when teachers evaluate essay tests or research papers in their disciplines. Papers with inaccurate information or unacceptable conclusions are then judged seriously inferior" ("Composition Theory" 413). When literature was a common content for composition classes, that focus would certainly have lent itself to a mimetic axiology, but literature was removed from many composition courses with the ascent of the process movement in the 1970s and early 1980s. Through the 1970s, 1980s, and well into the 1990s, the content of composition was commonly understood as "whatever is most interesting to students," the assumption being that writing courses are about *forming* arguments or crafting text independent of the *content* of those arguments or that text.

Fulkerson categorized the CCS axiology that became popular in the 1990s as a mimetic approach ("Composition at the Turn" 662) and argued that it reflected "content envy on the part of writing teachers" (663). While this approach seemed as though it might offer a resolution to the form/content dichotomy, Fulkerson argued that it did not. Rather, he felt that such courses nearly always focused on their content (declarative knowledge about culture and power) to the exclusion of focusing on writing or writing instruction (procedural knowledge about writing). CCS courses require that "students read about systemic cultural injustices inflicted by dominant societal groups and dominant discourses on those with less power, and upon the empowering possibilities of rhetoric if students are educated to 'read' carefully and 'resist' the social texts that keep some groups subordinated" (659). According to Fulkerson, this approach is appropriate for a writing-intensive history, anthropology, or sociology class, but it is not focused enough on writing to be considered (by him) to be a writing class. (A critique also offered some years earlier by Gary Tate in his book chapter, "Empty Pedagogical Space and Silent Students.")

Fulkerson's analysis, then, seems to suggest that composition has been largely understood as a "skills" course, and that the writing done in composition courses is (except in the case of CCS courses) separated from content because it is understood as nondisciplinary. Fulkerson's sense of the field suggests an underlying acceptance of the belief that composition courses are, by their very nature, content-less and cannot reflect a mimetic axiology, because the only disciplinary knowledge about which

students could write exists in disciplines outside of composition studies. According to this view, to demonstrate content knowledge, students
would have to write about some other discipline's content (for example,
sociology), but in such cases composition teachers are most often unable
to respond to inaccurate or off-the-mark information or conclusions
because those instructors lacks expertise regarding the content. (In this
example, sociology; for additional evidence of this problem, see Wardle,
"'Mutt Genres'" and "Cross-Disciplinary.") When content knowledge is
separated from writing instruction, the composition teacher is forced to
judge the quality of writing not by what it says, but by the process that
led to it (for example, number of drafts), adherence to specified forms,
grammatical correctness, specified style, or ability to persuade a general
audience. While all of these are important aspects of writing, they represent an incomplete set of concerns for a teacher to value. Instruction
toward rhetorically unified writing—with content, arrangement, style,
and delivery appropriate to specific audiences and discourse communities—appears to be unattainable for composition courses in which any
content and form are allowed but the teacher's expertise regarding all
the possible content and forms is realistically limited.

What Fulkerson's analysis suggests to us is that compositionists have
not recognized their own disciplinary knowledge as a possible content
for FYC courses. Understandings of FYC as a "skills" course have continued to instantiate a separation of form, content, style, and process
despite the fact that the field's cutting-edge genre, discourse, and activity theory shows why such separation is not actually possible (see, for
example, Bazerman, "Systems"; Gee; and Russell, "Writing"). Is it possible for students to write *about* a content (declarative knowledge) for
which the composition teacher is a qualified reader and which also
will not detract from but instead stress the writing-related (procedural)
knowledge that should be the focus of a writing course?

Recently, we have been among those developing research, theory,
and curricula that treat FYC as a content course in the specialized knowledge of composition studies. This approach diverges from those that
Fulkerson outlined by positing the content of composition studies as a
possible content for the composition course. Rather than write about
any topic, for example, students in such writing-about-writing courses
consider writing itself as a topic to consider. In particular, Writing-about-
Writing approaches ask students to consider their own relationships to
writing, their lives as writers, and how some relevant composition studies

research can help them change both their conceptions of writing and their writing practices. When we wrote about this approach in *College Composition and Communication* in June 2007, we gave a number of rationales for it, including the desire to change students' "understandings about writing, and thus change the way they write" (Downs and Wardle 553). We reasoned that learning *about* writing would change students' conceptions of, approaches to, and processes of writing by putting content, form, and process in harmony rather than constant tension. Our initial pursuit of this pedagogy was sparked by the needs of our own students and our concern that the common forms of FYC we had been trying to enact did not appear to be resulting in transferable knowledge about writing (556–57). Over time we both came to believe that some of the knowledge of our field might be helpful for students to read and consider directly. In other words, we began to feel that composition courses could serve as introductory "content" courses (554) in much the same way as do introductory courses in other disciplines.

Since writing that article, our own understanding of the potential of a writing-about-writing approach has grown as we have attended and helped facilitate a number of Conference on College Composition and Communication (CCCC) SIGs (special interest groups), participated on a listserv for those using the approach, worked with others to facilitate a CCCC workshop on the approach, chartered the Writing-about-Writing Network (WAWN) with founder Betsy Sargent, and created a related Ning with David Slomp. Our approaches have been enriched through dialogue between the many compositionists around the country who use writing about writing—some who have been quietly doing so for decades.

In the remainder of this chapter, we discuss the goals and rationale for the approach, describing how it attempts to overcome the form/content and procedural/declarative knowledge dichotomies, and what we know so far about whether the outcomes for the courses match expectations. Much of the discussion and work around this approach has yet to see publication, so our discussion here draws largely on the working groups mentioned above, as well as a small survey we conducted of those using writing about writing.

GOALS FOR WAW APPROACHES

Those using Writing-about-Writing speak of intertwining goals for students and the field of composition studies. We begin here with the three central goals that survey respondents and colleagues state for students, which are perhaps best summarized as a desire to create a *transferable* and *empowering* focus on *understanding writing as a subject of study.*

Understanding Writing as a Subject of Study

Faculty using the WAW pedagogy generally understand it in some way as a means to address the age-old FYC problem of trying to teach students "to write" without a content and common knowledge base and without working on many genres in transactional contexts (see Joseph Petraglia's edited collection, *Reconceiving Writing, Rethinking Writing Instruction* for more extensive discussion of this issue). In her response to our survey questions, Kathleen Yancey, current editor of *College Composition and Communication* and fellow contributor to this volume, noted that composition courses often "treat content as though it doesn't matter, but logically it must." While most of the approaches that Fulkerson outlines seem to accept the notion of composition as content-less skills course, Writing-about-Writing pedagogies actively resist that conception. Michael Murphy, director of College Writing at SUNY-Oswego, responded to our survey questions by arguing that composition courses "shouldn't have some gratuitous or incidental content that serves as a kind of alibi 'occasion' for writing."

In a WAW class, the subjects of students' writing are issues and questions related to writing, discourse, and literacy, in genres appropriate to their local learning objectives. They build common experiences and knowledge about writing that prompt them to actively learn more; their teachers, with expertise on writing as a subject, serve as better readers than students can on subjects they know less about. Students share what they learn with others, in forms appropriate to their ends—blogs, letters, conference and poster presentations, even articles for publication.

Debra Dew, director of the Writing and Rhetoric Program at the University of Colorado–Colorado Springs and coeditor of *WPA: Writing Program Administration*, noted in her survey responses that the WAW approach "sets up writing tasks and contexts with *content*-intensive experiences." By providing a relevant subject of study that helps students reflect on the very "skill" they are meant to learn, students can understand the study of writing as a form of intellectual work. As such, FYC can, as Heidi Estrem, director of the Writing Program at Boise State University, said in her survey response, "[C]omplicate something (writing) which many [students] see as only a skill." Yancey describes the

WAW content as a way of teaching not just procedural but also declarative knowledge, helping students gain "an understanding of composing that explains their current practices *in the context of a theory of composing.* The goals of the course thus include key concepts and their relationships in addition to successful practices and texts." Given the complexity of this issue, we think it is worthwhile to provide an extended example here of one way this works.

We each ask our first-year students to complete an auto-ethnography of their own writing processes. This assignment requires that they talk aloud and record themselves in a natural setting while writing a paper for a class. They then transcribe their own protocol and code it, using as a starting point a code the class invents together after reading studies by scholars such as Sondra Perl, Nancy Sommers, and Carol Berkenkotter. Coding categories might include "lexical revision," "conceptual revision," "writing without planning," "rereading," and so on. The students might discuss the form their papers should take, debating whether the task is entirely writing-to-learn and thus can take the form of an informal reflection, or whether it is also a learning-to-write activity preparing them to write about research in a more formal way. The students draft their papers in the genres agreed appropriate by the class, read and respond to one another's drafts in a structured workshop, and then revise for teacher feedback, which leads to grading in the end-of-semester portfolio.

In our view, the assignment represents a unification of three of the axiologies—expressivist, mimetic, and rhetorical. One purpose of the assignment is clearly to promote greater self-awareness and self-knowledge, an expressivist goal. But another purpose is mimetic—to use the terms and concepts in the course reading to help analyze and explain data. A third goal is rhetorical: to learn to write about research in ways that might be helpful in future writing situations. The style and genre are discussed at length, and students sometimes write quite innovative and alternative types of texts. The topic of the assignment is writing process; the readings are about writing process; and course pedagogy models a potential writing and revision process. The content is integral to the writing and learning, rather than gratuitous, to recall Fulkerson's taxonomic concerns.

Some critics of Writing-about-Writing worry that the WAW approach teaches declarative content about writing to the exclusion of procedural knowledge, or "craft." However, all of the WAW pedagogies we have seen, including our own, incorporate both. The focus on writing as content works seamlessly with discussions of craft, style, and revision, as we hope the above example illustrates. Doug Hesse, director of the Writing Program at the University of Denver and former chair of the Conference on College Composition and Communication, has argued that this approach does not allow for "writers [to] gain the floor by creating interest, through the arts of discourse" ("Place" 41). We wonder, however, whether it is ever possible to teach the "arts of discourse" (understood as style and craft) independent of content. How do writers know what sorts what stylistic options are usefully available to them unless they know to whom they are writing, about what, and under what circumstances? Discussing writing as craft and procedure as well as content adds another layer of rigor and complexity to the discussion while allowing students to make empowered and informed choices about their uses of discourse.

Hesse also suggests that placing writing at the center of a writing course creates a course in which student writing is "disciplined," only allowing rhetors to "develop given topics along approved trajectories" ("Place" 41) rather than allowing them to be limitlessly creative. The emerging WAW pedagogies we have seen and implemented ourselves seem to suggest two things: first, that WAW classes are not at all limiting in either their topics or their trajectories; any meaningful genre, form, writing-related content, and medium can make an appearance in a WAW class—as they are relevant to the learning outcomes related to writing. Since all writing classes inevitably have desired learning outcomes, the WAW approach is no different in this regard. However, because students in WAW courses are learning about the nature and possibilities of writing, they inevitably explore many content- and craft-related possibilities, perhaps more than they would in a traditional composition class.

Second, however, it seems to us that it is important not to conflate understanding that disciplinary conventions exist and how/why they work with forcibly "disciplining" or limiting student writing. As postprocess and genre theorists have noted, an exclusive focus on "individual expression and personal voice" can actually work to the disadvantage of students who are members of "culturally marginalized groups," because they never learn the "genres of privilege" and are thus denied access to "those in power" (Clark 22). In other words, knowledge about how texts work is empowering rather than limiting. Knowledge about how stylistic conventions and disciplinary genres work does not mean that writers are limited to using those; rather, such understanding allows writers to recognize what the expected options are and empower them to employ those options if they choose—or how to resist them usefully if they so choose.

Transfer

Many WAW teachers express dissatisfaction with students' transfer of learning from traditional composition courses to other writing contexts, and anticipate that WAW courses will significantly improve such generalization. Our respondent Laurie McMillan, for example, argues that "students are more likely to transfer what they've learned if they're not only practicing writing in first-year comp but also constantly reading and reflecting on writing/composition research." Some respondents, such as Scott Warnock, director of the Freshman Writing Program at Drexel University, distinguish between different probabilities of transfer: "While we may not be able to teach students transferable writing skills, we can provide them with transferable writing knowledge that they can take with them to help them work through any writing/communication assignment." As different writing situations offer different answers, the transferable knowledge is not the answers but the questions: not "how to write," but *how to ask about* how to write.

Transfer research has suggested that meta-awareness is one means for encouraging transfer (e.g., Beaufort; Perkins and Salomon, "Teaching"), and rhetorical understanding and metacognition are explicitly stated aspects of every WAW approach we have seen. Work on reflection, including Yancey's *Reflection in the Writing Classroom* and genre and activity theories, seems to have been influential in encouraging this focus on metacognition. Estrem points out, "Genre theory . . . gives us a framework for talking about writing—and, importantly, for doing *lots* and *lots* of reflection and meta-talk/writing." The fieldwriting that students do in Shannon Carter's approach is one way of reaching this end: Carter, codirector of the Converging Literacies Center at Texas A&M University–Commerce, wants students to develop a metacognitive awareness—which she calls *rhetorical dexterity*—"necessary to negotiate a variety of different writing tasks in a variety of different rhetorical contexts." Andrew Moss, coordinator of the Composition Program at California State Polytechnic University–Pomona, also hopes to help students acquire this rhetorical dexterity specifically within the university: "Writing-about-writing seems to offer students more direct, more explicit understandings of how writing and academic inquiry are interrelated. It provides them with a framework for understanding how writing works within the activity systems of a university. And it offers students sustained exposure to the texture and feel of academic writing—the language and rhythms of different kinds of academic prose." Having students learn concepts rather than general rules is also a road to transfer, and the rhetorical focus of WAW lends itself to such conceptual learning. McMillan says that in her class, "students end up seeing this as a particular genre of writing with particular conventions . . . associated with it rather than getting the sense that one set of rules exists for all occasions."

Critics of the WAW approach rightly wonder whether research will bear out the hopes regarding transfer (Kutney). Research to test transfer from WAW classes has begun, but is still in early stages, since such research is longitudinal and will thus take a number of years to conduct. Dan Frazier's recent discussion of transfer and WAW pedagogies suggests that transfer may hinge on "bridge" moments during and between courses. In other words, Frazier argues, one course is not sufficient to encouraging transfer, and educators and administrators must help create situations beyond and between classes that help trigger students to expand and generalize what they have learned.

We feel optimistic that the WAW courses are carefully designed for transfer in a way that traditional composition courses are not. However, if transfer researchers are correct in their belief that transfer depends not just on the initial learning environment but also on appropriate subsequent learning environments, then we may be frustrated in our pursuit of transfer until we can study WAW curricula within a carefully integrated vertical curricular experience.

Student Empowerment

WAW proponents as a group seem greatly concerned with student empowerment. They want students to have what Barbara Bird, director of the Writing Center at Taylor University, describes as "greater control over and investment in their learning/knowledge construction," and they want students to be what Heidi Estrem calls "the primary knowledge-makers and contributors." Most of those who responded to our survey see their WAW approaches as ways of helping students draw from their own literacy and writing experiences and research to generate real writerly authority. Andrew Moss notes that this pedagogy demands the same student engagement as that sought by critical theorists such as

Ira Shor, whose *Empowering Education* Moss finds useful in understanding what values, attitudes, and experiences students and faculty bring to classes.

In this regard, the WAW and CCS approaches have common ends, though they might be viewed as in opposition due to their differing sense of the source of student empowerment. The CCS approach tends to work toward empowerment by having the teacher instruct students to write through and write about issues of empowerment. In the WAW approach, the content and methodology of the course itself are seen as the sources of empowerment; in other words, students are empowered to better understand themselves as writers and users of language because the course treats them as authoritative speakers and asks them to own and take control of their own literate experiences, expertise, and questions.

HOPES FOR THE FIELD

Composition studies has a long and embattled history. After a long tradition of rhetoric as the foundation of Western education, that approach faded in favor of one or two composition courses primarily imagined as remedial skills courses. This movement did lead to research about composing and the reemergence of rhetoric as a field of study. However, the FYC course and many of those who chose to study in the emerging field of composition studies were often housed in English departments that did not allow these emerging scholars autonomy over their own courses. For a variety of political, practical, and disciplinary reasons, composition courses have proven difficult to change. They are often taught by adjuncts and graduate students with little if any training in the field of composition studies, a situation that reinscribes the understanding of those courses as "remedial" in nature, or "skills" classes that almost anyone can teach.

Most teachers and administrators advocating a WAW approach share a common goal for the field of composition studies: that by bridging form and content in FYC, the field itself might find sounder footing in the academy. Yancey notes that such an outcome is best seen as "a benefit, not the purpose" of WAW approaches. But survey responses like Dew's make a powerful case (as she also does in her 2003 *WPA* article detailing her WAW curricula) for this possibility: "We frame the course as an entry-level disciplinary experience—not as the *first* course in the major as in a sequence that leads to a rhetoric/writing major, but rather as a discipline-specific experience in rhetoric/writing theory [content] and practice [skills]. All fields work in both content and skills domains, and hopefully, they all will assess their efficacy in like manner." Explaining why framing FYC as a disciplinary experience seemed to her a logical next step for the field, Dew told us, "I reviewed FYC texts to better discern *what* content we could have them work with—I saw *myself* and *ourselves* in these books—language, rhetoric, writing—our content and our skills appeared everywhere. However, we were not naming the work as ours. I decided to reframe the content that was already within our WPA outcomes to make it visible and integral." In other words, we have the disciplinary knowledge, but we have not publicly claimed it *as such*, and in that choice have lost a key source of credibility in the academy and with our students. Framing what we know *as* disciplinary knowledge helps us gain authority to structure writing courses in ways that make sense given results of our research about writing and writers.

Warnock points out that there are benefits for teachers, too, in moving to a WAW approach because such an approach "provides us with a disciplinary foothold, helping to professionalize our faculty and the composition program." Such professionalization might help in our fight to improve working conditions for our teachers—an argument Dew has made repeatedly and eloquently. The results of early WAW assessment at the University of Central Florida (UCF) did aid in professionalizing the composition faculty, persuading the president to provide funding to convert all part-time and visiting composition lines to full-time positions so that faculty could participate in ongoing training and professional development. Framing composition as a class about writing and as only one of many writing opportunities necessary for students to grow as writers also helps to change inaccurate conceptions of writing and make a case for writing-across-the-curriculum programs. Such was the case at UCF, where the success of the WAW course was framed as only a necessary entry point to a vertical curriculum. This argument resulted in new funding to begin a writing-across-the-curriculum program (see "New Writing Department Goal").

CURRICULUM DESCRIPTIONS: WAYS OF WRITING-ABOUT-WRITING

While writing-about-writing adherents share many common goals, pedagogical possibilities for reaching those goals are nearly endless. While these curricula all are defined by making the knowledge of the field the studied and written content of the course, approaches around the country and even within programs are increasingly diverse. New teachers are often interested in knowing what WAW looks like. Here we want to emphasize that WAW can take many shapes. To be practically useful to new teachers, however, we will offer some examples of common ground shared by many WAW approaches, some ways in which WAW approaches differ, and then three sample "models" that demonstrate these variables in action.

Common Ground

WAW curricula generally imagine first-year students as smart, capable, and experienced, not tabula rasa or in deficit. As the goal of empowering students suggests, WAW demands a belief in students' ability to highly achieve. Bird, for example, has designed a demanding WAW curriculum specifically for basic writers, and has argued eloquently that such writers can and do rise to the challenge. The curricula in our survey responses set a high bar; everyone seems to be working in the spirit of David Bartholomae and Anthony Petrosky's *Ways of Reading*, a curriculum and textbook that became popular in the late 1980s (and remains so on some campuses today), recognized for its rigor and emphasis on placing authority in the hands of students. WAW curricula similarly assign difficult reading and expect that students can handle complex texts when given appropriate scaffolding and support.

Readings from composition studies is a second and related defining feature of WAW curricula. Readings, foremost, convey the content studied in the course. Beyond that, readings model the genre-related and intellectual moves of the academic discourses on which many WAW approaches focus. The readings also provide a platform for teaching strategies for reading intellectually challenging, complex, scholarly texts. In each instance of WAW in specific courses, at least those of which we are aware, these texts are at the center of the pedagogical approach.

Perhaps due to the WAW goal of transfer, these curricula place a high value and emphasis on metacognition and reflection, based on the premise that helping students become mindful of their assumptions and practices of writing and reading will yield greater control and better strategies. The WAW curricula with which we are familiar all stress reflection and use a variety of writing assignments, from literacy narratives to journaling to portfolio reflections, to prompt it.

Finally, we note that many (but not all) WAW writing assignments are analytical and/or research based. WAW courses emphasize interaction with texts that are themselves focused on writing and literacy, as well as interaction with a variety of actual scenes of writing. After reflective writing, the most common writing assignments are ethnographies and autoethnographies, interview reports, and other research reports in which students have observed some site of writing or literacy and have analyzed or theorized it.

The shared overall goal among WAW variants seems to be to change students' awareness of the nature of writing and literacy in order to shape the way they think about writing, with the expectation that how they write may change in turn. Toward this end, students in these courses engage a variety of sophisticated texts focusing (in writing) on writing and literacy, reflecting on their experiences and finding relationships and patterns between those and their reading. They often study some aspect(s) of writing and literacy in greater depth, relating the material and ideas presented in the course to actual scenes of writing and literacy.

Dimensions of Variation

While there is common ground across WAW pedagogies, there is also substantial variation. These variations include:

- The particular angle or perspective a course takes—what subjects it prioritizes and how student research is focused (if the course includes research);

- The end of student learning emphasized—a primary focus on personal growth versus a primary focus on contribution to the field;

- Types and number of readings; and

- Types and number of writing assignments.

The most obvious distinction among WAW curricula is that they may focus on writing and literacy from distinctly different angles. We see remarkable blends of subject matter, making it difficult to generalize without misstating what happens in courses. We can, however, distinguish three categories of approaches developing. The first focuses on literacy and discourse, how writing and language demonstrate community membership. The second focuses on writing studies itself—the existence of the discipline qua discipline, with its knowledge and expertise on writing, emphasizing rhetorical theory and its resultant strategies for writing. The third focuses on the nature of writing and writers' practices.

While these approaches ultimately focus on much of the same ground, they do so through significantly different lenses. Other approaches, like the one at UCF, try to cover all of this ground by teaching "units" with particular declarative knowledge that must be covered.

Another predictable source of differentiation among curricula is readings. These, of course, vary by curricular focus, as well as by the length of the course and how instructors decide to interweave readings with writing projects. Broadly speaking, we saw all of these kinds of readings in the survey: empirical research and theory on writing, writers' accounts of writing, empirical research and theory on literacy, literacy narratives and biographies, and even traditional textbooks integrated with scholarly and professional readings. Many WAW classrooms also assign student writing as classroom texts. In our own classes, for example, students read former students' work as well as selections from the national undergraduate rhetoric- and composition-focused journal *Young Scholars in Writing* and the local UCF student journal, *Stylus*.

While there is similar variation in writing assignments, some assignment types are quite common. For example, many courses assign a literacy narrative. Within the common category of reflective writing, a variety of assignments is given, the most popular being some form of reading journal. Most courses have students analyze readings in some way, most often through summaries, analyses, and responses. Writing with sources is almost universal, whether in short or long texts. Many courses use varieties of writing to support a research project: research proposals, bibliographies, literature reviews, summaries, presentations. Courses that included primary research tend most often toward interviews (with professionals and others, on the writing they encountered) and ethnographies, though some did not specify methods. And, as noted earlier, there appears to be great diversity in what students actually write about. If it has to do with writing, literacy, language, rhetoric, reading, communication, argument, persuasion, or the cultural functions or implications of any of these, a WAW curriculum has students researching and writing about it.

To offer a concrete sense of ways these variations can combine, we offer overviews of three possible curricula to consider as potential models for future WAW-focused FYC classes, one representing each of the three major approaches that we find represented in our survey—literacy/discourse, language/rhetoric, and writing/writers' practices.

Example 1: Literacy/Discourse

Shannon Carter, Texas A&M–Commerce

Carter's English 100-101-102 sequence is a mostly program-wide writing-about-writing curriculum based on ethnographic inquiry into in-school and out-of-school literacy practices—"the shape and function of literacy as a place-based, people-oriented, and socially mediated activity rather than an autonomous, neutral, standardized, portable skill set." Stated objectives in the syllabus include building researched academic arguments, awareness of the influence of context and audience on writing, rhetorical flexibility to negotiate various academic tasks leading to researched argument, an awareness of how research can be influenced by researchers' subject positions, and the creation of effective written reports of research findings. Students read work by Deborah Brandt, Beverly Moss, Christina Mirabelli, David Barton and Mary Hamilton, and Daniel P. Resnick, among others, and the 102 course then "invite[s] them to contribute to this ongoing scholarly conversation through their own ethnographic inquiry, including extensive field observations, interviews, and secondary research." Students write three assignments of three to five pages that build to an ethnographic project of ten to fifteen pages that may include text, aural, visual, and video components. The first assignment has students test Brandt's notions of literacy sponsorship against their own experiences; the second has students explore literacy *in place*; the third has them explore relationships between out-of-school and in-school literacy practices. Students usually draw their large ethnography project from one of these shorter assignments. The course stresses the content of the field *as* the content of a field, focuses directly on changing students' conceptions of writing, and emphasizes primary, contributive research to the field. There is mild emphasis on transfer; the curriculum gives little attention to disciplinarity or writing for other disciplines. Ultimately, the course seeks to "work against the literacy myth" that requires many writers to adopt notions and processes of reading and writing "that run counter to what research tells us about how literacy functions in the world and approaches 'expert writers' take when engaging in meaningful writing tasks."

Example 2: Language/Rhetoric

Debra Dew, University of Colorado–Colorado Springs

Dew's *Rhetoric and Writing I: Academic Reading and Analytical Writing* is required campus-wide and is the only authorized curriculum, which Dew sees as accomplishing disciplinary work: "The course . . . sets the disciplinary parameters for *what* rhetoric/writing is on campus and beyond." Students read rhetorical theory that gives them working concepts of rhetorical situation, appeals, stasis, and writing process; and then readings on language, including rhetorical performances (e.g., King, Standing Bear, Anzaldúa, Lincoln, Roosevelt), literacy autobiographies (e.g., Rodriguez, Baldwin, Tan), and essays that "define ethical and unethical language strategies and practices and complicate *rhetoric* conceptually" (e.g., Hirshberg, Huxley, Gerber on propaganda and advertising). Along with journal responses to readings, students compose four analytical documented essays with various aims: connecting the claims of a course reading to another text (film, advertisement, or video); positioning an argument within the ongoing discussion of a language issue; rhetorical criticism of a reading. Dew's curriculum is concerned that students recognize the study of rhetoric and writing as a discipline, which inherently carries some emphasis on changing students' conceptions of writing and showing disciplinary differences in writing (though these are not main emphases). No explicit attention is devoted to transfer, conducting primary research, or writing to contribute to the field. Rather, the course positions students primarily as writing-to-learn.

Example 3: Writing/Writers' Practices

Laurie McMillan, Marywood University

Laurie McMillan, writing coordinator at Marywood University, teaches a version of Writing-about-Writing that fulfills her institution's sole FYC requirement. It is specifically focused on promoting transfer of knowledge gained in the class through metacognition, reflection, and explicit discussion of writing processes and practices. Students read selections from Wendy Bishop's *On Writing: A Process Reader* and work through three units in the course: Why Write? How Writing Works, and Joining the Conversation (researched argument). They first focus on purposes and kinds of writing, with attention to style; their writing includes an e-mail to the professor and an interview narrative. They then explore more writing research and foundational concepts of writing, developing a comparative rhetorical analysis and a midterm reflection. The third unit, occupying the second half of the course, guides students through an extended research process, from proposing a research question to presenting findings. The course does not heavily

emphasize the disciplinary nature of academic writing, and its attention to changing student conceptions of writing as a specific project is
limited. Rather, it stresses the content of the course as the content of
a scholarly field, something that students themselves can contribute to
through primary research. Transfer remains the central goal: McMillan
hopes that "by practicing writing in a very self-conscious way, student
writers will improve in their ability to write effectively as they face new
writing situations."

CONCLUSION

Anne Beaufort, in her recent book championing a writing-focused
approach in composition, argues, "Freshman writing, if taught with an
eye toward transfer of learning and with an explicit acknowledgement
of the context of freshman writing itself as a social practice, can set students on a course of life-long learning so that they know *how to learn* to
become better and better writers in a variety of social contexts" (*College
Writing and Beyond* 7). In most cases, teachers pursuing WAW pedagogies are asking students to read and write about writing concepts themselves as a way to help them learn "how to learn" to continue to grow
as writers, by bridging the content/form/process gap that has plagued
FYC since its inception. Proponents of WAW pedagogies enact curricula
that suggest it is possible for students to write *about* a content for which
the teacher is a qualified reader and which stresses rather than detracts
from the writing-related knowledge that should be the focus of a writing
course. It would be unrealistic to assume that WAW approaches mark
the end of fragmentation and change regarding first-year composition
courses. What WAW does seem to mark, however, is a recognition of our
disciplinary history and an assumption that our disciplinary knowledge
can and should be shared with students in meaningful ways.

We are only beginning to see long-term assessments suggesting how
well WAW approaches overcome some other long-standing problems
with composition courses. Are WAW courses more effective in their
desired ends than traditional courses? And do they better encourage
transfer of writing-related knowledge to other situations? Recent end-
of-semester portfolio assessment results at the University of Central
Florida comparing WAW to traditional composition pedagogies suggest that the WAW curriculum can result in positively quantifiable differences in learning outcomes. For example, students in WAW sections
had significantly higher scores than students in traditional sections in

the transfer-encouraging behavior of self-reflection. They also demonstrated greater levels of global revision, and scored higher on ability to rhetorically analyze difficult texts and demonstrate college-level thinking. Whether these gains will result in better transfer remains a difficult and intriguing question, as we have discussed. Most reasonably, the research that informs writing-about-writing approaches suggests that one course (based on *any* pedagogy) is insufficient to teach students to write and about writing. Rather, we argue that WAW approaches serve as a more solid foundation to vertical writing experiences (whether in writing-across-the-curriculum programs, writing majors, or extended writing experiences within and outside the university) than traditional composition courses. Integrating writing-about-writing composition classes with rigorous cross-curricular writing experiences and supportive writing centers seems to us to be the most likely to result in college graduates who can demonstrate Shannon Carter's desired "rhetorical dexterity."

8

TRANSFER, PORTABILITY, GENERALIZATION
(How) Does Composition Expertise "Carry"?

Christiane Donahue

Transfer, a term with myriad connotations, has become key to recent discussions in composition studies. The process it names encapsulates deep questions about liberal arts traditions, professional education, general education, specialization, expertise, "useful" learning, and the very value of any educational frame in fostering students' development—all of the questions the field of composition has faced and will continue to face. The transfer discussion draws on historical phases of composition studies as well, tapping into old debates about the cognitive versus the social, enculturation and discourse communities, the nature of writing knowledge, even the research traditions of our relatively young field. This one word is nexus to intersecting points of thinking, teaching, and learning in contexts that often seem worlds apart.

While transfer is clearly at the heart of educational or training concerns, we don't yet know that much about how it works. We do know it is central to our field's concerns, in ways that call for much future attention and a revisiting of parts of our discipline's modern history. Perhaps most importantly, due to composition studies' interest in language and literacy and our recent trend toward longitudinal studies, we are in fact now in a position to contribute back to the broader cross-disciplinary research about transfer done in other fields.

In this chapter, I will review the essential literature from education, psychology, sociology and, more recently, composition studies, on transfer. In the process, I will describe what "writing" might be if we study it as "knowledge that transfers." Of course, the topic is far more evolved than one short chapter can manage to introduce. I will trace the main threads of transfer research in general and discuss the research as it relates specifically to composition, future research paths, and possible applications to composition instruction.

WHAT IS TRANSFER (AND WHAT IS BEING TRANSFERRED)?

The heart of transfer is "the personal creation of relations of similarity. . . [or] how the new situation is connected with the thinker's trace of a previous situation" (Lobato 18) in a way that enables something learned to be used anew. Note that the individual, the contexts in which the individual is working, and the individual's awareness of the work are included in this definition. The information and processes learned in one context, by solving one problem, *should* enable a learner to solve a conceptually similar problem in another context (Carter; Smagorinsky and Smith); "[H]aving never done 'X' before, the [novice] writer must decide whether any of the known strategies is relevant and, if they are, how to use them in some appropriate combination" (Smit 124). In some sense, transfer occurs constantly and naturally. One of the most influential studies of transfer recently (Tuomi-Grohn, Engestrom and Young) suggests that transfer in its most elemental form is equated with survival itself, enabling adaptation and evolution (1). We would not learn to speak or be able to navigate daily life without it. In educational settings, however, studies suggest that transfer is far less natural.

In many ways the contexts and principles identified in the education and psychology research are precisely what drive our composition teaching. For example, the role of metareflection in learning writing is part of the air composition faculty breathe. We might wonder, then, why composition hasn't had more to say in the broader transfer discussion, and why what has been said isn't read or cited in the scholarship outside the field. Composition is focused in particular on certain types of knowledge we hope will transfer. We want students—considering most of our outcomes statements—to learn strategies, processes, values, rhetorical flexibility, and linguistic knowledge not just for topic-specific gain but expressly for broader transfer, for use in new contexts. This is different in some ways from the knowledge that another domain might focus on. Writing teachers have tended to assume as a given the "transfer" of these writing abilities or skills, despite the fact that there is little evidence that such transfer commonly occurs.

At most universities (at least outside of composition programs), writing in general is always seen as transferable, reliant on skills-based models that emphasize acquiring "skills" to be replicated in all future classes.

Upper-level writing requirements, whether writing in the disciplines, technical writing, business writing or another model, are equally built on a sense of linear connected development across experiences. And yet—we know, after years of study, that no set of rules works everywhere (Ford, "Knowledge Transfer" 2004), that students do not recognize the connectedness we hope they will (see Bergmann and Zepernick), and that they see tasks in different disciplinary settings as different, even though the assignments are similar (Herrington). It is thus perhaps not surprising that transfer is described as unpredictable and hard to trace. Students may well recognize in new situations that they need to adapt previous knowledge, but if they don't know how to identify new demands and how to respond, there will still be no success.

In 1999, Alexander and Murphy suggested five "safe" generalizations we could make about transfer, based on available research at the time: it is essential to "competent performance in complex domains"; it occurs far less often than we might hope, at least in formal educational settings; it is supported in contexts that are "intentionally orchestrated to encourage cross-situation and cross-domain transfer," especially when success in this kind of transfer is rewarded; it is tightly related to analogical reasoning; it must be fostered by educators who take into account simultaneously the learner, the content, and the context (562–65).

A BIT OF HISTORY

All of these concerns with transfer may seem to be recent "discoverables," but they are not new. A century ago, the first studies of transfer (Thorndike and Woodworth; Judd; Thorndike) focused largely on understanding transfer as the central principles of a task transferred to another, similar task within school, that is from one domain or context to another. Much later work, partly influenced by interest in transfer from industry training sessions to workplace application, focused on transfer across school levels, and at transition points such as from school to the corporate world beyond or from secondary to post-secondary education. Barbara Rogoff suggested that "cognitive skills seem to fluctuate as a function of the situation, which suggests that skills are limited in their generality" (qtd. in Smit 120). This limitation caught the attention of those responsible for ensuring programmatic coherence or developmental models of college curricula.

Throughout that century, waves of interest—and controversy—rose and fell. "Transfer" itself was questioned, most notably by the work of

Jean Lave, suggesting that *all* knowledge is contextual and thus "transfer" is not possible, and D. J. Detterman and R. K. Sternberg, arguing for simply teaching explicitly what we want to see students produce rather than trying to create or imagine transfer possibilities. Within the field of psychology, conflict among cognitivists and situated cognition theorists added to the debate, the former accusing the latter of not being "scientific" and the latter accusing the former of being "culturally decontextualized" (Tuomi-Grohn, Engestrom and Young 2), a debate that rippled later through composition as we struggled with our own debates about the social and cognitive aspects of learning to write. Most of the interest in transfer was not, however, directly focused on writing or literacy.

Earlier definitions of "transfer" focused on how an individual carries knowledge, strategies, skills, or abilities developed in one context into another context, thus placing responsibility on the individual. It was designated as the essential piece and purpose of learning, but specifically of "good" learning. Acquiring knowledge is not enough; *using* it is the broader gain (Gagné; Perkins and Salomon, *The Science and Art of Transfer;* Bransford and Schwartz). But in this context, tensions surfaced between those who saw transfer as in the individual carrying something forward, and those who saw it as constructed, embedded, and situated. For some, "learners acquire an activity in response to constraints and affordances of the learning situation. Transfer of an activity to a new situation involves a transformation of the initial situation and an invariant interaction of the learner in the new context" (De Corte 557); the role of transformation is in the interaction. This point of debate becomes critical to a discussion of transfer within composition studies, as it allows us a frame for questioning whether first-year writing, as a type of knowledge, does, in fact, "carry" on to other courses in the student's career.

We might say that our field has operated under what Perkins and Salomon call the "Bo Peep" theory of transfer—it "assumes that knowledge and skill a person has learned anywhere will 'come home' to wherever it is needed . . . transfer will take care of itself" (*The Science and Art of Transfer* 4). We can look at our own well-documented resistance in composition to certain forms of empirical research (see Haswell "NCTE/CCCC's Recent War" and Charney) and deep suspicions about cognitive psychology as at least partly a factor in the absence of attention to studies of transfer in other fields. What attention was paid to questions of transfer was largely not tagged as such in the 1980s and '90s. Certainly the notion that literate activity might enable certain kinds of thinking or learning (Goody; David Olson; Langer; Bazerman, "Systems of Genre") is built on principles of transferable ability. Cognitive studies of schemata and mental models exposed principles of learning that parallel transferability (McCutchen, Teske, and Bankston). A schema, as "a hypothetical cognitive structure by which information and knowledge is thought to be organized and processed; new information is assimilated, learned, and interpreted in terms of relevant pre-existing schemata" (Haskell 82), frames the cognitive work also targeted by transfer research, although Haskell suggests that it does so "without articulating the precise structures responsible for the transfer" (83). This model is consistent with models of the affordances provided by genres.

TRANSFER AS WE KNOW IT

What do the different research strands tell us about transfer in terms of key overlapping interests? These interests include the relationship between the (cognitive) individual and her (social) embeddedness, and between instrumental and contextual learning, the novice and expert status of knowledge users, the models of activity theory and communities of practice, and the role of meta-awareness or metacognition in the transfers that matter to us.

Gavriel Perkins and D. N. Salomon, defining voices in the domain of transfer studies, have developed the useful categories of "high-road" and "low-road" transfer, and the qualifiers of forward and backward transfer. They concur with most scholars that while "everyday" transfer happens naturally, intentional education transfer is not common. How is previously learned material evoked, called on, and used? Low-road transfer draws on processes that are "automatic, stimulus-controlled, and extensively practiced." High-road transfer involves "mindful [nonautomatic] deliberate processes that decontextualize the cognitive elements which are candidates for transfer" (124). This metacognitively guided decontextualization of principles or procedures is the hallmark of high-road transfer, and sounds a lot like what we isolate as "critical thinking" in higher education teaching discussions. While it is difficult not to feel that "high road" is more valuable than "low road," this is not the case; each has a role in what we hope students will achieve. The "low road" produces "socialization, acculturation, and experience-based cognitive development, resulting in the acquisition of habitual behavior patterns, response tendencies, personality traits, cognitive strategies and styles, expectations" (122), certainly elements we would like to see develop in our students.

In fact, much of the research on working memory and cognitive load points to the need for automatized features of production, a question that is particularly important for our composition discussions. The much-criticized "autonomous" model of literacy, for example, is built on assumptions of transferability and uncritical reuse of writing "skills" in new contexts. While we are quick to argue against writing as that a-contextual autonomous skill, there may well be reasons to work harder as a field to identify what particular aspects of writing we would actually like writers to have acquired as "automated." Low-road transfer, building that automated set of skills, takes time, however, and instructional time constraints interfere with transfer (Foertsch 370; Bransford, Brown, and Cocking). Sufficient time for initial learning has been recognized as a key factor in transfer success, but education is "supposed to" accelerate learning, and high-road transfer is part of that acceleration.

Perkins and Salomon also distinguish "near" and "far" transfer as outcomes; the more similar the new task or context, the closer the transfer ("Transfer of Learning" 123). High-road transfer is, for them, a predictor of distant transfer, linked to greater abstraction (128). This matters to composition in particular in terms of our thinking about students' writing across multiple contexts, disciplines, situations, and years, and again for our thinking about the nature of writing as a complex, abstract intellectual ability or as a concrete set of skills.

The Individual and the Social Construction of Knowledge

Theorists in psychology and education have suggested that individuals and situations interact to produce transfer. Transfer is thus often seen as situated and sociocultural, which means that understanding how transfer works includes taking into account how individuals interact with situations, how individuals construct associations among various contexts, and how contexts and players enable these associations. While Lev Vygotsky's developmental theories of human activity may not have been labeled as part of the general evolution of transfer scholarship, his model certainly offers a way to understand the individual-social relationship at the core of successful "vertical" transfer.

Vertical transfer is what's learned in one context that is (re)used in a next-level-up higher function, acting in fact as a prerequisite for that next level, as compared to lateral transfer, in which what is learned in one context is simply (re)used in another parallel context (with a similar level of demand) (Gagné, cited in Teich 195). Vertical transfer shares a good deal with Vygotskian models of development; the known or acquired knowledge is used in "stretch" contexts in which new domains call on the existing knowledge in new ways. In terms of composition, this means that transfer is more likely to occur when teachers provide work that is appropriately challenging to students' current ability levels, drawing on students' zones of proximal development (Alsup and Bernard-Donals; Jaxon), and when the learning of new material is scaffolded (Dias et al.). The kinds of scaffolding required to support transfer, however, differ from student to student (Rogers).

Transfer is thus enabled by the new context in which knowledge needs to be reused as much as by the way in which it is learned in the initial context; this is commonly named the "affordance" provided by a new context (Tuomi-Grohn, Engestrom, and Young; Volet; Hatano and Greeno). The ability to transfer and the knowledge to be transferred are thus not carried "in" the individual but brought about by person-context mutual interactions and the way knowledge is presented in new situations.

In an attempt to uncover some of this interactive dynamic, Ford studied the relationship between general knowledge and local knowledge in technical writing in school and in the field. She found that in a new writing context, the writer draws on familiar strategies but must retool, and "must understand the ways in which these already-learned strategies play out in new contexts" (or do not) ("Knowledge Transfer" 302). Ford suggests that there are political and cultural influences on how knowledge is reused as well (303), influences we do not always attend to in our discussions of how writing can be reused knowledge, can transfer.

Novices to Experts

The notion of expertise has been particularly entwined with the transfer question. When spontaneous transfer *does* apparently occur, it is primarily in contexts in which "the problem solver has a wealth of experience in a particular field" (Foertsch 371). Nancy Sommers has shown that without deep content expertise, transfer of writing ability across college courses, even within the same major, occurs with difficulty. The issue with expertise is also one of cognitive capacity. Novices who "are still struggling to master the basic skills of a domain . . . may be too preoccupied with the intricacies of problem-solving to notice similarities between the current problem and ones they have encountered in the past" (Foertsch 372). This finding is echoed in composition research about what has, perhaps unfortunately, sometimes been called "regression." Scholars like Richard Haswell and Joseph Williams have shown that students taking on new writing tasks often manage previously acquired abilities poorly for a time, as they carry several layers of cognitive processing out at once. There is not as much room in the transfer scholarship for discussion of this kind of learning event as we might expect.

Activity Theory and Communities of Practice

Earlier understandings of expertise as "vertical" and linear in its evolution have thus been replaced by versions that include horizontal or lateral understandings appropriate to a fragmented and multiple-knowledge economy: "experts," say Tuomi-Grohn, Engestrom, and Young, "operate in, and move between, multiple parallel activity systems," (5) each with its own demands, appropriate tools, rules, and interactive patterns. Activity system theory was introduced in the 1990s to the U.S. field of composition, and has been used to theorize models of learning in general and literacy in particular; it posits learning as developing within activities and networked systems of activities (see in particular the development of activity theory applications to North American composition concerns: Russell, "Activity Theory"; Bazerman, "Systems of Genre"). What counts as expert knowledge and skill is different in each activity system, and experts expect to need to negotiate, to create hybrids, and so on. In addition, experts' attitudes are different; they are more willing to tolerate ambiguity, to learn from others, or to persist even when tasks are difficult (Bransford and Schwartz 84).

Writers, Smit suggests, fall back on general knowledge precisely when they find themselves outside their domain of expertise, while expert writers see analogies across genres and contexts that novices do not. And yet, writers learn the general and the specific together (134); Carter emphasizes as well that the general knowledge we learn about writing and the specific knowledge tied to a context are learned together, in interaction; neither can be isolated and worked on alone. This supports compositionists' stance that general writing strategies learned in isolation will not transfer—but neither will specific local knowledge if it cannot be used in generalized ways.

A strict "novice" versus "expert" dichotomy is thus simply less useful than it used to be. New contexts demand dialogic learning and problem solving, as experts are "increasingly involved in multiple communities of practice" (Tuomi-Grohn, Engestrom, and Young 3) rather than relegated to one silo of specialized knowledge. Paul Prior defines communities of practice, initially introduced by Jean Lave and Etienne Wenger, as "not defined by a discrete shared core of abstract knowledge and language that people internalize to become expert members; instead, a community of practice is an open, dynamic body, a 'set of relations among persons, activity, and world, over time and in relation with other tangential and overlapping communities of practice'" (21). The "community of practice" framing is supple, and depicts participation in practices rather than in fixed groups; activity is partially improvised by participants, partly collective context (20). This changes fundamentally our sense of how transfer—and in particular transfer of literacies—might work. Knowledge gained in one community will not only be dynamic in that community, it will also change in encounters with other communities of practice—and change the practice of that new community.

The emphasis on dynamic practice, rather than on more fixed discourse conventions, shifts us toward the more complex interaction Michael Carter has also suggested between the local and the general. He emphasizes the interactive balance between common underlying strategies and specialized knowledges, depicted by Lave and Wenger as "embodied, active, perspectival trajectories through multiple, interpenetrated and internally stratified communities of practice in the world, communities that are themselves dynamic, open, and evolving" (Prior 99). In this model, novices are not *initiated into* new settings, they negotiate them. The continuum of "relative newcomers" and "relative old timers" (xi) reworks the knowledge of the community regularly, and situated learning enables transfer through "legitimate peripheral participation" (Dias et al. 222).

If reciprocity of movement is key, transfer occurs only when the individual encountering the new context actually changes his relationship with the new activity (Tuomi-Grohn, Engestrom, and Young). This can be encouraged by varied practice, "forcing the cognitive element in question to adapt in subtle ways to each of these contexts, yielding an incrementally broadening ability that gradually becomes more and more detached from its original context and more and more evocable in others" (Perkins and Salomon, "Transfer of Learning"120). The emphasis, that is, shifts to transformative rather than applicative reuse. We come full circle to the model in which learning does not occur "in" the individual but in the *relationships* between activity systems as the individual moves within and between them.

Most of what we know that I have presented so far has focused on the kinds of transfer that are *not* taking place. Some of the earliest research studies of writing-related transfer focused on transfer from professional writing courses to other school writing or workplace writing. Yet, as Dias et al. have shown, the activity of university writing—and reading—is not the same as the activity of workplace writing or reading; one seeks to achieve the epistemic work of schooling, and the other seeks to instrumentally and economically carry out the work of an organization (223). Dias et al. establish that school writing seems to share little with writing in the world; it has a "learning purpose," useful in school only and in fact contradictory to the needs writers have beyond school (223).

This difference is a perfect location, then, for studying transfer, in particular high-road and vertical transfer. Each context incorporates fundamentally different stages and approaches. Dias et al. suggest transfer is hampered when students inappropriately bring school learning patterns and an individualist ethos (i.e., a focus on their own learning rather than task accomplishment) to highly collaborative, outcome-driven workplace contexts. Paré et al. suggest that students or new employees must "redefine the goals and criteria for their writing by locating it within an entirely different activity system" (231).

In an activity theory model, students who transfer writing ability successfully apparently begin "seeing texts as accomplishing social actions" and develop a "complex of activities" (Carroll, qtd. in Rogers 18), rather than a set of generalizable skills. In addition, writers are clearly influenced by motivational factors in their likeliness to transfer. They transfer when they are "supported to participate in an activity system that encourages collaboration, discussion, and some form of 'risk taking'" and when they "have opportunities to share and be inspired by a common motive for undertaking a specific learning task" (Guile and Young 74).

Meta-awareness

Successful transfer may also require a level of conscious or reflective activity. The learner needs to be aware of decision making, explicitly calling on earlier experiences in the new context, using cognitive and metacognitive processes (Haskell; Ford, "Knowledge Transfer"). Paying attention to context in the cases we study helps us to understand how this conscious generalizing happens, when it does happen (Rogoff). When learners can explicitly abstract principles from a situation, transfer is facilitated (Gick and Holyoak); learners who are asked to actively formulate principles from activities, even when what they generate turns out to be faulty, *notice* more in new contexts and develop the key ability to be critical about their own knowledge (Bransford and Schwartz). These learners engage in self-reflection and mindfulness (Belmont, Butterfield, and Ferretti; Bransford; Langer; Bereiter; Perkins and Salomon, "Transfer of Learning"). This is all welcome news to compositionists. Our practices—portfolio narratives, last-day-of-class responses, literacy narratives—are built on the assumption that self-reflection improves transferable knowledge.

While much has been made of this meta-awareness as one of the key components of successful transfer, however, some research is beginning to question its role. Conscious attention to transfer leads only to "near" transfer, according to Haskell (52). Unconscious processing is far more frequent, and fostering that kind of processing, through reasoning by similarity and analogy, is far more productive (58). Preliminary results from an ongoing longitudinal study (C. Donahue) indicate that mature practices might indeed develop without an accompanying meta-awareness. The student writers in this study do not evolve in their conscious understanding of literacy, knowledge, and disciplinarity ("disciplinary consciousness" as defined by Reuter and Lahanier-Reuter), although they do acquire a set of ways of articulating their experience. In their written texts, on the other hand, their relationship to knowledge, as represented in their source use and interactions, changes substantially. These observations suggest that expertise is perhaps developed with less meta-awareness than is usually recognized, at least in the U.S. context of undergraduate education, with its general and discipline-specific contours, in which students travel between specialization and broad introduction regularly, learning to translate across these landscapes. Bautier also suggests, based on several studies of student writing in French school contexts, that simply requesting reflection does not automatically produce "secondarized" knowledge (the term comes from Bakhtin's distinction between primary, in-the-moment genres and secondary, removed, metalevel genres).[1]

The focus in some studies has been on students' awareness of or explicit recall of knowledge that they need in new contexts. Jarratt, Mack, Sartor, and Watson call this "pedagogical memory"; their study, based on interviews and self-report by students, suggests that these

---

1.   Quite a bit of the U.S. literature on portfolios and self-reflection offers similar critiques.

memories can be useful in enabling transfer. Bergmann and Zepernick, however, note that students are quite able to articulate their perception of a thorough lack of potential transferability of what they learn in "writing courses" in their first year to what they need to know and perform in discipline-specific contexts.

When Transfer Fails

The transfer of writing knowledge can (and does) go wrong. Students who transfer abilities or strategies "as is" are not only unlikely to succeed, they may end up quite frustrated. They transfer problematically, for example, a strategy that in fact needed to be adapted, such as the five-paragraph essay (Smit 129). Students who focus on surface similarities rather than conceptual analog are equally handicapped (Gentner and Toupin; Novick). They lack sufficient knowledge (Haskell) or know one form so well that it interferes with another form needed in the new context (Bawarshi; Devitt).

What we do as teachers, what institutions shape, and what we define as writing can all obstruct successful transfer of writing ability. Much of the research just cited suggests that transfer doesn't happen easily in intentional contexts (either those studied or those set up for fostering transfer). In fact, it is clear that some contexts can actually hinder transfer: when individuals learn procedures without learning underlying concepts, or learning is overly contextualized, for example, when the classroom does not connect with everyday practices (Bransford) or details of the learned material are elaborated in one context and become attached to that context (Eich). Haskell suggests that learning can be "welded" to the topic and the place (47), and we know as well that transfer is hampered when material is taught in only one setting or context rather than in multiple contexts (Bjork and Richardson-Klavhen) or when home and school practices conflict. Students' preexisting conceptions of writing from other contexts can prevent transfer (Rogers; Devitt, "Antecedent Genre").

Most college teachers would prefer that some strategies and forms of research or writing *not* transfer to college tasks or across college contexts. Studies of students working cross-culturally have highlighted some kinds of transfer that do not serve students well. Simone Volet, for example, describes ambivalent transfer (such as cue seeking that works in one context but is discouraged in another), difficult transfer (such as learning that serves well in one context but may not be useful in a new one), and inappropriate transfer (such as acceptable or nonpenalized strategies in one context that are unacceptable in a new context) (631–36).

Studying student writing over time and young professionals' writing provides key insights into ways in which students might transfer unintended strategies in their work. Richard Haswell has noted in *Gaining Ground* that students who used complex sentence structures early in their undergraduate careers—with sometimes error-filled results— moved toward simply reducing their use of complex sentence structures later on, rather than toward mastery of those structures.

Current first-year composition approaches have actually been labeled potentially "anti-transfer" in discussions about composition's current crisis of purpose. Crowley critiques the current model for encouraging transfer as only a compliant way of being, and points to the deep humanist roots of first-year composition, which work against its potential as a starting point for transferable learning (242). Downs and Wardle build a suggested new model for the first-year writing course as a starting point for, indeed, understanding writing studies themselves. This approach, beginning in a discipline per se, turns on its head the problem of a-contextual learning about writing in the first year.

David Russell raised these precise problems with our programmatic versions of first-year writing versus writing in the disciplines, first-year writing being by its very nature anti-transfer, with his well-known analogy to "learning ballness" and learning specific ball-wielding strategies ("Activity Theory"). He further develops this question (Russell and Yanez) in a study of the difficult relationship that evolved between a history professor and his students around the writing in a general education history course. Russell and Yanez's work suggests that "general education" and specific disciplines are in fact different activity systems within the U.S. university, thus requiring different modes of participation; students are in lesser or fuller modes of participation in those systems. Initial models that depicted, in the 1980s and '90s, the university as a discourse community into which students must enter, and then disciplines as more specialized versions of that community, seem now to be reductive and overly linear understandings of the negotiation students take on.

These same scholars, however (Dias et al., among others) also suggest that what will foster transfer is thus a meta-awareness of the function of writing as a way of thinking in any activity (writing in its forms of note taking, sketching, and so on), and that enculturation into a new activity system (rather than transfer of school learning) is in fact the path to full participation (232). Dias's group adds that real "skills" are indeed likely to be transferable (keyboarding, using charts), but they—and the composition field in general—theorize writing as something much more than a skill.

Literacy and Transfer

The transfer of literate abilities is certainly a newer domain of composition research.[2] While current reviews of transfer literature in other fields don't generally reference the work produced by composition scholars on the topic, the example of literacy raised explicitly by Perkins and Salomon suggests that we tend to expect that literate abilities by their very nature will transfer. Both the natural acquisition of language itself and the fundamental role of reading and writing in schooling underlie this assumption. But the well-known Scribner and Cole study of literate activity among the Vai people pointed us decades ago to the lack of automatic cognitive advantages to literacy. This is not to say, as Goody, Olson, Barton, and others have profoundly demonstrated, that the ability to manipulate symbols in writing does not have unique effects on our cognitive processes and capabilities.

The recent attention to transfer might in fact be partly because our rapidly changing world demands it (Haskell 37).[3] New literacies are being studied for their effects (see Yancey "Made Not Only in Words"; Moje). Deborah Brandt notes that students in the future will require a "capacity to amalgamate new reading and writing practices in response to rapid social change" and will need "to develop a [new] flexibility and awareness" (651). Cultural anthropologist Michael Wesch suggests that these new cognitive structures must be the basis for our construction of a twenty-first-century educational environment. Some of the scholars studying transfer in these new contexts are proposing a theory of cognitive flexibility that will have ramifications for the way students will best learn and transfer knowledge (see Spiro and Jehng).

---

2. Perkins and Salomon explore, in what I find to be an intriguing juxtaposition, "puzzles" about transfer in literacy studies and in computer programming studies (1989).

3. There are many doctoral dissertations currently developing on the topic, and we are likely to see sweeping changes in the composition research landscape in the next few years. It will be welcome; this article is a mere opening of the door.

METHODS OF TRANSFER RESEARCH

What is perhaps most interesting of all is the fact that the single most important and agreed-upon tool for developing transfer—reasoning or learning by analogy—is the least-studied or referenced in composition studies. Analogy is, for most transfer scholars, at the heart of it all (Haskell). Hatano and Greeno point to analogy as the basis of everyday cognition (647)—that is, we use analogy to transfer learned knowledge all the time. Education's role is thus to provide a broader range of analogies—potentially more apt or more efficient—than what might be available by trial and error or the everyday. Material taught through analogy or contrast (Bransford) is most likely to have staying power. The way to understanding this gap between composition's attention to this issue and the rest of the available scholarship (along with the reverse gap, the relative paucity of transfer scholarship related to literacy outside of composition) is perhaps through a closer look at the research methods used in each domain. In composition, a recent growth in longitudinal studies of undergraduate writing has begun to shift our attention to explicit transfer issues, even though most of these studies did not necessarily set out to explore "transfer" as such. In fact, almost everything the field has learned about transfer has been from longitudinal studies, most often ethnographies or case studies.

The knowledge about transfer outside of composition studies that has been reported in this chapter has evolved out of very particular kinds of research. Much of the well-known scholarship is drawn from experimental research that sets up test situations with controlled variables (for example, testing children's ability to throw darts at underwater targets before and after explanations about how water refracts light), although some has drawn from looser, more contextual research (for example, studying children's reuse of knowledge in a classroom activity over time). Frequently, transfer is measured with what Bransford and Schwartz call "sequestered problem-solving," testing abilities in isolation. The effect of these methods on the knowledge gained is thus important to study.

While transfer is certainly hampered by some features of the learning context, it might also be happening more often than we realize. Hatano and Greeno suggest that education and psychology transfer researchers may be using overly narrow criteria of successful transfer (651). We might also be looking for the wrong thing; current transfer-testing tools identify "full blown expertise" but cannot capture the incremental steps in learning that will eventually enable expertise (Bransford and Schwartz). If, as Perkins and Salomon argue, "identifying a case of transfer requires no more than documenting the side effect of learning something on a different performance or context" ("Transfer of Learning" 116), how might that documentation look different in a longitudinal study versus a controlled experiment? We know that certain kinds of tests used are not able to tell us whether the subjects tested would transfer their knowledge if they were in a testing situation that allowed them to learn more during the test (Bransford and Schwartz). In terms of composition, as we will see later, the actual studies of transfer are done quite differently; experimental work and *in situ* research certainly offer different kinds of insight with different degrees of both reliability and generalizability. We do not know, for example, what each methodology allows us to see or tends to de-emphasize, what particularities it emphasizes. In addition, as Wardle argues, we cannot assume transfer did not occur—or an ability does not exist or was not learned—simply because the student does not use the ability in a later task (cited in Jarratt et al. 2). And because composition research rarely identifies the type or types of transfer being studied, comparative results are particularly hard to come by. Building a body of knowledge through cumulative research results is not equivalent to focusing on isolated studies.

THE FUTURE OF TRANSFER

The term *transfer* has been challenged as not sufficiently reflecting the complexity of the evolving world. Alternative terms proposed include "consequential transitions" (Beach), "expansive learning" (Davydov; Engestrom), "flexible applicability" (Prenzel and Mandl), "pattern-recognition" (Haskell; how close or far the new is from the original context, on a continuum), and "pedagogical memory" (Jarratt et al.). Additional, more flexible terms have included "generalization" (a term actually long in use in many fields) and "productivity" (Hatano and Greeno), each resisting the idea that knowledge is a static property of individuals. Perhaps most interesting is the proposal to study "preparation for future learning" as the best indicator of transfer likelihood; what constitutes optimal learning for transfer varies in this model, depending on the future domain in which a student will work and the types of knowledge that will be needed (Bransford and Schwartz; Spiro and Jehng). These recent developments fit quite well with the literacy-based questions of our field; the constructed, negotiated thinking and meaning making of "putting things into words" is a particularly important moment for understanding transferability.

I would like to suggest paths for ongoing attention to transfer in both research and practice. I believe that the field of composition is uniquely positioned, given its deep knowledge about literacy and its alternative methodologies, to go beyond using the transfer scholarship and to begin contributing to it.

In Research

We should focus our attention in the twenty-first century on how existing and future transfer research can help shape answers to our deep questions: Which writing instruction might be most effective, what competencies are reused in new contexts, how can that reusing be fostered, and who is or should be responsible for making sure transfer occurs? The first question may be: For how much longer will *transfer* remain the term of reference? While many of the other terms referenced in this article have been suggested, none has yet broadly replaced transfer, in spite of critiques of its implications. At what point might the term no longer service the discussion adequately?

A particularly significant research question that has been underdeveloped and matters a great deal to composition is: What are the features of "everyday" transfer that enable it, while transfer in educational contexts seems so difficult? For our work in writing, we might much more closely study initial language acquisition, move beyond long-established assumptions about the writing-speaking differences, and examine more closely—as many have already called us to do—the everyday literacies our students bring to school with them. The emphasis, however, of this attention needs to be on how students acquire and reuse those literacies, rather than what the literacies are. One of the well-known examples of a surprising lack of transfer is the Saxe study of Brazilian street children who are adept manipulators of mathematical concepts and processes in their daily interactions on the street, but do not see the math exercises presented to them in school as the same. How they acquire their "street" math abilities is particularly interesting to our desire to enable transfer in educational contexts.

Also interesting is the question of "forward" and "backward" transfer. Is the future situation (the new context) more responsible for affording transfer, or is the initial context more responsible for seeding transfer via the way in which the knowledge is learned? Is transfer "in" the student who carries knowledge, "in" the context and interaction? Imagine the effect of what we learn about these questions on individual classes and on programmatic planning in writing programs. It seems irresponsible to not be seeking these answers.

In many ways these questions are grounded in linguistics, at least in the kind of linguistics that treats language-in-use as its subject matter. The work on understanding the relationship between the individual-specific utterance and the generic or shared social fabric of language is quite relevant (François). Seeing each written text as what Beach calls transformative re-use rather than application of existing to new is powerful, but has not been the subject of extended analysis in composition. In this understanding, the application changes the use; François calls this reprise-modification, literally, re-taking-up-modifying, which is the irrevocable nature of all language production, whether spoken or written.

In this sense, and Bakhtin's way of thinking about utterances and genres is equally useful here, "transfer" is the very nature of language acquisition; we generalize (and in fact overgeneralize) linguistically as we acquire language. We might also call on Vygotsky's principles of learning to complete this frame for understanding transfer as active acquisition. For Vygotsky, abstractions must connect to, anchor in, real-life experience. The overlap between the known and the to-be-known must be sufficient for a learner to extend her current knowledge and strategies, but the "stretch" must be sufficient as well. His "zones of proximal development" serve in this case as zones that afford transfer. A much closer look at how that might work is essential. That is, studying all learning as movement from the known to the unknown, scaffolded in particular ways, and always understood as neither entirely the same (no movement) nor entirely different (a total breakdown in communication).

Another useful concept being developed currently in linguistics is that of "orientation" as the fundamental cognitive activity that enables what transfer studies have identified *as* transfer to occur (François). The ability to "orient" in a new context is the ability to read the signs, the cues, for what knowledge is being called on; it is equally the understanding that we *should be* reading those signs, that we need to read them. Every learner is "preoriented" by past experiences; every learner can engage in orientation, can recognize her orientation as well.

In composition work, we know writers need words and sentences (although of course that is itself rapidly changing); we know language users need a message to communicate; deep reading ability; research ability; finally, they need to know *that* they need to know more about potential strategies or approaches. These basic abilities, we also know, are transformed in every reuse. This concern for the interactive aspect of knowledge is evident in other composition-relevant areas of interest, such as assessment (is the learning "in" the individual? Can we assess it by interrogating the individual performance? Or is it constructed in contexts that must be part of the assessment?) The same questions must drive our inquiry moving forward.

We also need to begin carefully studying transfer in a different way, across media. While we believe that each new medium affords new ways of thinking and composing, we don't know this in any detailed way (Moje; Spiro and Jehng; Derry et al.). We also don't yet know much about the cognitive abilities that new media develop in the same way that other literacies do. Finally, we must, as a field, begin to compare methods and to understand the impact of any method on our findings about transfer. Remembering that much study of transfer in composition didn't even necessarily have "transfer" as its object, and that the methods used in composition and in other fields have differed extensively, we might imagine both new ways of studying transfer ourselves and new contributions we can make to the transfer discussion in other fields with our methods.

In Practice

Even as we pursue research, we must inform current practice with what we have understood so far. Transfer does not just take care of itself. Smit accuses the field of not institutionalizing "instruction in similarities between the way writing is done in a variety of contexts" (119–20). However, it is clearly not just a question of "teaching to transfer" (like "teaching to the test"). Some scholars decry any mention of "teaching for transfer" as even possible, because so much depends on the new context and its affordances. Teaching for transfer might really mean "teaching to invite transfer." Others, however, point to the feasibility of forms of teaching for transfer, especially in terms of "high-road" transfer (see Perkins and Salomon, "Teaching for Transfer"). Haskell suggests, "[T]eaching that promotes transfer, then, involves returning again and again to an idea or procedure but on different levels and in different contexts" (27), certainly something embedded in teaching practices such as the sequenced writing assignments structuring Bartholomae and Petrosky's *Ways of Reading.*

Perhaps the most important thing to understand about transfer generally—which will turn out to be also in fact particularly insightful in terms of our questions in composition—is that *what* transfers is a "subroutine,"

> developed in the learning context but also useful in the transfer context: an overarching principle abstracted in the learning context but applicable in the transfer context, a piece of factual knowledge useful in both but in quite different ways, a learning strategy that becomes useful in new domains, a cognitive style, or even a complex strategy of approaching new problems. (Perkins and Salomon "Teaching for Transfer" 116)

For writing, this suggests that both "skills" and other types of knowledge are subject to transfer, although this diversity is modified, according to Perkins and Salomon, by the "how" of transfer—how something transfers is connected to what is being transferred. Our understanding of writing and its teaching hinges thus on understanding what kinds of knowledge writing *is* and what we might foster according to each type of transfer.

We might be mindful, as well, of the ways in which instruction can in fact get in the way of transfer. Alexander and Murphy suggest that simple mention (we might call this the "coverage" model) of the content we hope will transfer is insufficient; on the other hand, ensuring that students engage in strategic effort tends to enable transfer (568–69).

In a more global sense, coherence in both program design and intellectual focus is essential:

> Teachers and students [must] share in the objective of "rooted relevance" (Alexander et al. 1996) whereby schooled information is not only meaningfully connected to learners and their worlds outside of the classroom, but also to the fundamental concepts and procedures that define particular domains or disciplines. (Alexander and Murphy 571)

Teaching should create "affordances" both within courses and across courses and programs. This can be done, in part, through attention to the types of memory in play; "contextual clues from [a] situation activate related items in memory that contain the same contextual elements" (Hintzman, cited in Foertsch 366). This works with different kinds of memory—both very specific "episodic" memory and more abstract "semantic" memory. The types of memory themselves should not, Foertsch insists, be seen as separate but as on a continuum between the most generic and the most context specific (367).

"Boundary-crossing" scenarios are also cited as particularly productive in promoting curricular transfer (Tuomi-Grohn, Engestrom, and Young). Bringing ideas, concepts, or instruments from one domain into another, apparently unrelated one demands "significant cognitive retooling" in these cases that appears to foster creative transfer (4). Several different scholars have explored this possibility: "boundary zones" (Karkola) outside of the usual convention-driven communities of practice, "think spaces" (Gutierrez, Rymes, and Larson) created by hybrid, polyvalent, polycontextual, multivoiced interaction among cultural groups; these necessary new forms might create new options. Intentional creation of "boundary-crossing" places for learning creates developmental transfer (Tuomi-Grohn, Engestrom, and Young 5).

Students whose teachers help them deconstruct the genres of their field transfer writing knowledge or ability more effectively. As Foertsch suggests, "[I]f teachers collaboratively assisted their students in uncovering the general principles that constrain composing in that and other academic contexts" (374), they might more successfully transfer abilities, although the counter-argument is that there *are* no general principles.

We do generally know what our students might need, and in fact much of the discussion here of "transfer-encouraging teaching practices" seems to be simply about good teaching. Consider, for example, Ford's outline of the key features of teaching for successful transfer: students need to know how to self-monitor; they need awareness of each discourse community to which they belong (within and beyond school); they need awareness of prior learning contexts; they need critical thinking (302). In a similar vein, Alexander and Murphy outline a three-pronged attack: developing dispositions toward transfer, fostering principled knowledge rather than an accumulation of knowledge, and creating systems that both model and reward analogical thinking (573).[4] In composition, at least, the second is self-evident; the first and third push our assumptions in new directions.

Our new ideas and approaches, or our attachment to existing ideas and approaches, should be confronted for evidence of their role in creating transferability. We must prioritize developing our collective knowledge about transfer, sharing our results with scholars in other

---

4.   See also Haskell's ten teaching principles, which seem to be almost self-evident.

fields, sharing and revising or informing methods for studying transfer, and using knowledge about transfer in our practice—individual and programmatic.

9

WRITING ASSESSMENT IN THE EARLY TWENTY-FIRST CENTURY
A Primer

Kathleen Blake Yancey

By definition, writing assessment is at the heart of composition studies: through pedagogically based assessment practices like responding to writing and introducing students to reflection and self-assessment, we assist students in developing as writers and develop our own writing/reading/teaching relationships with them. It's also fair to say, however, that compositionists often find themselves at odds with writing assessment and frustrated with it, believing with writing assessment scholar Pat Belanoff that such evaluation is "the dirty little thing we do in our closets" (ix). More specifically, compositionists often find writing assessment—especially when the assessment is external to our own curricula, as is the case with the so-called SAT test of writing, the Advanced Placement test of language, and the ACCUPLACER placement test—a reductive practice that is done *to* our students and us, one that misshapes and trivializes our learning and teaching work and thus threatens the potential for agency for our students and for us. In fact, the most antagonistic critique of writing assessment positions it at odds with the field itself, trumping more appropriate areas of study: "I would argue that the truly troubling direction in recent scholarship is an overemphasis on administration and assessment. These are important areas of concern, no doubt, but writing scholarship is severely limited in its potential when these concerns overshadow others" (Mayers).

Writing assessment is thus both hero/ine, the practice that brings us into relationship with our students, *and* villain, an obstacle to our agency. As important, how writing assessment has been central to the field of composition studies has varied across different periods. In this chapter, I trace those periods in three large moments—in the period leading up to the current moment; in the current moment; and (all too briefly) in the future moment. Moreover, in this tracing, we will see that the concerns of compositionists relative to writing assessment have changed and developed—depending on the definition of writing and the purpose(s) of writing assessment; on the power of given terms at different moments in time; and on the values and ideologies represented in those terms, especially and increasingly as they interface—or not—with the interests and directions of public policy makers.

A BRIEF HISTORICAL CONTEXT: THREE WAVES OF WRITING ASSESSMENT

During the last century, writing assessment, like other fields, has been defined by a set of terms. Initially the term was *testing*, the focus on the individual student, and the use to make high-stakes decisions, for instance, about whether the student could be admitted to college or enroll in the "regular" first-year composition course, the latter a kind of testing we still engage in: placement assessment. The tests were indirect measures, that is, a test that sampled something related to but other than the individual student's writing, typically a multiple choice test of editing skills serving as a proxy for writing.[1] Thus, while such a measure might seem low in terms of validity—that is, in terms of its ability to measure what it *purports* to measure, in this case the ability to evaluate a text an author composes; and in terms of its ability to allow us to make credible judgments—it did offer high reliability: the test could be scored consistently under all conditions, regardless of when it was scored or by whom, and cheaply. Thus, as I suggested in "Looking Back as We Look Forward," the most important question in this first wave of writing assessment was informed by an ideology located in a machine-like efficiency characterizing the early part of the century (Williamson; Yancey, "The Impulse to Compose"): "Which measure can do the best and fairest job of prediction with the least amount of work and the lowest cost?" (Inoue)[2]

The second wave of writing assessment, dating from the 1970s to the late 1980s, was prompted, at least in part, by the explosion of interest in writing process and in new pedagogies enacting the field's new understandings of process. In addition, researchers in writing assessment,

---

1.   And this continues to serve in some current measures, including the SAT test of writing.

2.   For these questions, I'm indebted to Asao Inoue, who adopted my historical framework for use in a graduate class.

working from both contexts—writing and evaluation/testing—had developed what has come to be known as holistic scoring, which is characterized by two important features. First, holistic scoring began with sampling student writing (as opposed to an indirect measure that samples students' editing practices on texts composed by others); it thus relied on a direct measure, or sample, of writing. Second, by developing and using scoring guides that provided for a reliability analogous to the reliability of indirect measures, holistic scoring was able to meet the standard for consistent scoring. Put differently, this method of writing assessment was still an individual assessment, keyed to each student's performance, but it was now a direct measure that was scored by adapting an earlier technology of testing to assure consistent ranking of writing samples. Perhaps as important, teachers, not testing experts, played a leading role in creating prompts and scoring essays (White, *Teaching and Assessing Writing*). The questions about assessment dominating this period were very different, then, than those driving the first wave: What roles have validity and reliability played in writing assessment? Who is authorized and who has the appropriate expertise to make the best judgments—teachers or testing experts? Who is best suited to orchestrate, design, and implement assessment—teachers or testing experts? What is the overall purpose of writing assessment, and what difference does purpose make? (Inoue)

The third wave of writing assessment, occurring from the late 1980s until the turn of the century, was characterized by attention to multiple texts, the ways we read those texts, and the role of students in helping us understand their texts and the processes they used to produce them. The vehicle for practicing assessment keyed to these principles was typically a portfolio of writing, generally defined as a set of texts selected from a larger archive and narrated, contextualized, and explained by the student him- or herself (Yancey, "Reflecting on Portfolios"). In part, as we see in the early work of Pat Belanoff and Peter Elbow, this shift was motivated by a particular kind of assessment: an end-of-program assessment intending to bring into the larger programmatic context the work of individual students as reviewed by program faculty. In part, this shift was also motivated by innovative classroom evaluation practices; portfolios provided a new method of classroom grading (Weiser; Yancey, "Make Haste Slowly") that included process but was not driven by it.

But two other features are important in this shift to portfolios. First, this shift was motivated by a new "construct of writing," which refers to the model or theory of writing that underlies an assessment. Previously, the construct of writing had been global: there was a working assumption that good writing was good writing was good writing—regardless of task or genre or rhetorical situation. In contrast, the assumption of portfolios was that writing is much more localized and differentiated and that it varies by rhetorical situation and genre: "[T]he ability to write one kind of document does not automatically guarantee the ability to write another kind of document; the successful completion of a generic 'research paper' does not ensure the successful completion of a journal article or business proposal or laboratory report" (Paretti and Powell 4). Portfolios, then, sought to sample a *range* of writing genres in an effort to tap a fuller representation of writing in a model of assessment keyed to a very different construct of writing—a construct of writing that is differentiated by task and one that is much closer to the way we think of writing now.

Second, and as important, we saw two new aspects of validity emerge, the first of which is often called "consequential" validity. This form or dimension[3] of validity refers to the power of an assessment to help the person tested learn; the principle here is that an assessment is valid to the degree that it helps a student learn. Perhaps not surprisingly, given their design, portfolios are possibly the best vehicle devised in terms of this dimension of validity because of the role of reflection and the power it has to help students learn in the process of assembling the portfolio: the ability to learn is *designed into* the assessment model. The second aspect of validity, following assessment scholar Samuel Messick, is located in two questions relating to the utility of the assessment: (1) To what degree are the decisions made about students (or teachers or programs) accurate? and (2) To what degree are the decisions made about students (or teachers or programs) appropriate? Assessment scholars today argue that without these dimensions of validity, a measure is not valid even when it measures what it purports to measure.

During this period of third-wave writing assessment, we also saw the beginnings of writing-across-the-curriculum programs, which seek in multiple ways—through writing-to-learn strategies employed in general education classes, for example, and in writing-in-the-disciplines classes at the junior and senior levels—to foster writing development inside

---

3.   Different theorists understand this component of validity differently, with some seeing the ecological or consequential as aspects or dimensions of validity, and others seeing validity itself dependent on its function of enhancing learning.

a vertical curriculum for the entire life of the college student. As Sue McLeod explains, often designed into the WAC model, even from the very beginning, was a second kind of assessment—program assessment—which focused not on the student, but rather on the program itself:

> Many WAC programs, my own first program included, started with grant money and had to have an assessment component to show the granting agency that we did what we said we would do. Let me state up front that I am for assessment; when I began consulting at other institutions that wanted to start WAC programs, I always included assessment as part of what I recommended they should do, a feedback loop into the program that would let them know what they were doing well and where they needed to improve. I recommended, and still recommend, gathering data of all sorts—numbers of students and faculty involved, specific changes made to assignments and syllabi, documents produced by faculty to explain the writing conventions of that discipline (like those at Oregon State and George Mason University), evaluations of faculty workshops, and so on. ("Future")

As defined by Yancey and Huot, program assessment has three purposes: (1) to see what the program is doing well; (2) to determine how the program might improve; and (3) to demonstrate to others why the program should continue or should be funded. This assessment, then, is keyed to program issues and is intended to assure that the curriculum designed for students is in fact the curriculum students experience and that the curriculum prepares students in the way it claims to. Where the assessment shows a discrepancy between goals and accomplishments, analysis of such discrepancy can lead to corrections supporting a stronger curriculum. A program assessment thus directly addresses curriculum, and it does so, ordinarily, by sampling a subset of work from the entire student population. Yancey and Huot outline equally important assumptions guiding program assessment in WAC that apply to other programs (such as first-year composition), among them that such assessment calls on diverse and often multiple methods and that it focuses on the point of interaction between teaching and learning with the goal of enhancing that interaction (7–11). During this period of writing assessment development, then, the questions at the center of the field shift again, with the dominant ones asking, "Whose needs does writing assessment serve?" and "How is it a political and social act?" (Inoue)

A final feature characterizing writing assessment during all three waves of assessment—which is also when composition incorporates attention to process into its agenda—is the addition of *formative assessment* to the terminology. Previously, assessment had been largely summative: focused on final assessments like grades and scores. But during this larger period, formative assessment—which, like response to students and program assessment, is used to *help* students and programs while they are *in formation*—is added to the mix (NCTE, "Fostering High-Quality Formative Assessment").

THE CURRENT MOMENT

The current moment in writing assessment is complicated, dynamic, and, at least in some ways, in flux, although we can identify five minor and three major themes. Here I quickly note the minor themes, which may become more prominent in the future, before detailing each of the major themes; as we shall see, they continue to focus the attention of compositionists and of the nation.

One of the minor themes, as we see in the work at Washington State University, considers how assessments of writing and critical thinking are related (Condon and Kelly-Riley); this project found that without the work of critical thinking included in a writing assessment program, the writing assessment may ask too little of students. A second theme examines how writing assessment reproduces social inequities, especially racial inequities (Inoue and Poe); such reproduction, these critics claim, challenges a validity that claims to be racially blind. A related theme, the third, has to do with the construct of writing when the assessment involves students from another culture whose native language may or may not be English: there is, according to Sandra Murphy, another construct involved, what she calls a cultural construct. A fourth theme focuses on the construct of writing in a world where many compositions are digitally mediated: it asks, is there a different construct for digital composing, even if only the word-processed variety (Sandra Murphy and Yancey)? And a fifth theme has to do with the validity of directed self-placement, a placement mechanism allowing students to determine the best course for their entrance into college (Blakesley, Harvey, and Reynolds; Gere et al.).

In the intervening decade plus since the late 1990s, we have seen as well three specific changes of note occurring in the writing assessment world—and the assessment world more generally. First, as we shall see, learning outcomes, especially as linked to assessments, have become increasingly important, if controversial. Second, with groups like the

Spellings Commission leading the way, the federal government has taken a surprising interest in postsecondary assessments, leading to a new emphasis on program assessment, but of a regressive kind. Third, the field has turned its critical attention to earlier forms of assessment, like portfolios, that it earlier touted, with the result that we have a more sophisticated understanding of what's at stake in portfolios and of their effects, at least, if not agreement on their definition or their value. Moreover, taken together, these issues carry forward the themes characterizing earlier periods of writing assessment as they raise important questions that continue to vex us even today, chief among them (1) who controls the writing assessment; (2) what the construct is that is being tested; and (3) how we define validity and how that matters.

OUTCOMES AND OUTCOMES-BASED WRITING ASSESSMENT

In 2000, the Council of Writing Program Administrators adopted the "WPA Outcomes Statement," the first time a group representing postsecondary writing interests had attempted to create a common set of outcomes for first-year writing programs generally. Outcomes, they agreed, were not objectives: rather, they are statements about what students know and can do, in this case at the conclusion of a first-year writing program of any variety—first-year seminar, first-year composition, first-year "stretch" composition, and the like. The authors of the outcomes statement also agreed that while the outcomes might be used to link to standards or benchmarks, the outcomes themselves were independent of such evaluative norms; more properly, if such benchmarking were to occur, it would take place on a given college or university campus. Not least, the collective authorship of the WPA outcomes agreed that the outcomes themselves would function as a boundary object: individual campuses could take them and revise them toward local outcomes, thus providing both for local mission and intent and at the same time for articulation with a larger context.

More specifically, the 2000 WPA Outcomes stipulates four kinds of knowledge: (1) rhetorical; (2) critical reading, thinking, and writing; (3) processes; and (4) knowledge of conventions. Some institutions have adopted them as is; others have used them simply as context for developing their own programs; and still others have used them with adjustments—Arizona State University, for example, emphasizing argument in its WPA statement and Minnesota Community and Technical College including in its adaptation the making of meaning through multiple contexts. And in 2008, the WPA Outcomes were adjusted themselves to include a fifth outcome, use of digital technologies in writing, thus illustrating another aspect of these outcomes: they can and should be revised. Thus far, although the WPA Outcomes Statement has been used primarily to create language and outcomes for the assessment of individual student work, it can be also used for program assessment.

In its creation of outcomes, the Council of Writing Program Administrators anticipated a larger movement across the country that soon followed, one focused on outcomes developed over the last decade especially. ABET, for instance, which is the accrediting body for engineering programs, has a set of outcomes that programs need to satisfy, as does NCATE, the accrediting body for teacher education. Outcomes, then, typically lead to assessment of one kind or another. Moreover, outcomes—and outcomes assessment, typically of the program assessment variety—are increasingly being required of all disciplines, as we see in this announcement for a 2010 conference focusing on outcomes and assessment for humanities disciplines:

> If you are affiliated with an English department, you probably realize that many humanities faculty are apprehensive about the national, state, and institutional imperatives for assessment. They ask how the truly distinctive humanities learning outcomes can be evaluated using the quantitative methods that assessment seems to demand. Attempts to measure these qualitative educational outcomes, they fear, are more likely to eviscerate than to enhance their programs. The Symposium will address these practical and theoretical concerns from the perspective of humanities scholars who advocate assessment. It will provide you and your institution with new ways of conceptualizing assessment in the humanities. . . . By supporting academic programs as they address the challenges of assessment, you can broaden understanding of the centrality of your program to institutional mission. The relationships you build can be long lasting. *The goal of assessment is to highlight strengths in a program and specific areas in which the programs might be made even better.* (Anderson; emphasis added)

The promotion here states the case well for the moment in 2012 the challenges, the opportunities, and the possibilities that can emerge from an outcomes-based program assessment.

Still, it's not the case, as seems to be suggested here, that the writing community at large has embraced outcomes and outcomes assessment: far from it. In the first place, it's probably safe to assume that many if not most teachers of first-year composition are only vaguely aware of outcomes or outcomes assessment. And in the second place, not all those who are aware are pleased. Derek Soles, for instance, responded to the idea of outcomes negatively quite apart from their potential for assessment. He objected that the WPA Outcomes Statement failed to endorse specific philosophies of composition, from expressionism, with its "self-hyphenated words" (378) to the "radical agenda[s]" (377) of feminism and Marxism, and he noted (rightly) that such a statement would not likely whet the appetites of upper-level administrators for student "academic and career success" (378). His point: that as has been true historically, the individual teacher's composition philosophy should trump the curricular commonality of the outcomes statement, a point of contention that continues today. James Zebroski, in "Composition and Rhetoric, Inc.," expressed the same opinion, but from another perspective. In discussing the role of knowledge making in composition, he refers readers to the "recent[ly] vetted" WPA statement endorsing a "limited notion of knowledge in composition and rhetoric" (179). Although the point is not elaborated, one inference of Zebroski's critique is a concern that in trying to speak to such a broad mandate and set of conditions, the authors of the statement have diluted the substantive purposes of first-year composition in unacceptable ways.

At this point, it's not clear that anything like a majority of writing programs is engaging in outcomes-based program writing assessment, if we use the 2008 NCTE-WPA White Paper on Writing Assessment in Colleges and Universities project as evidence. Seeking to document outcomes-based assessment, the white paper included links to a gallery of models and resources; included are only seven models in a context of nearly three thousand institutions of postsecondary education in the U.S. Moreover, the gallery is largely inhabited by the usual suspects, that is, the programs that are already documented in the literature: Carleton College, the University of Seattle, and George Mason University, to name three of the seven. That said, what the models showcase *is* instructive and points us toward what is possible: enhancing curriculum on the basis of the review of student work. Some of the programs, like the one operating at St. Joseph University, represent an assessment model with twin intents: assessing individual student work *and* assessing the program. For the first purpose at St. Joseph, faculty read portfolios of student work.

> Assessment results are [then] reported directly to students via a written evaluation. In addition to the score sheet and narrative, students are encouraged to meet with evaluators and writing center staff, as well as advisors, to discuss portfolio results and writing skills in general. In the past, students have been surveyed to capture their perceptions regarding the portfolio process. Findings revealed overwhelming support for the continuance of the program and the evaluative techniques, particularly the commentaries. (NCTE-WPA White Paper)

But the program isn't satisfied with helping individual students only. In addition, it uses the portfolio program to inquire into how well it functions for the student population at large:

> Collective program results are communicated through an annual portfolio report disseminated to members of the college community. These reports not only give results of student performance but also include recommendations for curricular reform and areas of focus for classroom instruction. For instance, annual reports have led to increased attention to teaching research skills, as portfolio results evidenced a significant number of students struggled in this area. ()

This model, which has been operating since 1989, receives generous institutional support, has become a part of the culture of the institution, and has motivated considerable curricular reform. In sum, the St. Joseph model provides one instance of what a successful model of writing assessment might look like.

Another model, at a very different kind of institution—the University of Kentucky—also keyed to program assessment, but to program assessment exclusively, is much more recently developed, but likewise illustrative in showing how program assessment can assist us with curricular enhancement. One of Kentucky's first steps was to develop a scoring guide based on outcomes, which it decided to create locally "through an extensive process of structured discussion and revision"; the five outcomes are:

- Ethos (engaging with issues, demonstrating an awareness of intended audience, using distinctive voice and tone);
- Structure (arrangement that complements the writer's purpose, logical structure, awareness of rhetorical moves);
- Analysis (taking a stance, considering multiple perspectives, avoiding easy conclusions);

- Evidence (selecting and incorporating appropriate sources, presenting evidence in a balanced way, using sources to advance ideas); and

- Conventions (use of appropriate citation methods and conventions of Standard Written English and attendance to sentence-level concerns appropriate to the project's purpose). (Kendall, Thoune, and Kirkman)

These outcomes were then designed into a four-point analytic scoring guide that was used to see how students fared on each of the five criteria according to a given "level of mastery: scant development, minimal development, moderate development, substantial development." Given that the purpose in this model of assessment is to see how the students fare generally, the review of the scores isn't to help individuals, but to see where the curriculum is working well and where it might be revised, which is precisely how the results were used:

> Initial findings from the direct assessment . . . suggest that students completing first-year writing at UK are well versed in how to use Standard American English and general documentation conventions. However, students appear to be less able to engage in sophisticated analysis, to establish a strong sense of ethos, to use supporting evidence effectively, and to evince an awareness of multiple perspectives on a given topic, all elements associated with good writing in our UK context. These factors speak to the need for the writing program to foster the development of our students' critical thinking skills. A revision to the ENG 104 curriculum supports this development by promoting academic inquiry and the discovery of knowledge through experiential, collaborative learning. (Kendall, Thoune, and Kirkman)

In this model from the University of Kentucky, one can see all the elements of a strong program assessment: a plan for assessment; collective definition of terms and development of processes; collection of data, including student work; analysis and evaluation of data; interpretation of data; and plan for revision, which in the assessment world is called a "feedback loop," referring to a feeding-back into the curriculum based on the insights generated in the assessment process—which is the ultimate aim of all program assessment, i.e., improving the program—and which in this case involves enhancing students' critical thinking skills.

Outcomes, and outcomes-based assessment, seem at this moment a permanent part of the assessment landscape, and as we will see, they may offer protection from larger, nationally based standardized efforts also focused on program enhancement.

THE SPELLINGS COMMISSION, THE VALUE PROJECT, AND TENSIONS BETWEEN GLOBAL AND LOCAL

Not long after compositionists voluntarily moved to outcomes and out-comes assessment, program assessment specifically was receiving new attention in the national postsecondary arena in response to twin politi-cal and policy pressures emanating from the Spellings Commission—and both writing and the technologies of writing assessment are at the heart of the issues connected to such assessment.

Created in 2006 by the then secretary of education, Margaret Spellings, the commission focused on what Spellings called the four A's of post-secondary education—access; affordability; accountability; and assess-ment—that together provided a lens for inquiry into an educational sys-tem already deemed inadequate. In addition, the commission was inter-ested in a system of comparability that would allow potential students and parents to discern differences between institutions. Although the motivations of the leaders of this effort may have been benign—and the leaders represented both of the major political parties—several in the composition community—including Kristie Fleckenstein; Brian Huot, "Consistently Inconsistent"; and Chris Gallagher—have provided strong analyses of the assumptions and weaknesses of the commission and its recommendations. In contrast, higher ed responded more favorably to the call of the commission, possibly in an effort to head off a postsecond-ary version of No Child Left Behind (which many thought was the goal of the commission as Spellings had imagined it). Gathered together, institutional leaders—as represented in higher-ed organizations like the Association of Public and Land Grant Universities (APLU)—endorsed a new kind of program assessment they called the Voluntary System of Accountability (VSA), keyed to what was now called "value-added." The questions such assessment sought to answer were: What value have col-leges and universities "added" to students? and How does this value com-pare across institutions?

Despite its name, the VSA itself is not a system nor an assessment, but an acronym referring to three commercial tests that can be adminis-tered to a sample of students, who typically either volunteer or are paid to sit for the exams (on my campus, for example, they are paid $75 to take the exam). The exams can influence what happens at the institution, but not what happens to the students, raising interesting questions about the role of motivation in performing well on such a measure and *its* impact on the validity of the measure. Moreover, it is not the same set of students that is tested, but different classes of students; an institution can determine, for instance, that a group of first-year students performs at one level and a group of seniors at another, preferably higher, level and thus, through the difference in scores, that "value" has been added. More critically, how the results of the exams could lead to enhanced curricula—which, as earlier indicated, is the point of program assessment—has yet to be explained or demonstrated.

Two of the three tests, the MAPP and the CAP, are multiple choice tests; the third option, the Collegiate Learning Assessment (CLA), is an essay test and thus the option of choice for many institutions precisely because (1) it includes writing; (2) it is thus a direct measure; and (3) it seems closer to what students might be asked to do in classes. The CLA, which is gaining international reach—the government of Australia, for instance, is mandating its use for Australian tertiary institutions in 2013 (Oliver)—claims to test a diversity of skills including writing and critical thinking: put simply, it requires students to complete a set of essays responding to so-called real-world tasks. A sample question asks students to recommend which plane to buy from a given set of options and criteria. The creators of the CLA call it a performance assessment akin to asking a law student to write a brief. Upon closer analysis, however, the comparison doesn't hold: the legal writing task, at least in terms of content and genre, is a good match of prelaw to law school to law career, whereas the percentage of students who will after graduation or later recommend the purchase of a plane is (laughably) small. The match is weak and the validity of the assessment questionable. In other words, what precisely is being directly measured isn't entirely clear. As important and more troubling, the CLA scoring mechanism is leveraged on individual students' performance on the SAT: the reported CLA score is a product of the difference between a student's SAT score, which functions as a baseline assumed to be a valid predictive measure of how a student will perform in college and is used to predict the CLA score the student *should* earn, and the CLA score the student in fact earns. That difference in these scores *is* the reported CLA score. Accordingly, a student's writing score—his or her development—exists and is determined to be adequate *only* to the extent that it speaks to the SAT, which makes the SAT the principal determiner of student development and of what any college contributes to that student's development.

Universally, if we are to judge by the kinds of published responses of compositionists cited above, the VSA is deplored, but to date no professional organization—including CCCC and WPA—has issued a position statement opposing it. And the activity around writing assessment supplies a mixed data set about our interest in and commitment to program assessment: on the one hand, the WPA Assessment Institute hasn't been held for several years now, and on the other hand, we've seen a cottage industry of new books on writing assessment (Huot; Huot and O'Neill; Lynne; Elliot; Broad et al.), and *CCC* is currently publishing several articles on writing assessment annually, from quantitative analysis of placement assessment (Peckham) and assessment of prior learning (Leaker and Ostman.) to theoretical critiques of the neoliberalism informing current federal policy (Gallagher). As important as these studies and analyses are, they aren't presenting models for the program assessment that could talk back to the Spellings-influenced program assessment initiatives that are in the process of becoming policy. And at the same time, there has been resistance in some composition circles to the one national movement seeking to create a more qualitative assessment that might compete with the VSA on its own terms: the Association of American Colleges and Universities (AAC&U) VALUE project.

The AAC&U's FIPSE-supported (Fund for the Improvement of Postsecondary Education, a government funding source) VALUE project focuses on faculty assessment of student work, ideally inside electronic portfolios, but more practically of any single text; as AAC&U explains, the VALUE project

> seeks to contribute to the national dialogue on assessment of college student learning. It builds on a philosophy of learning assessment that privileges multiple expert judgments of the quality of student work over reliance on standardized tests administered to samples of students outside of their required courses. The assessment approaches that VALUE advances are based on the shared understanding of faculty and academic professionals on campuses from across the country. (Kendall, Thoune, and Kirkman)

This model of assessment thus understands validity in yet another way, as a function of (1) embedded assessment—that is, assessment drawing on work samples created in authentic contexts like classrooms and service learning sites; and (2) faculty expertise. To tap this expertise, the VALUE leaders invited faculty from around the country to create scoring guides that could be used to assess electronic portfolios, the basic idea here borrowed from the WPA outcomes work (Rhodes). More specifically, this faculty-led, boundary-object approach was exactly that adopted by AACU when in 2007 it invited faculty—some one hundred volunteer faculty from nearly one hundred institutions working in fifteen areas (including quantitative literacy; team work, integrative learning)—to participate in an iterative rubric-creating process: after the rubrics were created, they were applied to both individual pieces of student work and to electronic portfolios. The first completed scoring guide was in written communication, created by a five-person team filled with compositionist credentials, including Linda Adler-Kassner, then of Eastern Michigan University and now of the University of California at Santa Barbara and past president of CWPA; Susanmarie Harrington, the WAC director at the University of Vermont; and Carol Rutz, whose WAC assessment work at Carleton College is standard reading for anyone interested in WAC assessment. Compositionists, in other words, had several hands in this effort.[4]

Interestingly, despite its commitment to faculty expertise and its homegrown character, this model of assessment informing the VALUE project is not going unchallenged. Put simply, on the composition side, there are concerns about what is perceived as a global effort in a writing world where the local is valued. Thus, according to the leaders of the AAC&U effort, the writing group was the least satisfied of all the groups with the completed guide: generally, the members of the writing group believed that the generalized rubric template, given its limitations, precluded their creating a meaningful guide (Morgaine). It's also likely that the group was reflecting concerns raised by others in the composition community. For example, both Brian Huot and Bob Broad, enacting Huot's emphasis on assessment defined by five characteristics—writing assessment as (1) site based; (2) locally contextualized; (3) context sensitive; (4) rhetorically based; and (5) accessible—argue for a completely local system of rubric development and application that would be at odds with any national model, including the AAC&U model. Bob Broad has interpreted the local in terms of inviting campuses to reject values that are "given" to them so that through a process he calls dynamic

---

4.   I served on the steering committee for the VALUE project.

criteria mapping, they might identify the values important to them, which is precisely the process used at the University of Kentucky's program assessment, as the leaders of that effort explain:

> Disenchanted with the rubrics that were available to us from outside sources even with modification, the committee sought another approach to the formation of a rubric that could be more responsive to local needs and dynamics. We ultimately took our lead from Bob Broad's *What We Really Value* and his notion of "dynamic criteria mapping" as the process by which we would identify the values that matter most to our UK first-year writing community, and thus would help us define the criteria for the scoring rubric. (Kendall, Thoune, and Kirkman)

This tension between local control—which for many compositionists is a first principle of good assessment—and a national approach, even when adjustable as in the case of both the WPA outcomes and the VALUE project, is one that continues today. One danger of going completely local, of course, is a lack of larger context: if the program assessment results were at odds with what others expect, it would call into question the program of assessment itself. Were, for instance, all the students in a given institution to be rated, in Garrison Keillor's formation, as above average but were then to find their writing substandard—as evidenced in graduate school rejections or failure to be hired—the institutional assessment would have scant defense given its disconnection from any other system or set of outcomes. A second danger is also related to context: without being in articulation with a large context, or within an ecology of some kind, institutions can find themselves at odds with good practice, not intentionally, but as a default simply by virtue of being disconnected and uninformed. Moreover, situating one's work in multiple contexts—be that work scholarship or assessment—helps us see more and better, and in fact is one argument in favor of efforts toward globalization, which in composition, at least, are gaining considerable interest. A key question for writing assessment going forward, then, is how to balance an institution's interest in developing local values and practices while remaining in dialogue with a larger context in order to benefit both contexts as they inform each other.

PORTFOLIOS: PRINT AND ELECTRONIC

When portfolios were initially introduced into composition studies—within a three-month period between 1991 and 1992, there were three anthologies explicating different uses of portfolios: Belanoff and Dickson; Graves and Sunstein/; and Yancey, *Portfolios in the Writing Classroom*—they were adopted almost uncritically. But as Sandra Murphy and Yancey point out, given the diversity in their definition and use, it was almost predictable that they would not provide the perfect assessment technology. And at bottom, given those differences in assumptions and models, was a difference in the construct of writing, a theme we have noted previously. Because portfolio programs, like other assessment measures,

> reflect curricula and the web of beliefs, goals, and assumptions that undergird education, [they] vary widely in ways that are theoretically and educationally important (Murphy, 1994; Murphy & Underwood, 2000). In some projects, students are encouraged to choose what their portfolios will contain. In others, teachers assume that responsibility. In some projects, students submit only final versions of work; in others they submit drafts, notes, and other evidence of the processes they engaged in as they produced the work. In some projects, students are asked to reflect on their work, their learning, and/or their processes for producing work. In others, not. All of these basic differences in assessment design reflect at some level different views about the construct of writing that the assessment purports to measure as well as differences in the construct of writing assessment itself. (373)

In terms of an assessment, then, a portfolio is not a portfolio is not a portfolio, and the construct of writing it samples likewise varies.

In addition, two critiques of portfolio practice in particular are worth noting: first is a difference between intent and effect. One benefit of portfolios is assumed to be what students learn as they compile them— reviewing their own work, reflecting upon it, and in the process understanding themselves better as writers. As explained earlier, such reflection acts to provide a kind of ecological validity. But interviews with students—conducted by Gail Cummins and Liz Spalding, for example, as well as by Tony Scott ("Creating the Subject of Portfolios")—suggest the opposite. According to their data, creating the portfolio—which, according to portfolio theory, provided students with an opportunity to see themselves anew, acquire agency, and influence the assessment of their work by composing their own account of learning and development—was a task that the students perceived as "not useful." At the same time, given that the students interviewed were all high school students or recently graduated high school students reflecting upon their experience in the same state-wide, large-scale, fairly depersonalized assessment system where the portfolio itself was almost invisible, it's a good question as to how widely such a view of portfolios is shared, especially where the students are college students composing in a more hospitable environment.

The second critique, often issued through a Foucaultian lens, is related: it points to the considerable opportunities for surveillance offered by portfolios, especially given their capacity for making learning visible and thus available for inquiry or review. In other words, the very practices that make portfolios useful—the ability to show process and student context, and thus make both available for intervention—also make the student and those practices something of an object. A response to this issue—which, rather than being portfolio based is created by any situation where students self-assess—was invoked by Huot and Yancey when they argued that students need to be genuine participants in the process of assessment, not objects of it. Still, the field hasn't fully developed ways to accomplish this aim.

A third issue connected with portfolios is, once again, related to the construct of portfolios, the construct of writing, and specifically to the role of reflection in both. Stated simply, we are still in search of a definition of reflection and of its role in writing assessment. Early on in the portfolio literature, Chris Anson ("Portfolios for Teachers") made the distinction between primary sources for assessment and secondary sources, arguing that reflection was a secondary source that provided additional or confirmational evidence for judgments rendered through reviews of the primary texts. Somewhat later, and especially after the literature on reflection widened outside portfolios—as we see in sources as various as Yancey's *Reflection in the Writing Classroom* and Kara Taczak's "The Sixth Knowledge Domain: A Theory of Reflection"—reflection was understood as complementary to other writing texts but not subordinate to them; indeed, Taczak argues that it is its own domain—or construct. Meanwhile, in 2005 Ed White introduced what he called phase 2 portfolio scoring, a practice in which reflection is removed from the portfolio and "graded" as a single text, in part for the sake of efficiency (i.e., to save costs), and in part because the reflective assignment he recommends, one that asks students to argue that their work demonstrates a set of outcomes, requires the very outcomes they are required to demonstrate ("Scoring"). Working with electronic portfolios, however, Doug Hesse and the University of Denver have found that this kind of very focused reflective assignment—one that asks for argument and demonstration—isn't in fact very reflective but rather narrows students' focus (Campbell et al., "The Value"). The UD findings suggest that in such an assignment, students are less likely to see what is at odds with such an argument—with the summative assessment acting as a powerful motivator, such that any opportunity to learn is forfeited, understandably enough, in the rush to secure the grade. From this vantage point, the phase 2 model functions not in support of but rather in opposition to the kind of nuance and thoughtfulness that many associate with reflection.

Recent work by portfolio researchers in the Inter/National Coalition for Electronic Portfolio Research[5] (Jennifer Campbell et al.) brings several other perspectives on reflection into consideration. One finding suggests that reflection is likely very discipline specific, which would mean that we might be on the cusp of developing very different models located in a more robust theory of reflection, probably a hybrid between the Taczak domain-theory and the UD thoughtfulness version. Likewise, the sixth cohort of the I/NCEPR, inaugurated in September 2010, which includes writing programs from several institutions—including the University of Mississippi, the University of Michigan, the University of Georgia, and Northeastern University—is focusing on the assessment of electronic portfolios. More specifically, the coalition is considering how reflection might function as a site for consideration of (rather than argument on behalf of) multiple artifacts and how comparability could be achieved without the standardization so prized by the Spellings Commission approach.

In sum, the current attention to reflection as both theory and practice suggests that it will play an increasingly vital role in writing assessment, although how that role will be defined is still an open question.

FUTURE CONCERNS

As this primer suggests, we have seen innovations in writing assessment—new theories, new practices, and new understandings—flourish during the late twentieth century and into the twenty-first. Increasingly, we have also seen the role of the federal government move from a benign disinterest to a focused effort to encourage a certain view of institutions and to influence their practices: encouraging an

---

5. With Barbara Cambridge, I founded the coalition; we codirect with Darren Cambridge.

outcomes-based, standardized assessment model pointing toward comparability across institutions with no interest in local contexts or values.[6] At the same time, compositionists have developed local program assessments enhancing their curricula, and other institutions including compositionists—like the Inter/National Coalition for Electronic Portfolio Research—are developing new models of assessment that honor the local, that rely on a sophisticated construct of writing, and that provide new evidence of validity. These changes are not stage bound; rather, they

---

6.   One major reform initiative not addressed here is the implementation of the Common Core State Standards, a set of standards that states have been invited to adopt and whose implementation has been fueled by Barack Obama's Race to the Top funding. As I explained on WPA-L,

>   The Common Core Standards are keyed to college and workplace readiness; although they are "voluntary," their development is funded in part by Obama's Race to the Top funding, which (among other things) is dedicated to the efforts of two consortia developing new comprehensive assessment systems. One of the systems is alleged to be better (i.e., less controlling) than another, but the little I've seen suggests that they do a pretty good job of continuing to de-professionalize teachers, the teachers, you'll remember, that do not need graduate degrees qua our Secretary of Education Arne Duncan. <sigh>

>   NCTE has worked very hard to help make the Standards better (or less bad) while not being entailed: a *very* delicate act. To see what this looks like, you can begin with [then-NCTE president] Kylene Beer's carefully crafted letter http://www.ncte.org/standards/commoncore/response—and follow along on the NCTE page. There you'll find other letters, analyses, and so on. It's worth noting that even conservatives like Diane Ravitch and Sandra Stotsky oppose them, although for very different reasons.

>   There are many concerns we in writing might have about the standards: here are two.

>   The first is how *college readiness* is being translated: in the weaker version, given that the Standards folks are hoping to create a seamless transition from one educational context to another, the idea is that the scores students earn on high school exit tests would be used for college placement—or even for college credit.

>   The second is that these standards are leading to college credit itself—and quite a bit of it. This week, for example, Leon County (where Tallahassee is located) announced that it had been awarded $3.4M Race to the Top funding "to accomplish some of the district's goals by 2015, including increasing the graduation rate to 85%, cut achievement gap in half, and increasing the percent of 9th graders who eventually earn at least a year's worth of college credit from 34 percent to 56 percent."

>   That last item—increasing the percentage of students who eventually earn a YEAR'S worth of college credit (my caps)—to over half the class? And precisely which classes will they be exempting, and precisely what evidence do we have that this is in the students' best interest?

>   I have no doubt that the CCSS will affect postsecondary writing curricula and possibly their assessment, but at this point, it's not clear entirely how.

occur in waves, with one change, like portfolios, introduced while the earlier forms of writing assessment—such as the SAT multiple choice "test of writing"—continue.

If past is prologue, the future of writing assessment will be shaped similarly, particularly with an emphasis on outcomes and outcomes-based assessments; on program assessments; and on portfolios—all of which will continue to raise questions about construct(s) of writing, about validity, and about ways through writing assessment we can best foster students' development as writers.

10

STUDYING LITERACY IN DIGITAL CONTEXTS
Computers and Composition Studies

Gail E. Hawisher and Cynthia L. Selfe

In a twenty-first-century world shaped increasingly by digital environments for creating and communicating meaning by electronic workplaces, homes, and online businesses, and by computer networks that extend across linguistic, cultural, and geopolitical borders, it has become rare to find a writing program or a composition classroom that does not incorporate computers or rhetoric and composition faculty who do not recognize some level of responsibility for preparing students to read, write, and communicate effectively in digital environments. Digital environments also provide crucial environments for reading and composing activities that take place in WAC programs, writing and learning centers, community literacy programs, libraries, ESL, and professional and business writing programs. In fact, digital environments are so ubiquitous as communication spaces in our world that they are, arguably, an integral part of composition studies. Studying almost any aspect of rhetoric and composition without acknowledging the significant roles that digital environments play as people make meaning in their homes, in schools, in communities is, in sum, to be blind to the realities of contemporary communication.

No longer the new kid on the block, the field of computers and composition studies is now well into thirty years as an intellectual force within the larger discipline of rhetoric and composition/writing studies.[1] It is also difficult, however, to ignore the fact that in the larger scheme of disciplinary knowledge, computers and composition

---

1. Published in 2000, an early book in which we attempted to bring the global into our field of vision is Hawisher and Selfe's edited collection, *Global Literacies and the World Wide Web*. See also Hawisher and Selfe's *College English* article with Yi-Huey Guo and Lu Liu, "Globalization and Agency: Designing and Redesigning the Literacies of Cyberspace."

still counts as a relatively recent area of scholarship that has been dated variously from 1975, with the publication of Ellen Nold's "Fear and Trembling: A Humanist Approaches the Computer" in *College Composition and Communication*, or from 1979 with Hugh Burns's historic dissertation, "Stimulating Rhetorical Invention in English Composition through Computer-Assisted Instruction." Since the 1970s and 1980s, the range of research and scholarship in this maturing field continues to change in dramatic ways. This work can be characterized, in part, by its roots in composition studies, social theory, feminist theory, and technology studies; by its commitment to the educational spaces of classroom and literacy programs; by its continued attention to issues of race, class, gender, representation; by its related interests in language studies, particularly in the teaching of reading and composing in the broadest sense of these terms, often in contexts not limited to alphabetic representation; and, most recently, by its turn toward the complex issues of literacy and globalization.

Inspired by the recent MLA report *Evaluating Scholarship for Tenure and Promotion*, in this chapter we focus primarily on multimodal digital research that allows for the increasingly rich representation of language and literacy practices in digital and nondigital environments. This research—inflected by feminist studies, new literacy studies, critical theory, and digital media studies—provides scholars a promising set of strategies for conducting studies and for representing research and scholarship in digital contexts. Moreover, and unsurprisingly, this scholarly work has been increasingly taken up as digital tools have made their way into the academy and beyond. But there are other issues to address as well. As the field has matured over the years and as digital media have become ubiquitous in our professional, pedagogical, and everyday lives, it has become incumbent upon those of us who study digital media and literate activity to name what we do while at the same time ensuring that the departments we inhabit recognize the field of computers and composition and its research as worthy of scholarly inquiry. As women and senior scholars in this rather unusual area of the humanities, we have made it our goal—as much as is possible—to make certain that the scholarly work of emerging scholars counts when it comes to matters of tenure and promotion.

As the MLA report points out, there is often departmental resistance to new forms of scholarship. Understandably, many academic units retain long-standing historical and cultural values and sometimes go so far as to oppose new forms of knowledge production, especially those situated within digital environments—among these, a value on the scholarly and research performance of individuals rather than teams; a value on conventional forms of information exchange, particularly printed books and journal articles; and a value on models of scholarly production tied to institutional capital in university presses and professional journals. For those scholars who recognize the strengths of both conventional and emerging forms of knowledge production, this situation is becoming increasingly problematic to negotiate, especially for junior scholars working toward tenure. Thus through our work as editors of *Computers and Composition*, the Hampton book series New Dimensions in Computers and Composition and as founders of *Computers and Composition Online*, along with our newest project, Computers and Composition Digital Press, we have attempted to provide venues that extend the possibilities for scholarly publication within our field.

In this chapter, we argue for a "more capacious notion of scholarship" (MLA Task Force 5) as we describe recent representative publications we've supported through our editorial work, along with some of our own research, in which we have increasingly made use of digital media as we've turned toward the global. With these discussions, we intend to capture prominent approaches to inquiry that mark the field of computers and composition in the early twenty-first century.

THE RISE OF MULTIMODAL COMPOSING IN DIGITAL CONTEXTS

> Multimedia composition is the craft of inventing, shaping, producing, and delivering text, audio, video, and images purposefully. As a craft (or art), it is a set of skilled practices for integrating content that may appear in various forms—words, sound, moving and still images, even physical objects—all in the interest of communicating, entertaining, or persuading.
>
> David Blakesley and Karl Stolley

Noteworthy developments in the field of computers and composition must include the appearance of multimedia composition and multimodal texts as they relate to literate activity. As Blakesley and Stolley point out, multimodality has to do with moving away from an exclusive reliance on alphabetic texts and often using images, audio, and video "purposefully" to produce and shape meaning. Moreover, scholars such as Gunther Kress (*Literacy;* "'English' at the Crossroads") argue that any single mode of communication, including the alphabetic, can represent only a portion of the meaning that writers might want to convey to audiences. Hence, writing professionals across the country have begun to offer students opportunities to experiment with other modes of expression in conjunction with writing. As multimodal composition has become popular in writing classes—we're thinking of our own universities and newly introduced courses such as Writing with Video and Writing across Media at Illinois and Digital Media and English Studies at Ohio State—it has also taken center stage in much of the scholarship emerging today.

There is, of course, a rich history even in this relatively new turn to multimodal composing. In 1996, the New London Group published a groundbreaking article in the *Harvard Educational Review* explicitly naming this approach and connecting it to teaching literacy. Variously termed "multimedia composition," as represented in the quotation at the start of this section, "multiliteracies" (Cope and Kalantzis), or "multimodal literacy" (Jewitt and Kress), its theoretical base attempts to accommodate the rapidly changing social, economic, linguistic, and technological demands of complex and globalized environments. This theory acknowledges that contemporary authors, faced with complex rhetorical situations, need the ability to draw on an increasingly varied set of design resources and representational modalities to make meaning and create texts—among them, still photography, video, audio, alphabetic, animation, graphical drawings, and color. As noted, a theory of multimodality draws, at least in part, on the research of Gunther Kress (*Literacy;* "'English' at the Crossroads"), who continues to document the increasing importance of visual information as a semiotic channel in the twenty-first century.

Given its emphasis on rhetorical understanding and innovative pedagogies for literacy instruction, this work resonated with related research and scholarship in computers and composition studies. As Diana George points out in "From Analysis to Design," visual modes of representation have a long history of being used in U.S. composition courses as support for writing assignments and instruction, but they have generally been considered the handmaiden of alphabetic texts—a less sophisticated, less precise mode of conveying semiotic content than written language. As a result, George notes, the visual has traditionally in writing studies been given short shrift as a composing resource that students could draw on to create their own compositions.

In recent years, digital media increasingly have provided not only students but also computers and composition researchers access to environments within which they could draw on multiple semiotic channels to study and produce effective multimodal texts. Work on visual modalities of representation became, throughout the late 1990s and into the new century, a rich area of research. Carolyn Handa contributed to research in visual rhetoric—editing two special issues of *Computers and Composition* and publishing the first "critical sourcebook" on the subject *Visual Rhetoric in a Digital World*—both projects aimed at studying the intersection of rhetorical theory, visual representation, and digital environments for composing. In an extended study, Gail Hawisher and coauthor Patricia Sullivan explored the visual representations that women provide in online contexts, examining how women in the U.S. and abroad create complicated identities shaped by multiple rhetorical and sometimes ethnic concerns. Hawisher and Sullivan connected their explorations to the cyborg studies of Donna Haraway and sought connections that might change conventional ideas about how women make themselves known on the Web. With the recent popularity of social network sites, attention to visual representations has become all important as photos are posted and tagged to reveal our many selves and people are invited to join various groups in which they may actively participate. Collective identities, such as membership in a Facebook group as one of many fans of the *AFLAC* duck—or one's taking on a more serious role as a group member advocating for the repeal the 2008 California ban on marriage equality—are possible as well.

Turning to aurality, Cynthia Selfe, in a recent *College Composition and Communication* article, "The Movement of Air," argues for a reconsideration of the role of sound as a composing modality. Exploring the history of aural composing modalities (speech, music, sound) within composition as a profession, Selfe points out how aurality was subsumed by the discipline's privileging of print in much of the twentieth century. Selfe argues that the history of aurality, along with that of visual modalities, has limited our profession's understanding of composing as a rhetorical activity and has helped deprive both faculty and students of valuable semiotic resources for making meaning. Further, in light of scholarship on the importance of aurality to different communities and cultures, she argues that the current adherence to alphabetic-only composition constrains the semiotic efforts of individuals and groups who value multiple modalities of expression and compose hybrid texts. Selfe maintains that teachers and scholars of composition need to adopt an increasingly thoughtful understanding of aurality and the role it—and other modalities—can play in contemporary communication tasks.

The increased attention to digital and multimodal literacy practices not only continues to generate new research projects, but also encourages academic journals to represent research in new ways using photography, visual elements, text, video, sound, animation, hypertext, and multimedia. In 1996, for example, the groundbreaking journal *Kairos*, focusing on rhetoric, technology, and pedagogy and today edited by Cheryl Ball and Beth Hewitt, stipulated in its submission policy:

> *Kairos* publishes "webtexts," which means projects developed with specific attention to the World Wide Web as publishing medium. . . . [W]e invite each author or collaborative writing team to think carefully about what unique opportunities the web offers. Some projects may best be presented in hypertextual form, others more linear, and in some instances multimedia and graphical architecture may be critical, while other projects may be less suited to such approaches.

Kairos's invitation attracted a wide range of academic texts, from those such as Jonathan Alexander's "Ravers on the Web: Resistance, Multidimensionality, and Writing (about) Youth Culture," which used a hypertextual organization of alphabetic writing, and Anne Wysocki's "Bookling Monument," which explored visual possibilities of representation.

Other journals, too, took up the challenge of representing new forms of scholarly texts. By 2005, *Computers and Composition Online*, under the editorship of Kristine Blair, featured the following policy:

> Submissions for *Computers and Composition Online* need to be web-aware, meaning that they not only use the World Wide Web as a medium, they also take advantage of the benefits of this kind of publishing. Rhizomatic structures that disrupt traditional linear forms are welcome. Artful use of graphical interfaces and hypertext are also encouraged. Multimedia use, including digital video and audio, is also welcome.

Research and scholarship on multimodal literacy has continued in traditional print forms as well. Nancy Allen edited *Working with Words and Image: New Steps in an Old Dance*, and Anne Wysocki, Johndan Johnson-Eilola, Cynthia Selfe, and Geoff Sirc authored *Writing New Media: Theory and Applications for Expanding the Teaching of Composition*.

Both books attempt to apply research in visual rhetoric and multimodality to the teaching of composition. The authors' own *Literate Lives in the Information Age: Narratives of Literacy from the United States*, along with Adam Banks's *Race, Rhetoric, and Technology* and Heidi McKee and Danielle DeVoss's *Digital Writing Research* collection have continued to rely on print venues for publication—a practice we envision as extending into the future even as we turn increasingly to digital publication. It is no accident that we ourselves continue to edit both a print journal and a book series that we claim as critical venues for scholarship in the field of computer and composition studies.

RESEARCHING SITES OF WRITING AND LITERACY: COMPUTERS AND COMPOSITION DIGITAL PRESS

> In academia, specifically, all writing is increasingly computer-mediated; all writing is digital.
>
> Danielle DeVoss, Heidi McKee, and Richard (Dickie) Selfe

We recognize, of course, that the changing environment of electronic publication refuses to stand still for any journal, regardless of its commitment to innovation. As noted, the 2007 MLA Task Force calls for new forms of innovative digital scholarship resembling books in their intellectual heft, but departing from these conventional publications in their digital and often multimodal formats. This report cites a converging set of trends that favors digital publications: among just a few of them, the increasing expense of library acquisitions, the declining funds available to university presses, and the expanding power and reach of online scholarly networks.

At the same time, scholars in computers and composition studies who often were more familiar with new forms of digital media had already in 2007 begun to understand that the flattened spaces of printed pages, while privileged by the academy and its traditions, were less than ideal in their representational potential than the multidimensional landscapes that digital media could offer, landscapes in which video, audio, and multimedia representations, as well as alphabetic text, could be combined in a variety of ways.

Within this changing context, in 2008, we founded Computers and Composition Digital Press (CCDP), an open-access academic press committed to publishing scholarly, multimodal e-books and digital projects that explore new genres and formats that go beyond those associated with conventional printed books.[2] To a great extent CCDP has been designed to address the converging set of challenges we've discussed while building on the work of the journal *Computers and Composition*, the book series New Dimensions in Computers and Composition, *Kairos*, and *Computers and Composition Online*. The press projects, for example, are freely available to both faculty and to the public, and do not, thus, contribute to the rising acquisition costs currently plaguing libraries. In addition, the projects published by the CCDP carry the imprint of a university press, Utah State University Press, while drawing only minimally on the resources of that press. Finally, Computers and Composition Digital Press offers all of its projects online, using the Web as the primary means of extending the reach and scope of its intellectual effort.

Perhaps the most difficult challenge of all for the new press has been the delicate balancing effort it must continue to enact between convention and innovation, tradition and change. On the one hand, for instance, if CCDP hopes to attract colleagues who have scholarly projects to publish, it must make sure that such projects are appropriately valued within the context of their home departments and institutions, and vetted against the traditional academic value on rigorous peer review, scholarly excellence, and intellectual reach so prized by departments of English. On the other hand, however, the press is committed to publishing and circulating digital projects that extend the boundaries and forms of innovative scholarship.

To address this last challenge, we have taken several steps. With an eye toward tradition, the editors formulated an internationally recognized editorial board, one consisting primarily of senior scholars with extensive knowledge about both the existing values of academic departments and the potential innovations characterizing digital media environments. Members of the editorial board make recommendations to the press editors in much the same fashion that such boards function within conventional presses, although projects are reviewed online instead of on paper. In addition, the partnership with Utah State University Press makes a crucial contribution to establishing the conventional authority of CCDP efforts within the broader environment of the modern

---

2.   Richard Selfe, H. Lewis Ulman, Jason Palmeri, and Karl Stolley serve as valued editors of Computers and Composition Digital Press. Patrick Berry and Melanie Yergeau are the CCDP's creative directors; and Stephanie Vie is project director. See <http://ccdigitalpress.org/>.

academy. As part of this partnership agreement, all projects published with CCDP also undergo editorial review by the Utah State University Advisory Board. Within this partnership structure, once projects are accepted for publication, they will carry the imprint of both Computers and Composition Digital Press and that of Utah State University Press, an important credential for faculty facing tenure and promotion in many English departments around the country.

Perhaps of greatest interest to the CCDP editors, however, are those scholars who have begun to focus on the benefits of using audio and video not only to *conduct* their research, but also to *report on* and *present* their research, producing texts that are more informative and richly descriptive than those that rely on the alphabetic alone. Although video and audio have been used for a number of years to collect and report on data in disciplines such as anthropology, biology, and political science, for example, such methods have not seen widespread use in other humanities disciplines like rhetoric and composition, in part due to the limitations of possible publication venues. With the advent of digital media publications, however, it is now possible for scholars and researchers to expand their research reports beyond the range of the alphabetic.

In our own research, for example, we have begun to use digital video and audio to collect and report on the literacy life histories we have collected from students and colleagues with transnational connections, narratives that detail various uses of digital technologies to maintain relationships with family, friends, and coworkers and to author their own productions. Rendered in a more conventional form—that is, through transcripts and quotations—such narratives can become mono-dimensional and less complete, accurate, and informative. Printed accounts of these interviews, for instance, contain participants' words but often fail to convey other important information: the dialects of speakers from various regions and parts of the world, the rhythm and pace of their voices as they talk about particular incidents, the vocal emphasis they place on some words and phrases as they tell their stories, the revealing gestures and facial expressions they use to accompany a specific narrative or part of a narrative, the bodily presence they invest in communicative exchanges as they relate a story. In other words, they tend to be bereft of the social cues that we value in face-to-face contexts.

Like a growing number of scholars, we argue that digital photographic images and media clips can add additional semiotic information to alphabetic representations of research. We also, however, agree with Roy Pea and Jay Lemke that digital media representations of research *should* be used in tandem with written descriptions. This collaborative engagement around shared digital representations of research evidence, we believe, provides a powerful argument for a digital press like Computers and Composition Digital Press that can publish multimodal scholarly work. Potentially, these kinds of digital media publications—hybrid mixes of alphabetic text, audio clips, and video reports—could challenge the ways in which departments of English typically understand research and the knowledge that accrues from it, prompting questions about who owns data, and at what stage of the research process; how scholarly knowledge is produced and by whom; and how scholars engage with the findings of their colleagues.

Our initial call for proposals recognized that the digital press would be publishing book-length texts and projects in a wide variety of forms, ranging from primarily alphabetic to integrated multimodal projects. In fact, the first Computers and Composition Digital Press volume to appear is *Technological Ecologies and Sustainability* edited by Danielle DeVoss, Heidi McKee, and Richard Selfe. In itself, the collection is a wonderful example of a project that brings together primarily alphabetic chapters with others that incorporate video, image, and sound. The e-book itself, like more conventional books, consists of seventeen chapters with titles that reflect current interests in the field. A sampling includes Peter Fadde and Patricia Sullivan's "Video for the Rest of Us? Toward Sustainable Processes for Incorporating Video into Multimodal Composition"; Kristie Fleckenstein, Fred Johnson, and Jackie Grutsch McKinney's "A Portable Ecology: Supporting New Media Writing and Laptop-ready Pedagogy"; and Beth Brunk-Chavez and Shawn Miller's "The Hybrid Academy: Building and Sustaining a Technological Culture of Use." These chapters all trace to some degree the introduction of multimodal texts into programs, institutions, and research, often drawing on multiple semiotic channels to make their arguments. At the same time, we note that eleven of the seventeen chapters have been crafted by at least two authors. While the collaborative spirit has long marked the field of rhetoric and composition, the most recent move to texts that demand expertise across a wide variety of domains tends to require more than the lone author so often prized in the humanities. Thus this first volume, through its range of semiotic channels, penchant for coauthorship, and indeed its process of digital dissemination, reflects approaches to scholarly inquiry and publication that the field of computers and composition studies is likely to attend to far into the future.

A BEGINNING

In sum, the emerging vision we offer of computers and composition studies celebrates a young, changing field that exists itself in a larger, dynamic field of rhetoric and composition/writing studies. This vision, as we hope our chapter captures, recognizes the ongoing, groundbreaking influences of digital media and new literacy practices, but also values conventional forms of knowledge production and circulation. It argues for collaboration and the acceptance of the turn toward the multimodal in academic texts, and it argues against our profession's single-minded focus on single-authored, mono-dimensional texts that remain confined to the printed page. With hope for the productive future of those who would publish in our multifaceted discipline of rhetoric and composition—and with the expectation of ongoing discussions of digital media, literate activity, and electronic publication—we offer this chapter to the consideration of readers and scholars seeking new ways of authoring in this newest of centuries.

11

"WHAT GOES ON HERE?"
The Uses of Ethnography in Composition Studies

Elizabeth Chiseri-Strater

"What is the postmodernist critique of ethnography?" was a question posed to me by a member of the search committee on a campus visit for a compositionist job I thought I desperately wanted. As a newly minted doctorate who had written a dissertation that was an ethnographic study of undergraduate reading and writing practices (that would become *Academic Literacies*), I knew I should be able to answer this question since one of the strengths of my interdisciplinary graduate program was my coursework in ethnography, a research approach to the study of cultures,[1] including the subculture of schooling.[2] In answering this question, I was hyperaware of how skeptical an English department

---

1. My thanks to Beth Campbell of Indiana University of Pennsylvania for her insights into the connections between ethnography in anthropology and its translations into composition studies. Her dissertation, "Being and Writing with others: On the Possibilities of an Ethnographic Composition Pedagogy," will be of great value to our field.

2. Culture can be defined in many different ways. Definitions include the following, which can be found in Chiseri-Strater and Sunstein, *Fieldworking: Reading and Writing Culture* (3):

   > Culture is local and manmade and hugely variable. It tends to be integrated. A culture, like an individual, is a more or less consistent pattern of thought and action (Benedict 46).

   > A society's culture consists of whatever it is one has to know or believe in order to operate in a manner acceptable to its members. . . .[I]t does not consist of things, people, behavior, or emotions. It is rather an organization of things" (Goodenough 167).

   > Cultures are, after all, collective, untidy assemblages, authenticated by belief and agreement (Myerhoff 10).

   > Man is an animal suspended in webs of significance which he himself has created. I take culture to be those webs (Geertz 14).

   > Culture is an invisible web of behaviors, patterns, rules, and rituals of a group of people who have contact with one another And share common languages. (Chiseri-Strater and Sunstein 3).

might be about hiring a faculty member who could be viewed as a social scientist in English studies clothing. So, discarding my newly acquired knowledge of the ongoing critiques of ethnography by anthropologists and feminists, I stumbled through a response about how ethnographic approaches provided composition researchers with a methodology for examining reading, writing, and language practices within specific contexts such as their own classrooms, a pedagogy for teaching students to observe, reflect, and write about cultures and subcultures, and theoretical grounding for engaging in activist fieldwork, all ideas that skirted the question asked of me.

Reader, I did not get the job.

And yet that question haunted me, as all failed interviews are apt to do, so I will begin here by addressing that query about postmodern critiques of ethnography, mainly leveled by anthropologists at their own field during the late 1980s and early 1990s but relevant to composition studies both then and now. I'll argue that the epistemological debates going on in other disciplines at the time were largely ignored by compositionists because our novice field was challenged by a methodological merry-go-round of competing research options (cognitive studies, case studies, teacher research, ethnographic fieldwork) that were largely undertheorized and were vying for dominance in our rising field. Further, because the discipline itself was in the process of developing, with one foot in the humanities and another foot in the social sciences, many compositionists had little contact with the ongoing conversations in anthropology, folklore, or feminist studies about the postmodern challenges to ethnographic methodology. Much like the lure of postcolonial theory[3] in our field today, composition studies was both attracted by yet resistant to the need to adopt yet one more approach into our already-hybridized discipline. It seems useful, then, to go backward before coming forward

---

3. In their introduction to *Crossing Borderlands: Composition and Postcolonial Studies,* Andrea Lunsford and Lahoucine Ouzgane define the agenda of postcolonial studies as seeking to "expose the mechanisms of oppression through which 'Others'— aboriginal, native, or simply preexisting cultures and groups—are displaced, eradicated, or transformed into obedient subjects" (1). They suggest that their collection wishes to make a connection between the field of postcolonial studies and composition by addressing several like themes: "resisting the urge to speak for students, valuing student voices and student writing, a focus on access and agency, attention to material conditions, and attention to the role of English and to the ways in which Americans can be said to be postcolonial" (5). I am suggesting that the same epistemological issues arise in ethnography that are also addressed in postcolonial studies.

to map the incorporation of ethnography in composition studies now, split as it often still is among different fieldwork approaches, some closer to qualitative studies than ethnography. It is my hope to argue for the continued usefulness of ethnographic research as a way of acquiring a holistic view of the behaviors, beliefs, rituals, and interactions of groups of people, particularly with respect to literacy, but also for us as reflexive researchers who gain much knowledge about ourselves in the study of others, particularly when that involves collaborative partnerships.

WHAT WENT ON IN ETHNOGRAPHY IN THE PAST?

The postmodern critique of ethnography in anthropology was marked by the publication of Clifford and Marcus's book, *Writing Culture: The Poetics and Politics of Ethnography*, which challenged the idea of ethnography as a neutral and transparent social science, a process and product that could be considered in any way objective, valid, comprehensive, or complete. One of the strengths of this essay collection was that it posited the argument that ethnography had always been about writing, not just researching cultures, whether anthropologists recognized this or not. Articles in this collection, written by scholars such as Geertz, Crapanzano, and Rosaldo, showed that any ethnography is always a textual and rhetorical construction rather than an objective description, signaling postmodern thinking about the fragmented view of the observer into the field of anthropology. After the publication of *Writing Culture*, suggests folklorist and ethnographer Beth Campbell, "ethnography could no longer speak (or write) for Others, it could no longer discern the truth(s) of Others from its distanced observation points (even if those Others were participating), and it could no longer imagine itself outside of its own historical, disciplinary, and cultural environments" (4). What happened at this juncture in anthropology, then, became an epistemological shift away from the realistic, representational writing grounded in positivism that had advanced the colonial agenda as it moved toward experimental writing that attempted to capture and evoke the fluidity and fragmentation of the ethnographer's postmodern experiences within everyday culture(s), more local than global.

The cross-disciplinary scholarship in both anthropology and feminism had provided me with an understanding (if not a complete ability to articulate it) of the shift in a field I was newly becoming familiar with while studying rhetoric and composition. I was then learning ethnographic field methods as they were being newly critiqued by anthropologists and in particular by feminist anthropologists (Wolf; Lawless; Behar and Gordon) who launched a postmodern critique that challenged issues of voice, power, representation, reciprocity, agency, ethics, and authority, all ongoing debates in feminist ethnography today.

While those critiques by scholars outside our field might have provided a good answer to the interview question asked of me, I might also have called upon a scholar within composition studies who was struggling with the array of competing research approaches that challenged our disciplinary cohesion, mainly with the dominance of cognitive studies at the time. Stephen North, in his ambitious and pessimistic book, *The Making of Knowledge in Composition: Portrait of an Emerging Field*, devotes a chapter to what he describes as the "embattled Ethnographic community," whose future, he writes, "cannot be all that bright." North argued that composition ethnographers are confused about their terminology, their source of authority, and their overall "methodological integrity" (312). And while North does a good job of overviewing the range of qualitative inquiries in composition at the time, a cluster of early studies about writing, many of which are often mistakenly called ethnographies, it is noteworthy that he does not reference any work by anthropologists or feminists writing about the crisis in ethnography—except for Clifford Geertz—and in reviewing his book's bibliography, it seems unlikely that North had read this other scholarship. Whereas North views ethnography's problem in composition as "not having enough scholarly authority," (57) as scholar Beth Campbell rightly points out, the real issue at stake was the dissolution of scholarly authority altogether in many disciplines at the time, an argument North had either overlooked, ignored, or was not familiar with.[4]

These early reprisals of ethnographic studies in composition, like North's, mainly center on anthropology's former positivistic, scientistic paradigm: that studies are not replicable; that they offer no cumulative knowledge; that they are not hypothesis driven. Such criticisms reveal

---

4.   The notable exception to understanding the crisis in ethnographic authority would be the work of Linda Brodkey, whose essays "Writing Critical Ethnographic Narratives" and "Writing Ethnographic Narratives," both written in 1987, reveal her reading of both anthropology and critical theory. Brodkey believed the goal of critical ethnography to be connected to writing practices and researcher activism, suggesting that the researcher's challenge was to interrupt both the monologic ethnographic narrator and to transform hegemonic social practices, a goal that remains current for ethnographers working out of the humanistic model today. Brodkey was clearly way ahead of her time in our field.

a limited understanding about the type of epistemology undergirding ethnographic methodology after it had rejected empiricism and began to read more like literature than like social science. To be fair to North, whose work was published over twenty years ago, he was challenged to interpret a wide range of writing research that at the time included both experimental and cognitive studies in a field that had not yet made its "social turn" and certainly not its "ethical turn." The uncritical adoption of ethnography as a neutral methodology by many compositionists, I would argue, reveals the lack of cross-disciplinary fertilization within our young field as well as a split that remains today between social science ethnography (that which begins with questions and focuses on discovery from data and leans toward generalization of knowledge) and humanistic ethnography (that which values interpretation over analysis as well as the researcher's self-reflexive experiences).

The ethnographer in our field who moved attention away from the stronghold of cognitive studies in writing (Shaughnessy, *Errors and Expectations*; Rose, *Lives on the Boundary*; Emig, *The Composing Processes of Twelfth Graders*; Flower, "Cognition, Context, and Theory Building") to its subsequent and contemporaneous embrace of ethnographic work is Shirley Brice Heath. Heath's *Ways with Words* was published in 1983, three years before *Writing Culture*, and became the ur-text in literacy studies; for the rich findings she gathered about language and literacy in context, it should remain so. For a decade Heath worked as an anthropological linguist who collected literacy data from two communities within the Carolina Piedmonts about their reading, writing, and speaking habits. In her detailed analysis of how the language practices of two southern mill communities, one white, Roadville, and one black, Trackton, differ from that of the mainstream townspeople, Heath is able to show how their "ways with words" are embedded in their daily habits, literacy performances, and the values of the community members. As rich and detailed as Heath's study is, it did not respond to the postmodern/feminist critiques in anthropology at the time, which would suggest her work was rooted in the empirical research method, or what anthropologist Van Mannen would categorize as a "realist" tale. The imprint of the realist tale, according to Van Mannen, is "the almost complete absence of the author" from the text (46). Heath's writing style, while beautifully descriptive, does not experiment with any way of showing how the ethnographer is influenced by her positionality or access to her field sites, nor does it reveal her power/

materiality relationship to the two economically disadvantaged communities she researched.

Nonetheless, Heath's landmark work became a model for a number of important sociocultural literacy studies that emphasize language in context over previous studies of writing (mainly cognitively informed) that had stripped context. Taylor's *Family Literacy*, Taylor and Dorsey-Gaines's *Growing Up Literate: Learning from Inner City Families*, A. Fishman's *Amish Literacy*, Bishop's *Something Old, Something New*, and Lofty's *Time to Write* all address the ethnographer's key question, "What goes on here?" as they investigate how people acquire and use language inside and outside of academic contexts—within families and communities. Even though these literacy studies (among many others) reflect a positivistic view of ethnography as a transparent methodology of description and analysis, they have been useful to composition studies in providing an understanding of how language practices are tied to larger social, political, and economic influences beyond classroom and school.

And it is curious that early ethnographic research in composition studies was not marked either by experimental writing practices or by our understanding of collaboration, two key theoretical areas of study within our field. Certainly, as composition teachers working with our students to produce a range of both academic and personal writing, the notion of a multigenre ethnography that would include the writer's experience and voice alongside that of her informants should have been a close fit. Attention to collaborative practices would suggest the importance of bringing our consultants into the conversation about how to shape their words and meanings together with us, since fieldwork is not just a personal but rather an intersubjective experience wherein both the ethnographer and her consultants are affected by the research process and products. As writing teachers and proponents of the social construction of knowledge, it is interesting, then, how some of our most powerful ideas are missing in our earliest ethnographic studies. Gradually, essay collections such as Mortensen and Kirsch's *Ethics and Representation in Qualitative Studies* would take up the conversation about the methodological, ethical, and composing complexity of writing ethnographic narratives. It is my purpose that this brief backward look at ethnography's entrance into composition studies will reveal the yearning of our field to achieve status through adoption of a social science methodology that in anthropology, folklore, and feminist studies had moved beyond our field's translation of it.

WHAT GOES ON IN ETHNOGRAPHY AND COMPOSITION
STUDIES NOW?

This part of my discussion argues for the continued value of ethnographic approaches in our field, motivated by the "ethical turn," which revolves around what we can mutually learn from those cultures and communities we study to promote an enlarged worldview for ourselves, our students, and our consultants. Ethnography has kept a strong presence in composition studies because of its adaptability and hybridity, which allow for its very different uses: one, as a methodological tool for investigating writers, writing classrooms, and rhetorical/literacy spaces beyond school; two, as a pedagogy and curriculum for writing classrooms and social justice projects; and three, as a new genre of writing that invites self-reflexivity and experimentation. In attending ethnographic and qualitative research strands at national conferences (CCCC, NCTE), we are likely to find panels made up of all types of research. Some ethnographic studies still adhere to a positivist epistemology of neutrality, holism, and depth, whereas others move in the direction of postmodern humanism, critical praxis, and feminist approaches. We may affiliate with the feminist pragmatist ethnographers, whose focus is on whether the study is an "adequate" account of the literacy practices of others and, more importantly, whether the study has benefited those others (Sullivan 98). Or we may be more engaged with the work of critical ethnographers,[5] whose goal is to explore the effects of race, class, and gender on both the researcher and the researched (see essays in Stephen Brown and Dobrin). And still in many ethnographic studies in composition we may find traces of the classical empirical methodology alongside subjective interpretive reflections. As scholars in the field, it is important for us to locate those tensions that can often be found in the fieldworker who borrows from both research paradigms and then make decisions for ourselves about the worth of the study. As Min-Zhan Lu reminds us, it is our responsibility to understand the aims, purposes, and positioning of the ethnographic researcher and her consultants rather than merely critique the research methods and ethics involved since, as

---

5.   In their essay collection, *Ethnography Unbound,* editors Stephen Brown and Dobrin write, "Unlike traditional ethnographic practice, critical ethnography shifts the goal of praxis away from the acquisition of knowledge about the Other (either for its own sake or for the service of the ethnographer's career) to the formation of a dialogic relationship with the Other whose destination is the social transformation of material conditions that immediately oppress, marginalize, or otherwise subjugate the ethnographic participant" (5).

she writes, "How we labor as readers of ethnography matters" ("Ethics of Reading Critical Ethnography" 296). When reading contemporary ethnographies, we need to ask ourselves what we have learned about ourselves or others that is of value to our understanding of researching literacy (methodology), of our teaching practices (pedagogy), and/or of ways of representation and experimental writing (genre).

There continue to be valuable ethnographic studies that focus on college writers and classrooms, writing programs, and writing-across-the-curriculum programs: Beaufort, *Writing in the Real World*; Bishop, *Something Old, Something New*; Chiseri-Strater, *Academic Literacies*; Durst, *Collision Course*; Stephen Fishman and McCarthy; Hunt; Paley; Perl and Wilson; Seitz; Sunstein; Walvoord and McCarthy. Such studies tend more toward analytic than interpretive methodologies but often cite the work of those anthropologists breaking the positivist model of research (Behar; Clifford and Marcus; Crapanzano; Geertz; Marcus and Fischer; Rosaldo), revealing the researchers' awareness of the changes taking place in ethnography in other disciplines. Many of the ethnographic studies on writing reflect the theoretical and methodological under-pinnings of Wendy Bishop's influential handbook, *Ethnographic Writing Research: Writing It Down, Writing It Up, and Reading It*, a guide for conducting research on writers and writing classrooms. Bishop also provides a range of classroom studies conducted by her own students, some more ethnographic in intent and design than others.

In her text Bishop positions herself as a teacher of research methodology, ethnography in particular, and a scholar of critical theory who, she says, is often unable to unbraid these two strands of her thinking. She suggests that in the past compositionists with humanities training may have resisted the positivist ethnographic research in the field, but that currently "ethnography may be moving composition researchers closer to their English studies colleagues—in literature and creative writing" because "the writing researchers' textual practices and evolving theories about texts have more in common with those who use critical theory . . . than they do with those building theoretical models in the natural and social sciences (*Ethnographic Writing Research* 147). The tension in Bishop's book comes from her outlining a positivist approach to methodology while valuing postmodern and other critical theories. And yet for Bishop and many other supporters of ethnographic methodologies for studying writing classrooms, the overall goal is not just to produce what Bishop calls "micro ethnographies" but to change teaching practices, to make us better at what we do in our classrooms through close observation of and reflection about our students and ourselves. Teacher-researchers who study their own classrooms, not those of others, have adopted and adapted ethnographic approaches for their own ends[6] (see Ray).

Ethnographic studies by composition and rhetoric researchers who look beyond the classroom include the work of Moss, who has studied the literacy practices of African American churches, Lindquist, who looked at the rhetorical strategies of patrons of a working-class bar, Cintron's study of gangs, Schaafsma's research on an inner-city summer writing program, and Purcell-Gates's ethnography of a mother and son who are learning to read and write. Further, there are ethnographic studies of the workplace, such as Doheny-Farina, "Writing in an Emerging Organization." The enormous range of studies in our field reflects its close alliances with sociology, communication studies, and anthropology.

Another move toward change in our field comes with doing ethnographic studies out in the community, not "on" others but "with" them, which is part of the activist research often associated with service learning and community outreach projects. Nowhere do we see this goal more strongly played out than in Ellen Cushman's *The Struggle and the Tools: Oral and Literature Strategies in an Inner City Community*. Cushman spent more than three years researching and advocating for African American residents of an economically marginalized community. Even though Cushman professes to employ a "traditional model" of participant observation, she is not the neutral observer in her study but rather allows textual space to reveal herself as both dialogic and reciprocal in her relationships with her informants. She finds herself uneasy with the strict limitations of participant observation and breaks the boundaries by becoming involved with her informants' lives, using her writing skills to serve a civic purpose. Others have followed Cushman's field

---

6.   As an example of ethnographically oriented teacher research, when I directed composition at UNCG, I had the teaching assistants conduct mini-ethnographies on each other's classrooms, giving them an opportunity to have another observer, less threatening than their supervisor, write field notes, conduct interviews with students, collect classroom artifacts, and write up a report to share with their colleague. These observational, linguistic, and reflective skills were valuable since our teaching assistants often became directors of composition themselves who would be in charge of writing teaching observations. In no way were these mini-ethnographies evaluative; instead they were descriptive and reflexive on the part of the researcher.

methodology in doing community-based writing projects with their students (Deans Adler-Kassner, Crooks, and Watters; Ervin). And while there are critics of using writing classes to teach civic rhetoric, there are many proponents who teach fieldworking skills in an effort to help students connect with their local communities. Such partnerships projects bring student researchers face-to-face with a range of ethical issues involved with studying others: race/power dynamics, representational challenges in writing, and self-reflexivity being among them. It is clear that in-service learning-outreach projects, the empathy gained by field researchers who enter communities outside the academy should not be the only goal but rather the specific observational, reading, writing, listening, and ethical skills posed by the experience by looking at how literacy informs contexts and contexts inform literacy practices.

When students themselves become full researchers of sites they chose to investigate, not necessarily working for the communities of the sites, as with service learning, ethnography can become an innovative pedagogy for teaching research writing, often the curriculum for second-semester first-year writing courses. Since the field site is of their selection, student ethnographers confront how knowledge is constructed as they become participant-observers, take fieldnotes, interview, collect artifacts, and do background research on a given subculture. Moreover, this approach emphasizes writing process and rhetorical skills as the fieldnotes become research memos that in turn become part of the final research project as students make specific choices about voice, audience, and data selection. Students learn about issues of ethics of representation as they write up their findings and share those with their informants. This pedagogy can turn students into active participants in their own learning as they struggle to render their field experiences into text and do justice to what they have observed, heard, and felt in the field. Writing teachers who adopt this approach are most often already familiar with anthropology's critiques and teach research methodology from an interpretive rather than purely analytic stance, with the final projects reading more like humanities papers than social science reports. Since clearly students can gather only a limited amount of data in a semester, their mini-ethnographies are more about gaining a sense of authority, agency, self-reflexivity, and cultural awareness than in producing a completed explanation of any given field site (see Chiseri-Strater and Sunstein for sample student ethnographic projects and methodology; see Mack and Zebroski and Kahn for arguments toward having students use ethnography in writing classrooms).

The ethnographic essay (as opposed to a fuller ethnographic study) represents a new genre that has much in common with creative non-fiction in its emphasis on detailed observation, thick description, and in-depth interviewing. Both also foreground the positionality of the researcher in terms of what she has brought to the study of another person or subculture. A whole strand of ethnographers argue along with me that one of the goals of ethnographic inquiry is self-reflexivity; "what we learn about the self as a result of the study of the 'other'" (Chiseri-Strater, "Turning in upon Ourselves" 119). This "turning inward" might result in an essay that is more about the researcher than the researched (Ruby), or a post-ethnographic reflection (Massey). It might also take the form of autoethnography, a genre somewhere between autobiography and ethnography, as Hanson explains: "[A]utoethnography is a personal experience narrative that distinguishes itself from traditional autobiography (and ethnography for that matter) because the author does not conceal the practices that she seeks to counter or disrupt" (185).

These textual experiments reflect the uneasiness that some ethnographic researchers feel about the limitations of representation and the ethics of using the words and experiences of others to create texts. Other solutions to this quandary include incorporation of multiple voices within the ethnography, resulting in multi-or polyvocality rather than a dominant narrative voice. Another option is actual collaborative ethnography or coauthorship, in which the researcher and the informants work together to produce a field project. An example of such a study is Lassiter et al., *The Other Side of Middletown*, an ethnographic study of the African American story of Muncie, Indiana, collaboratively researched and written by faculty, community members, and students, or a recent community-action project for completing and publishing oral histories of a town called Glassville, described and critiqued by Stephen Parks. While full collaboration is not always feasible or achievable, as Lassiter points out, "co-interpretation" is what makes an ethnography qualify as collaborative (146). No longer is it possible to ignore the consultant's perspective on the written ethnography, even though it is not always important to him or her (see Behar's *Translated Woman* for an example).

The continued experimentation with writing ethnographies represents how composition studies has caught up with the postmodern critique of ethnography in ways that make it more, not less appealing to composition researchers for its versatility as a research method, as a pedagogy, and as a genre of writing. The current trends within the ethnographic community clearly reflect a disruption with modernity and an independence from colonizing approaches to studying "others." While important in the history of composition studies and particularly to qualitative researchers, many of the earlier epistemological debates about ethnography's authority no longer seem as important as understanding the usefulness of this approach and the different types of knowledge gained from it. As Beth Campbell puts it, "What matters is not whether a particular version of ethnography is more or less scientific or humanistic, or for that matter, more or less theoretical or storied. Rather what matters is the recognition that all of ethnography's proliferations and multiplications inhabit and enact different bodies of knowledge and ways of being" (6).

Rather than the failed community that North predicted over twenty years ago,[7] ethnographers have helped sensitize compositionists into ways of studying their own and other cultures and into their own reflexive lens in doing so. Ethnographers have embraced the ethical turn in the field that has turned researchers into activists, collaborators engaged in critical praxis. Ethnography, feminism, and postcolonial theory intersect in their desires to challenge textual authority and power and to experiment with issues of representation and otherness. More than a methodology, a pedagogy, or an experimental genre, ethnography offers a way of seeing and being in the world with others that enlarges our vision of both ourselves and "others."

---

7.   According to Beth Campbell, who did a search of the ProQuest Dissertation Abstract Database, ethnographic dissertations have gained in popularity over the last ten years. She reports that 5.51 percent of dissertations written since 1998 have the term *ethnography* or *ethnographic* in the title, whereas in the ten years previous to that, only 4.38 percent included either of those terms (personal correspondence).

12
ARCHIVAL RESEARCH IN THE FIELD
OF RHETORIC AND COMPOSITION

Barbara L'Eplattenier and Lisa S. Mastrangelo

As researchers in rhetoric and composition, we are drawn to the pursuit of information that is revealed only in archival documents—the letters between administrator and teacher or teacher and former students, the writing assignment that reveals a previously unknown strategy, the transcript that shows that meetings between various colleges occurred. We find "things" that allow us to make connections with our other research, and we find there are "things" we wish we could find to verify our suspicions. We like the never-ending chase to find old documents and artifacts.

Thus, throughout the course of our careers, we have pursued archival research through a number of projects.[1] We've visited large and small archives, written dissertations based on archival research, and published work that uses archival documents as primary source materials. Both of us have amassed our own collections of documents that we have photocopied from other locations. We see our field of research as a romantic one, full of promise and mystery.

For a long time, researchers in this area worked without much information about how to do what they wanted to do, or even information such as that which is offered in this collection about what defined this particular area of the field. We were pleased, then, when this collection asked us to define our area of scholarship as it stands today and discuss its importance to the field. We would like to offer some definitions of

---

1. For a number of years, rhetoric and composition did have the *Longman Bibliography of Composition and Rhetoric,* edited by Erika Lindemann from 1984 to 1986. After that, the bibliography became the *CCCC Bibliography of Composition and Rhetoric,* edited by Lindemann through 1990, when Gail Hawisher and Cynthia Selfe became the editors. Gail Stygall and Kathleen Murphy became editors in 1995; this edition was published in 1999. An online version was developed by CCCC, edited by Todd Taylor from 1997 to 1999 (http://www.ibiblio.org/cccc/). (Our thanks to the WPA listserv, and especially Rich Haswell, for helping us piece together this small history.)

the area of archival research, as well as some discussion of their current status.

DEFINING ARCHIVES AND ARCHIVAL WORK

Rhetoric and composition tends to call any collection or stack of documents "an archive." Archives, according to rhetoric and composition researchers, can be anything: a well-funded "top ten" University Special Collections Archive, papers stored in the basement of the town hall, a box of papers found in an attic or basement, the contents of an office, or an actively used filing cabinet for a writing program.

The nature of such groupings of artifacts is radically different. So too is the nature of how they came to be in their physical location and order and the reasons they were saved at all. The word *archive* has specific disciplinary conditions applied to it, as do all words, and as a result, how we label where we found the artifacts we find and use is an issue that we feel needs to be explored in greater depth. (We use the word *artifact* deliberately because what we find includes more than just documents.) What we label the groupings of artifacts we find can and should tell readers specific things about them.

An archive, according to the *Glossary of Library and Internet Terms*, is a "repository holding documents or other material, usually those of historical and/or rare value" (Fowler). Traditionally, archives have been part of a formal institutional structure—federal/governmental archives, libraries, universities, historical societies—although the levels of funding and formality can differ radically. Archives typically include single copies of artifacts—letters, photographs, old syllabi, course notes, students' notebooks, and rare books. These are organized and catalogued by archivists and made accessible to researchers. Artifacts in an archive are often irreplaceable, hence the restricted access and regulations surrounding the use of them.

Archivists play a significant role in the creation of the archives that we work with. As a discipline, we have perhaps been *too* unaware of what Morris and Rose call "the invisible hands" of archivists and the implications of having those invisible hands work with collections. It is to our benefit as researchers and historians to understand how and why archives are constructed in the way they are; these constructions have serious implications for helping researchers develop research plans, locate materials, and understand connections between artifacts. For example, in rhetoric and composition historical work, historians often make use of university and/or college archives. While university archives may seem like gold mines because they have so much information, this may not be true. Or rather, while they may have a lot of information, much of it may not be available to the researcher. In contrast, college collections may have more material available to the researcher, but they may have more restricted hours, fewer staff members, and fewer amenities. Other archives may be specialized and include information only from a specific movement or group. Again, like collegiate archives, these may vary in size and may vary in terms of the facilities that are available. Happily, the field has recently begun to publish work that discusses such facilities and the ways their collections are processed (see Morris and Rose and Ramsey, for example). More of such work, and more cross-disciplinary training and research in archival theory, would benefit our discipline immensely.

Just as researchers may find artifacts in many different places, they also work under many different kinds of conditions. Lisa once worked in a university archive where she had to put her laptop on a table made from a door on top of two sawhorses; Barb once worked in a university archive where the wiring in the basement could not support a photocopier, and so she did her own photocopying of fragile and old documents right next to library students photocopying biology notes. Lisa has researched in a local town archive that was actually housed in the back of the hardware store. The local historian/archivist had papers piled from floor to ceiling, and unceremoniously plopped piles of papers here and there while searching for a particular document that Lisa was sure only he knew the location of. We should recognize, though, that all groupings of artifacts have different organizations, and different groupings can mean different research strategies are required. Working closely with the archivist or person in charge of the collection is often necessary.

Another significant issue for rhetoric and composition archival researchers is the lack of bibliographic information on specific archives and archival materials.[2] Unlike many other disciplines, rhetoric and

2. However, the existence of CompPile has superseded these efforts. Edited and organized by Rich Haswell and Glenn Blalock, CompPile (http://comppile.org/) indices 306 journals into nineteen different scholarly areas; historical work is slotted under "Rhetoric: Rhetorical Analysis, History" with seventeen journals listed as being indiced. Five of the seventeen journals have volunteers who regularly update the database. None of the seventeen are devoted primarily to archival work— *Rhetoric Review* devotes the most amount of space to articles based on archival research. Other bibliographic rhetoric and composition resources include Rebecca

composition has not yet compiled bibliographies of archival resources to help guide young researchers. Instead, researchers often stumble across pamphlets in attics (Sharer) or collect books in used bookstores (Johnson) or discover connections through their families' literacy stories (Hogg). The lack of archival bibliographies often causes researchers to redo work or spend time hunting down basic sources. Generalized and discipline-specific databases and bibliographies on other subjects or disciplines do exist. However, as rhetoric and composition's search terms are not commonly used or recognized, using these can be a difficult, frustrating task. Because we do not have our own database of primary sources, rhetoric and composition scholars must brainstorm "around the circle," in bibliographic sources and archives, finding new key words and search terms and working continually to winnow down the search, as Ritter describes in *Working in the Archives.* Cross-disciplinary and collaborative work with archivists can help archivists see the value of and need for search terms related specifically to rhetoric and composition.

Chris Warnick's "Locating the Archives: Finding Aids and Archival Scholarship in Composition and Rhetoric" goes into significant detail describing print bibliographies that might be useful to rhetoric and composition scholars, including *Archival Information: How to Find It, How to Use It,* edited by Steven Fisher, *Articles Describing Archives and Manuscript Collections in the United States: An Annotated Bibliography,* compiled by Donald L. DeWitt, *A Guide to Archives and Manuscripts in the United States,* edited by Philip Hamer, and the National Historical Publications and Records Commission's *Directory of Archives and Manuscript Repositories in the United States.* Elizabeth Yakel's "Searching and Seeking in the Deep Web: Primary Sources on the Internet" does the same for electronic resources.

Until recently, it has been hard to even search for documents that a particular archives might have without either contacting the archives directly or visiting in person (sometimes both). However, *ArchiveGrid*

Moore Howard's bibliographies at <http://wrt-howard.syr.edu/> and the EServer Technical Communication Library (http://tc.eserver.org/), which is maintained by Geoffrey Sauer.

Examples of non–rhetoric and composition bibliographic sources include *Genderwatch,* a full-text database of popular and scholarly material on women or gender from the late 1970s on and *America: History and Life,* which covers the history of the United States and Canada from prehistory to the present and indices about two thousand journals. These indices focus on scholarly publications rather than original sources.

and the *National Union Catalog of Manuscript Collections*, electronic databases that search national archival holdings, are particularly valuable for locating archival sources, but again are not specifically dedicated to rhetoric and composition documents. For example, with the development of *ArchiveGrid*, collections that have been electronically indexed and placed online can be searched. In general, due to the overwhelming cost, collections that have been digitized are often highly trafficked and highly visible collections. (Student and faculty papers are rarely highly trafficked and visible, unless the person was particularly well known.) In addition, *ArchiveGrid* maintains a database that colleges and universities must belong to (there is currently no individual subscription available) and to which many smaller colleges have no reason to belong. Some progress has been made in recent years in making archival documents available to researchers in print documents. Some presses have begun to issue collections of primary sources, often printed in conjunction with another book; some examples are Carol Mattingly's *Water Drops from Women Writers: A Temperance Reader*, published shortly after *Well-Tempered Women: Nineteenth-Century Temperance Rhetoric*.

These collections are usually made up of edited, selected archival materials that may come from a single archive (as do the majority of pieces in JoAnn Campbell's *Toward a Feminist Rhetoric*) or from multiple archives (Brereton's *The Origins of Composition Studies*) or from a variety of public documents (Bizzell and Herzberg's *The Rhetorical Tradition*). Documents are both public and private texts: reports, speeches, columns, school papers, love letters, excerpts from lectures and articles. Each selection—or section—is usually prefaced by a brief (one hundred to five hundred words, but rarely more than a thousand) introduction that describes the author, the historical time period, and the importance of the author/text. Usually, one or two pieces by the authors are presented. These are often "significant" pieces or pieces that are seen as representative of the author's rhetorical strategies, ideological stance, and abilities. Sometimes, pieces are canonical pieces, such as Sojourner Truth's "Ain't I a Woman," or were highly influential during their author's lifetime, such as Ida B. Well's "Lynch Laws in All Its Phases." An important thing to remember is that the editor may or may not have edited or condensed the materials, due to limitations of publication space or for contemporary comprehension. These texts make significant amounts of archival material readily available to researchers, teachers, and students, and the discipline rightly highly values these texts; John Brereton's *The Origins of Composition Studies in the American College, 1875–1925* won the 1997 CCCC Outstanding Book of the Year award.

In essence, there are a huge number and variety of types of archives and ways to find them, and it can be a difficult and arduous task. In recent years, these facilities have become much more important to historians in composition and rhetoric as we work to reclaim our past, to broaden our definitions of the sites and locations where rhetorical activity has occurred, and to use this history to fill in our own gaps.

CURRENT METHODS OF ARCHIVAL RESEARCH IN COMPOSITION AND RHETORIC

We currently find that there are two sets of "advice" out there for doing composition and rhetorical history in the archives. The first is methodology or historiography. The second is methods. There is a distinct difference between the two, but they are both important for any researcher in the field to consider. Until recently, most publications have focused on methodology rather than methods. Methodology is an interesting and valuable theoretical category, but does little to help the researcher who is looking for practical advice on how to enter the archives and what to do once he or she gets there.

Historiography

In *Rhetoric Society Quarterly*, Hui Wu points out that methodology—more commonly known as historiography—for rhetoric and composition researchers is about theorizing how and why archival work is done, not about *how* to collect or access archival information.

As L'Eplattenier points out, archival methodology—historiography in rhetoric and composition history—focuses almost exclusively on the researcher. These are the works that

> theorize the researcher's stance, ideological bias, definitions of rhetoric, the non-neutrality of historical presentations, the plurality of histories, or the theoretical constructs that inform our work. Such research addresses why we study *what* we study, why we study *who* we study, and how the theories we have read influence our writing and our perception of the world. (68)

These are articles meant to contextualize the researcher and present to the world his or her biases, as Cheryl Glenn's description in the introduction to *Unspoken* demonstrates:

I am white, female, heterosexual, feminine, feminist, hearing, well-educated at a Big Ten school, fully employed at another Big Ten school. Thus it is that this volume bears the ideological weight of my own perspective, and while I cannot reduce it, I can acknowledge it. (xix)

In part, such historiography discussions allow rhetoric and composition to play with the big boys—these sections show that we can do "high" theory, we understand postmodernism, and we can speak in ways that are more traditionally valued within English studies and the academy. Historiography in rhetoric and composition allows us access to the higher-status field of theory and philosophy—another version, if you will, of the theory/practice split of rhetoric and composition history.

For a field that values context, postmodernism, and the fluidity of truth, these declarations of methodology give credibility to the types of history we have decided to tell. Sharon Crowley reminds us in her "Tisias, Corax, Plato, Aristotle . . . AMEN!" prayer that the previous dominant model of rhetorical history limited rhetorical activity to the white, male-dominated *polis* ("Straight" 18-19). But a solid grounding in philosophical and theoretical methodologies gave rhetoric and composition scholars the expertise, credibility, and, more importantly, the legitimacy, to expand beyond the white, male-dominated *polis* into areas such as women, students, civic groups, and others who are not on top of the patriarchal heap. Like the development of the feminist journal *Signs*, rhetoric and composition historians have had to show they could work within the system before breaking out of the system. Theorizing methodology allows us to do that.

This focus on methodology prompted Linda Ferreira-Buckley to publicly state that "ten years ago our histories were under theorized; today I fear they are under researched" (28). Since that 1998 statement, the field has continued to focus on methodology over method and the pedagogy of methods. While historiography is undeniably important, it is also just as important that historians in the field, or those who would become historians in the field, have the background information that they need in order to successfully, thoughtfully, and ethically work with archival materials. In other words, while we need to think about methodology, we also need methods.

Archival Methods

In "Octalog II: The (Continuing) Politics of Historiography," Linda Ferreira-Buckley famously said, "[W]e lack the tools of the historian's trade" (28). Her worries have often been noted, but rarely systematically addressed. Speaking about issues such as training and access to finding aids, research grants, and tenure clock issues, Ferreira-Buckley rightly noted that our discipline has paid little attention to the practical aspects and training involved with the development of histories. Just as important as methodology, researchers need good methods. While this is an area that composition-rhetoric has begun to explore, it is still very much an up-and-coming area in the field.

Since Ferreira-Buckley's (repeated) statements, little has changed, an unfortunate situation, because as any empirical researcher knows, methods strongly impact the development and construction of any research project. They are

> the means by which we conduct our research, how we locate and use primary materials, and for historians, how we recover materials for our histories. Methods are about achieving access to information, about finding aids, about reference materials, about archive locations and restrictions, about the condition of the materials, about the existence of evidence or the lack of evidence; about the triangulation of information—all the factors that impact our "systematic method of gathering evidence" and our interpretation of that evidence. . . . methods allow us to contextualize the research process or the researched subject and materials. (69)

Publications that focus on methods are limited: Gesa Kirsch and Liz Rohen's *Beyond the Archives* looks at the emotional entwining researchers have with their research subjects and indirectly addresses methods. *Working in the Archives,* edited by Alexis Ramsey, Wendy Sharer, Barbara L'Eplattenier, and Lisa Mastrangelo, explicitly offers advice to the researcher new to archival work. The Donahue and Moon edited collection, *Local Histories,* incorporates brief descriptions of how and where the researchers located sources, as well as a note that identifies the archive and collections visited. Importantly, the collection also includes a specific bibliography at the end identifying archival sources separately from other primary or secondary sources. However, most published histories do not reveal their methods. How did these researchers find their topics? Which archives did they visit? Through the more explicit statement of methods, future researchers will have greater tools at their disposal to locate similar materials. Like bibliographic listings of archival sources, the *how* of doing research in the archives is an area that needs scholarly attention.

THE LARGER PICTURE

Within the discipline of rhetoric and composition, research that draws on archival sources, supported by methodological arguments, has been instrumental in expanding the definition of "rhetorical activity." Traditional rhetorical topics such as the classical rhetors, the Scottish rhetors/philosophers, and the *polis* have long been the focus of both rhetoric and composition and speech communication. However, our discipline has also explored and embraced as appropriate research material the composition classroom (particularly in the nineteenth and early twentieth century), the rhetorical activity and impact of women's groups, African American groups, labor groups, and religious groups, as well as various sites of literacy, civic discourse, and propaganda. This expansion has allowed rhetoric and composition to claim nearly any area of discursive activity as an appropriate subject for historical (and contemporary) study and has given our discipline a vibrant collage of work.

This body of work focuses on the *analysis* of primary source materials, rather than the presentation or retelling of primary sources. Rhetoric and composition histories tend to have a pragmatic focus; they must make explicit connections to the present and discuss how said histories are useful to the teacher, researcher, administrator, or what rhetorical lessons can be learned from the actions of the studied.

It is important to note that this work with primary sources has experienced a shift in recent years. Many of the early histories of the field, for example, sought out textbooks as ways of looking at trends in education or secondary publications—Berlin (*Writing Instruction; Rhetoric and Reality*) and Kitzhaber (*Rhetoric in American Colleges*), for example. While textbooks are important for looking at market trends, they do not offer information about individuals' pedagogy, their relationships with faculty and students, their participation in social movements or in their local community (Bordelon 418). And because these textbooks are now archival documents, rarely found in circulating libraries, this focus has given us a limited sense of the field as a whole. As contemporary practitioners know, textbook publication is more subject to the whims of the publishing industry than it is reflective of actual pedagogical trends. Over the past several years, rhetoric and composition histories have begun to look to primary sources to fill in the gaps in our histories—the historical gaps where other scholarship tells us that there simply *is* no history or the gaps where we suspect there might be more going on than we first realized.

More recently, work like that done in Donahue and Moon's collection *Local Histories* has sought other primary sources—newspaper publications (including student newspapers), yearbooks, scrapbooks, student papers, syllabi, course notes, departmental papers, annual reports, student publications, letters written by colleagues and students—in order to investigate rhetoric and composition's history. This variety of primary sources often presents a very different perspective on the topic under study, and in unexpected ways. For instance, rather than discussing what students learned, looking at tributes that students have written about their teachers can actually help us re-create pedagogies. Looking at letters that students have written home may reveal course assignments, attitudes toward assignments and teachers (see the students' comments in "Controlling Voices: The Legacy of English A at Radcliffe College, 1883–1917" by JoAnn Campbell, for example). And looking at syllabi or final exams can offer a potentially very different picture of how instructors actually used those textbooks. Recently, research has focused on a more complicated "retelling" of our history. Part of this is due to the fact that many researchers are often using a much more diverse collage of materials than "just" textbooks or "just" articles.

DIFFICULTIES OF ARCHIVAL RESEARCH

There are, of course, some very real difficulties to archival research. Despite a stronger and ever-growing Web presence for documents, very little archival information specifically in the discipline of rhetoric and composition is available without actually traveling to archives. (For the researcher looking at rhetorical activities of groups or well-known individuals, materials may be available online.) This means paying for travel, often paying for lodging and food, and paying for extras such as photocopying. Archival research can be very expensive, especially for underfunded graduate students. While some archives offer travel funds, these are unusual. Some institutions offer research support while some philanthropic groups offer financial support for research. This support tends to be focused on the topic rather than the discipline. Other groups offer prizes for the "best" whatever published or presented or completed on the "whatever" topic. For example, the Baltimore City Historical Society offers the Joseph L. Arnold Prize for Outstanding Writing on Baltimore History, a $500 prize awarded to the writer of the most interesting and well-researched paper on some significant aspect of Baltimore City history. Discussing a research project with the university grants office may give researchers access to data-bases that compile grants.

Archival research can also present other difficulties for a researcher. Dissertation committees, for example, may not willingly endorse archival projects because they are risky—there is always the risk of students not being able to find what they need to complete a project in a finite amount of time. Likewise, many tenure-track professors choose other types of publications because they are simply more easily researched, written, and published.

While there is currently an audience for scholarship based on archival work, some of it still remains difficult to publish. As we mentioned earlier, we are often told that our histories must *do* something—it is not enough for them to be interesting and to tell fascinating stories in and of themselves. They must connect somehow to current teaching practices or current interests in the field. This point was driven home early in the discipline's development. The 1988 CCCC presentation "Octalog: The Politics of Historiography" presented a diverse group of historians: James Berlin, Nan Johnson, Bob Connors, Jan Swearingen, Sharon Crowley, Richard Enos, Victor Vitanza, and Susan Jarratt. They didn't agree on much, but they *did* agree that, regardless of their subject, histories were supposed to be "doing" something—whether that was in terms of pedagogy and the contemporary class or in terms of shaping and changing the present or representing the past and thus impacting the future. (Connors agreed more reluctantly than the rest, but all of the speakers agreed that there was a *point* to their history—whether to challenge current ideology or, as Connors put it, simply to "to try to make my world a better place, to try to brighten the corner in which I live and work." [12].) Histories that do not make such connections—that simply present stories—are considered suspect.

We object strenuously to this stance, but it is certainly one with which new researchers in the field should be familiar. Instead, we think it is important to remember that sometimes history has value in and of itself, and sometimes the archival material that we have cannot, for one reason or another, be connected to current practices, or even held against them. As Lynée Gaillet notes, "I believe storytelling—with a purpose, based on painstaking research, tied to a particular cultural moment, making clear the teller's prejudices—is the real task of the historian, regardless of the negative connotations often associated in academia with storytelling. Although many historians have looked to the past to understand the present, that goal is not universally embraced and has recently fallen out of favor in the wake of charges of 'presentism'" (36). Students and faculty who currently undertake archival research in rhetoric and composition should be forewarned of the fact that currently their research must show some connection to the present day.

Another problem with archival research and publication is that it is nearly impossible to factually verify what is being published. Because the editor of the journal or edited collection cannot double-check facts without going to an archives him- or herself, or requesting copies of the materials from the author (which we've never seen done), editors are left to trust that the author's materials are "real." These histories tend to be a close reading and explication of primary source materials not always readily available to the reader, which can become an issue for future scholars who are trying to verify information, as archives are not always easily accessible to people.

Archival research in the field of composition and rhetoric remains a minority among the types of research being conducted. However, those of us who have undertaken Connors's August mushroom hunt know the frustrations, the goals, and the rush of discovery that archival research can bring.

13

WRITING PEDAGOGY EDUCATION
Instructor Development in Composition Studies

Heidi Estrem and E. Shelley Reid

Why, then, is there a need to study teacher learning? If even ordinary people know all about teaching, and if teaching seems to change so little from generation to generation, what possible questions about teacher learning could be of interest? . . . [W]hile most of us feel we know what teaching and schooling are all about, few of us are satisfied with what we know.

Mary M. Kennedy

Within composition studies, the work of mentoring writing teachers inhabits a curricular space that is similar in significant ways to that of first-year writing. But while the teaching of first-year writing has enjoyed close, careful, thoughtful attention within our field over the past fifty years—and while composition programs often practice more college-level teacher education than any other place on university campuses—writing pedagogy education (or WPE, as we'll call it throughout this chapter) is still a diffuse, emerging area of inquiry. What writing pedagogy education "is" takes multiple shapes as it responds to local needs and disciplinary influences.

Writing pedagogy education, as we see it, encompasses the ongoing education, mentoring, and support of new college-level writing instructors: most often—although not exclusively—graduate teaching assistants. The heart of WPE, the seminar for new teaching assistants (hereafter TAs), bears a strong resemblance to another central location of composition studies: first-year writing. Like first-year writing courses, the TA seminar is introductory in nature and often a required course (sometimes it is a graduate TA-only required course), taken by students with a range of interests in and commitments to the subject at hand. Sidney Dobrin notes that the TA seminar is "the first contact with and initiation into composition studies that graduate students face and . . . it reaches professionals that do not identify themselves as compositionists specifically" (21). In another parallel to first-year writing, the vast majority of the intellectual energy and research in WPE has centered on the TA seminar. We will argue in this chapter, though, that the reach of progressive WPE extends well beyond the TA seminar—just as writing instruction does not begin, or end, with one class in an undergraduate student's first year of college. Questions about how we as composition specialists get this important work done—how we mentor, educate, and nurture new instructors within composition studies—have been attended to by many in our field; these efforts are documented more thoroughly in the next section of this chapter. TA education is also a practice steeped more in thoughtful lore than in systematic research—a challenge that we will also address here.

Writing pedagogy education in its richest form is a complex, ongoing, evolving process in which instructors of writing are encouraged— through multiple venues and in multiple contexts—to teach, reflect, innovate, and theorize about the practice of teaching writing in college. This particular kind of education permeates composition programs through a blend of mentoring, coursework, practice, and leadership; it resonates perhaps more readily than many areas of composition studies with Joseph Harris's contention that composition is a "teaching subject." Even so, writing pedagogy education has in practice too often relied on approaches that are locally self-evident or based on "common sense," rather than growing deliberately from the work of a formal subfield with theories and practices that are steadily reflected upon, critiqued, researched, and refined. With this chapter, then, we hope to explore WPE's current place within the context of the field and to enrich our collective understandings of the kinds of research and analysis that writing pedagogy educators still need. To that end, we map out the key issues, concerns, and controversies within WPE, analyze its scholarly location(s) in composition studies and higher education, and end with recommendations for research possibilities and strategies for building on our current body of scholarship. We believe both that the broad prevalence of WPE within composition studies makes it a useful subfield for all compositionists to be familiar with, beyond any personal experiences we may have with WPE as novice teachers, and that new and continuing scholars will find increasingly fruitful opportunities to focus their attention on this crucial area of study.

TAKING STOCK: THE SCHOLARSHIP OF WRITING PEDAGOGY EDUCATION

While we have taken college-level writing pedagogy education as our focus—that is, the educating and mentoring of teaching assistants who are teaching first-year writing courses within university writing programs—WPE operates in overlapping spheres, and any review of the research in this area necessarily draws from multiple areas. Because of space constraints, we have largely focused on research and accounts related to college-level WPE, but we also highlight relevant research conducted on instructor development in English education; later, we also explore the disciplinary connections between WPE and English education.

Two recent bibliographic essays commissioned for Betty Pytlik and Sarah Liggett's 2002 collection *Preparing College Teachers of Writing: Histories, Theories, Programs, Practices* (*PCTW*) offer strong starting points for scholars in the field. Pytlik's "How Graduate Students Were Prepared to Teach Writing: 1850–1970" provides a clear view of how many questions and issues in TA WPE have stayed the same, even as practices and institutions change. She identifies several recurring themes: "the inadequate writing skills" (8) of TAs, the need for writing programs to educate students whose own writing is "deficient," the struggle to provide cost-effective WPE within time and budget constraints, and the complications of providing WPE within English departments that primarily saw their mission as preparing literary scholars, not writing educators. It's both reassuring and a little disheartening to see that as far back as 1956, workshop participants at the College Composition and Communication Conference (CCCC) were recommending that TAs be supported by inservice training, syllabus guidance, staff meetings, supervision, and "a course in the teaching of composition/communication" (qtd. in Pytlik 11), issues that still pose challenges for WPE scholars and practitioners today.[1]

Stephen Wilhoit picks up the contemporary threads of this story in *PCTW* with "Recent Trends in TA Instruction," noting that he finds "general agreement concerning the structure of TA instructional programs but ongoing debates over which institutional procedures to employ and concern about the working conditions of TAs" (17). Wilhoit's

---

1.   Recent books by Shari Stenberg (*Professing and Pedagogy*) and Margaret Marshall (*Response to Reform: Composition and the Professionalization of Teaching*) provide broader narrative histories of the education of teachers in English and composition.

article provides an overview of late twentieth-century scholarship that addresses key program structures: preservice orientation, in-service practica, apprenticeship and mentorship programs, and the placement and education of TAs as writing center tutors. He also reviews materials that address programmatic practices and the content of TA education efforts: classroom observation, role-playing, teaching journals and portfolios, reflective practice, research and publication, and writing program administration. Scholars seeking an overview of issues and publications in WPE can quite usefully begin with these sources. Alternately, one can begin by viewing the work of the field through its major modes of scholarship: narratives of local experience, descriptive analyses of pedagogy education, or framework analyses of WPE programs.

Narratives of Local Experience: Reporting Successes

Within individual studies in WPE, one popular mode of scholarly writing is characterized by straightforward descriptions of (usually successful) local experiences in teaching or learning writing pedagogy. While these are common—and important—in WPE scholarship, they will receive less attention in this chapter than broader analyses, because they have less power to move scholarship in the field forward. As Mark Dressman helps us to understand, such local narratives can be intimidatingly upbeat: pressure to demonstrate success can limit scholars' ability to investigate open questions, discuss results that are inconclusive or contradictory, and conduct broader, richer research studies. We mean it as no criticism of the writers included to point out that many pieces in *PCTW*, *Teaching Writing Teachers of High School English and First-Year Composition* (edited by Robert Tremmel and William Broz), and Dobrin's *Don't Call it That!*—not to mention chapters and articles in the ever-increasing supply of "How to teach first-year writing" books—fall into this category. These collections have been tremendously helpful to us as instructors and writing program administrators. Within these collections, contributors describe various aspects of their teaching or mentoring, and readers are left with new pedagogical strategies for consideration. Writers of numerous articles throughout the literature of English education take a similar approach, exploring the effectiveness of various techniques within a "methods" class for preservice teachers (from videotaping teaching to service learning, for example, as reported by scholars like Basmadjian and Kaufman). In both areas, these kinds of accounts of classroom strategies are useful in giving all writing educators additional possibilities and perspectives. But while public, thoughtful first-person testimony is crucial for increasing awareness and creating a sense of a national conversation, the lore-like and success-focused approach of this mode of writing has limited power to expand scholarship in WPE.

DESCRIPTIVE ANALYSES OF WRITING INSTRUCTORS: REFLECTION AND GROWTH

A second mode of scholarship in WPE emphasizes descriptive analysis of what new or in-training writing teachers do, say, write, or think, and why. Often this scholarship draws on surveys, interviews, readings of teaching-related documents such as journals or reflective essays, and/or ethnographic observation, and often it focuses on relatively small, local populations. Throughout these descriptive analyses, *reflection* is key for both the researchers/instructors and for the new instructors/research participants. Wendy Bishop's 1990 book *Something Old, Something New* documents how reflection and growth occur for five new composition instructors. Elizabeth Rankin's 1994 monograph *Seeing Yourself as a Teacher* and Sally Barr Ebest's more recent *Changing the Way We Teach* (2005) further demonstrate TAs' recursive pathways toward establishing a teaching identity and disciplinary confidence. Scholars in English education have also produced careful accounts of new instructors' development, and similar key issues—the importance of reflection, for example—are echoed in these accounts. Jane Danielewicz's *Teaching Selves: Identity, Pedagogy, and Teacher Education* is a narrative, case-based study of "how students become teachers": how six students begin to grow into (or claim) the role of teacher (2). Such accounts focus on providing a thick, richly narrativized description of new teachers learning to teach—an apt and necessary scholarship for a field dominated in practice and theory by complex human experiences.[2]

While not always providing specific program-level recommendations, these close, careful accounts of instructors in development productively complicate the picture of WPE that surfaces in local success-story narratives. They help give composition teacher-scholars a pastiche view of the enormous challenge that new instructors of writing face every year, and of what we, as educators and mentors of those new instructors, also

---

2.   Works by Farris, Hillocks, Ray, Reid, and Winslow, among others in the past twenty years, also incorporate the voices and perspectives of individual pedagogy-learners at the college level, and McCann, Johannessen, and Ricca do the same at the high school level in their analysis of new teachers' experiences.

face. Mary Kennedy, an education researcher, notes that "[t]he nature of teaching practice . . . is such that teachers can be unsure at any given moment what should be done, and can be unsure, once they have done something, of whether their actions were successful" (3). Case study–based projects illuminate instructors' moments of doubt, revealing both their actions and decisions (or moments of indecision). This strand of research raises many good questions about the nature of WPE—but, due to the local, detailed methodologies used, cannot usually go further than simply raising those questions.

PROGRAMMATIC FRAMEWORKS: MENTORING WITHIN AND BEYOND THE TA SEMINAR

A third mode of written accounts in WPE—one that has generated the most attention in the last few decades—gives less space to individual teachers' voices and instead focuses on reasoning out the exigencies and plausible frameworks for writing pedagogy education. Calls for better, broader, or alternate forms of WPE fall into this category: Catherine Latterell's 1996 survey of programs supported her call for more discipline-related education; Irene Clark examines the benefits of starting WPE in writing centers; and Jo Sprague and Jody Nyquist draw on research in learning and psychological development in recommending steps that new TAs should move through. Sometimes these curriculum- or program-design proposals foreground analysis that is based on closely observed local experience ("what works for us"): Shirley Rose and Margaret Finders carefully describe how they have enacted a "reciprocal model of reflection" for new TAs (83), while Wanda Martin and Charles Paine articulate how practices in their peer-mentoring program are designed to support "autonomy of practice" and "new people [bringing in] new ideas" among their TAs (231). In other cases, these accounts develop by analogy to related situations—teacher education, education in writing or rhetoric, administrative negotiations—or through more theoretical lenses. Thomas Recchio links WPE to first-year writing and proposes seeing pedagogy learning as requiring an "essayistic" frame of mind ("open, receptive, adaptable, curious, responsive, and self-aware" [255]); Susan Kay Miller et al. frame WPE as parallel to and involving broader forms of professional development; Rebecca Rickly and Susanmarie Harrington outline feminist approaches for WPE, drawing on their own experiences as administrators and mentors.

Another common thread of inquiry within framework-oriented accounts addresses the tension between practice and theory in the preparation of new writing teachers. One can trace this particular line of inquiry from mid-twentieth-century writers such as Albert Kitzhaber through analyses by Richard Gebhardt, Tori Haring-Smith, Douglas Hesse ("Teachers as Students"), and Robert Parker, among others. Gebhardt's 1977 article "Balancing Theory with Practice in the Training of Writing Teachers" articulated several kinds of "theoretical" knowledge that writing teachers should have (basic understanding of rhetoric and of history of the English language, along with more methodological frameworks); when we read it alongside ideas such as Parker's call to foreground and value TAs' already-present "theories-in-use" (413) and Hesse's careful unpacking of the difficulties new teachers find in entering into unfamiliar disciplinary conversations, we can start to piece together a picture of the fraught relationships new practitioners may have with "expert" theories about pedagogy. Recent articles by Ruth Fisher; Anthony Michel; Mary Lou Odom, Michael Bernard-Donals, and Stephanie L. Kerschbaum; and Michael Stancliff and Maureen Daly Goggin tease out possible strategies that contemporary WPE scholars might use in easing new teachers' learning in this area. Indeed, the tension between practice and theory as it is played out within the space of the seminar for new TAs forms the very impetus for Dobrin's recent collection of essays, *Don't Call It That*, so titled because of the "desire for the practicum course not to be perceived as a how-to course, but as a richer, more academically sophisticated and rigorous course" (2). The question of how, when, and whether to introduce or "balance" theory—whatever "theory" might mean—and practice permeates much of the scholarly analyses in these pieces, reflecting the individual uncertainties uncovered through case-study research as well as larger disciplinary anxieties that we take up later in this chapter.

A major strength of framework-oriented pieces is their ability to address the challenge of envisioning (and enacting) WPE as a sustained, systematic effort. For example, Kathleen Yancey argues that while local exigencies mean that "a common model [for WPE] seems neither possible nor desirable" ("Professionalization of TA Development Programs" 63; see also Stancliff and Goggin), several components of WPE recur in a range of programs. Yancey's heuristic for WPE program design asks program administrators to consider such elements as the characteristics of local TAs, departments, and first-year writing programs; the sites and leaders available for WPE; issues of ethical treatment of TAs; and questions about assessment.[3] Similarly, Kennedy's book-length study of eight different teacher education programs in English education employs diverse methodological approaches—scenario-based interviews with preservice teachers, contextual and cross-institutional analysis—in order to trace the impact of teacher education programs on developing instructors and to emerge with recommendations for teacher education program design. Because her research is so broad and carefully contextualized—drawing from substantially different *kinds* of programs, employing similar and standardized interview protocols, yet resisting easy recommendations based on program features (like number of courses or kinds of field experiences)—Kennedy's work is useful in demonstrating for us what a variety of research methodologies might add to our field.

Another genre of programmatic-level research takes the form of descriptive collections of curricular materials. For example, the 1995 special issue of *Composition Studies* focused on doctoral training in the field and included the syllabi for seventeen graduate courses (from a variety of institutions) in writing pedagogy. The grouped syllabi provide insights into the nature of such courses, but are presented without any overall conclusions. A scant few additional studies of the curriculum of English methods courses for preservice teachers also exist. In *How English Teachers Get Taught*, Peter Smagorinsky and Melissa Whiting focus on the methods course for preservice K-12 teachers through examining eighty-one syllabi. They note a similar lack of research-based knowledge within English education; they point out that we have "surprisingly little knowledge about the manner in which students in methods classes are taught . . . our knowledge has always been informal, much like the 'lore' North (1987) has described" (1–2). Their book provides a window into the texture of the methods course: the greatest number of courses were what they labeled "survey-based," reflecting an overwhelming number of objectives and goals—a kind of "coverage" approach sometimes paralleled in WPE (see Reid, "Uncoverage"). A similar recent study of three different methods preservice courses in California (again using interviews and textual analysis) also helps provide insights into how (future) English teachers are being taught to, in turn, teach writing; in this study,

---

3.   See essays later in *PCTW* by Goleman, Powell et al., Gottschalk, Martin and Paine, and Thatcher for analyses that address both local resources and field-wide goals in WPE program design.

Sarah Hochstetler's findings, like the recommendations made by many within WPE, center on the complexity of reading syllabi beyond the context of the course itself, the diversity of local program features, and the diffusion of writing instruction beyond the official methods course. These kinds of themes are echoed in college-level WPE literature as described above.

Interestingly, perhaps because of a felt sense that all WPE is locally constituted, or perhaps, as Robert Tremmel argues, because in composition, as in English studies generally, we are accustomed to a certain amount of "tribalism" as a core operating principle ("Pig Iron"), we as yet have no book-length articulations of WPE principles (though Shari Stenberg addresses writing pedagogy in her monograph on English pedagogy education). Even so, framework scholarship is likely to be crucial in upcoming years for creating continuity within and across the disciplines that anchor WPE. Tremmel's article "Seeking a Balanced Discipline" (published in 2001, in *English Education*—notably not in *CCC* or in any other journal more commonly read by compositionists) proposes a newly rejoined field of "writing teacher education" that would encompass both composition studies and English education. Extending the work of WPE scholars like Gebhardt and Yancey, Tremmel outlines key recommendations guiding *both* methods courses and programs for TA development, discussing their overlap and intersections.[4] A paucity of similar wide-reaching articles or field-defining monographs may signal an important opportunity for growth in the field as we try to "unify diversity" (Gebhardt, "Unifying Diversity") in the field in order to more powerfully "set our own agendas [and develop] a fully theorized discipline" (Tremmel, "Pig Iron"). And as we explain in more detail below, we may also be on the cusp of an expansion in *approaches* to research on the teaching of writing teachers: calls for more data-based, multisite, or longitudinal research across composition are also being heard by

---

4.   Building from and informed by the work of Tremmel, Broz, and others, recent efforts have been made to systematically and visibly reconnect English education and composition studies. The "English Education–Composition and Rhetoric" SIG meets at CCCC, and the CEE-sponsored Commission on Writing Teacher Education meets at NCTE. These overlapping groups are made up of methods instructors, writing program administrators, National Writing Project site directors, and others interested in the connections between teaching writing teachers for K-16 placement. Variously, the meetings attract composition specialists who have been asked to teach methods courses for preservice teachers K-12 and English education specialists who find themselves working as writing program administrators, WAC coordinators, or TA mentors.

pedagogy researchers: as we add more data to our descriptive and analytical scholarship, a more complete picture of WPE is likely to emerge.

THE PLACE AND SPACE OF WRITING PEDAGOGY EDUCATION IN COMPOSITION STUDIES

Writing pedagogy education scholarship is unusually positioned in relation to composition studies as a whole: in some ways, it occupies a central location in the "town commons," while in other ways it remains on the margins, as visible to and present for outsiders as it is to composition specialists. It is also a scholarly field that, like many in composition studies, overlaps with and makes room for knowledge and inquiry modes borrowed from other academic locations. Understanding the current place of WPE scholarship helps us envision how it might grow—where the scholarly "gaps" are, why they exist, and how to address them. Similarly, understanding the challenges and opportunities that WPE scholars may encounter as they map out their pathways in the field can help us prepare to foster and direct that growth.

For better and for worse, one might begin by characterizing WPE as the "general education" node of composition studies: introductory, required of most learners in the field, and wide-reaching in its intended effects. Nearly every contemporary composition studies scholar has been the recipient of formal writing pedagogy education, and many of us have continued to take some role in our school's pedagogy education efforts through teaching, mentoring, or related curriculum or committee work. And just as most composition faculty know a little about what happens in WPE, WPE faculty are usually familiar, at least in passing, with work going on in many of the subfields noted in this collection, a familiarity we need in order to help new and continuing teachers "translate" that scholarly work into daily practices. Research about FYC curricula, basic writers, second language learners, and plagiarism are crucial areas for WPE practices and research, but so are theories and practices related to assessment, writing centers, WAC, new media and other technologies, and administrative negotiations. Moreover, for scholarship in all these other areas to gain a broad audience and effect significant change in the scholarship and practice of composition studies, pedagogy education seminars must succeed as a central site for introduction and recruitment to the field. In claiming fertile ground not far from the central rapids of first-year writing programs, WPE scholars have the opportunity to work across disciplines and even institutional boundaries in their research and their daily practices.

At the same time, though, WPE scholarship can appear to be caught up in eddies outside the mainstream of composition studies—or, equally, enriched by overlap with other disciplines, as are areas such as new media and WAC. In its close ties to FYC (and to English education and methods courses) and thus to the aspects of composition studies that may seem more like "service" or "application" than sophisticated university research, WPE scholarship may carry some stigma. After all, it was just a few decades ago that rhetoric or composition faculty were hired on the tenure track in many English departments with the sole field-related duties of choosing FYC textbooks and supervising teaching assistants. The field of composition studies professionalizes these days, in large part, by moving away from pedagogy education—just as individual graduate students often conceive of themselves as professionalizing by moving out of the pedagogy seminar and into more "advanced" classes and fields of study. Chapters in sourcebooks for writing program administrators make clear how frequently the practices and even the theories of WPE are merged with the administrative, managerial, and political work of a WPA (see Morgan, Ward and Perry, and Carpenter). Meanwhile, acquiring scholarly expertise in pedagogy requires study in (and knowledge of research methods from) education-related disciplines that are at the very least institutionally distant from, and often frowned upon by, English departments and even some rhetoric/composition scholars. Yet WPE is at many institutions part of the most public face of composition programs—a role it shares with writing centers and WAC programs, both of which are also key sites of pedagogy education though they are not often thus described. Most of the immediate beneficiaries of WPE are not and will not themselves become scholars in the field, giving it something of a Jerry Lewis complex: more popular abroad than at home, or at least equally (and surprisingly) visible from points outside the field.

Indeed, seen from abroad, WPE scholarship is clearly linked to several national trends: an increased focus on preparing college faculty for teaching and then supporting them through newly expanded campus teaching centers (sometimes headed by WPE experts); ongoing research in the education and continuing education of adult learners; increased interest generally in the scholarship of teaching and learning (SOTL); increased interest in assessing the effectiveness of educational endeavors. As we begin to understand more about how to teach in higher educational contexts in the twenty-first century, those concepts can in turn be applied to WPE. Of course, it is clearly not a straightforward effort of translation. For example, while the trends within higher education and the concerns of our brethren in related fields (like English education and teacher education more generally) sometimes parallel the trends in college-level WPE, they do not exactly match up. English educators prepare *future* writing teachers to teach within a K-12 educational framework; WPE practitioners work with *in-practice* writing teachers teaching within a higher education framework. The more we understand both the convergences and the gaps between learning to teach writing to 160 fifteen-year-olds in literature-based high school English courses and learning to teach 50 first-year college composition students, the stronger our scholarship will be. Likewise, the more clearly we can envision all the multiple spaces in which WPE practice and scholarship operate, the better prepared we will be to engage with the most challenging issues in the field.

The multiple and extensive placements of WPE as a scholarly field provide both opportunities and challenges for the individual practitioner: the options for cutting-edge and immediately useful scholarship abound, but it's simply not possible to follow and understand the research in all of these various fields. Scholars in the field need to be able to embrace a highly specific, specialized view of WPE while humbly leaving the doors wide open to all we can learn from research in other areas: research about teaching, about learning, about adult education, about writing, and so on. We need to be ready to cross boundaries—within composition studies disciplines and across other disciplinary lines—and to establish local and national networks to foster wider understanding of practices and theories in the field. Scholars in WPE can best serve the immediate needs of those seeking to work fairly, ethically, and humanely with new college-level writing instructors *as well as* serving the fields of composition studies and related fields like English education by establishing collective, cohesive research agendas and developing robust, principled WPE programs.

Frankly, it can be challenging even to locate and define a feasible, focused area of study or a particular research question, since pedagogy scholarship takes many different forms (educational reports, case studies, descriptive analyses, and so on) and legitimately addresses so many questions within and beyond composition. Like the teachers of first-year writing themselves, WPE practitioners must make many, many decisions based on their disciplinary knowledge, the characteristics of the instructors with whom they work, the culture of their local graduate program, the culture and curriculum of the first-year writing program, and the expectations of the university. These decisions about what teachers should know and when (and how!) may need to be informed by theories of (writing) learning and (writing) instruction, by analysis of the needs and abilities of the teachers themselves, and by awareness of the affordances of an institution and a program. It follows that scholarship regarding pedagogy education decisions needs similar broad-based background information—and that choosing a question to pursue can be an overwhelming task. How does one theorize generally about educating such a range of teachers for such a range of educational endeavors? On what element(s) of WPE does one focus: seminars, workshops, mentoring, coteaching, teaching? With what tools, frames, methods, and/or standards does one assess the results of pedagogy education? Since the subfield is still so young as a site of concerted research—and so intricately connected to other subfields—it can take time for a WPE scholar to get her bearings.

Another challenge for WPE practitioners lies in the mixed messages and uneven expectations that pervade both first-year writing courses and WPE programs. Within composition studies, we value first-year writing highly and teach it carefully. Yet we constantly face the challenge of legitimizing this piece of curricular landscape when it is, in turn, taught by our very newest instructors in higher education—and very often, by those without much background in writing or writing pedagogy. The pedagogy education work of WAC programs can raise the additional question about who is qualified to teach writing, and how they gain such qualification; the questions and scholarly research thereon are no longer centered solely in an English department. Additionally, new graduate TAs themselves conceive of first-year writing in substantially different ways, and they also conceive of a "TAship" as dramatically different things (is it a teaching job? a reward for academic prowess? a necessary purgatory?). Demonstrating our commitment to a thoughtful, systematic WPE program disrupts these kinds of (mis)conceptions of what it means to teach college-level writing while also providing grounded instruction for college writing students. But doing so is not always easy, and not just because of our familiar concerns about resources, personnel, or institutional commitment (although these matter too).

Committing to sustainable WPE is challenging because of what we do not know and how dispersed our knowledge and practices are. It is thus likely to take a combination of chutzpah, perseverance, networking, and continuing tolerance of ambiguity to gain expertise in WPE, to initiate and complete high-level scholarship in the field, and to gain recognition for work in it. Yet the field is also, *because* of its multilocality, rich in opportunities for a variety of research projects, using a range of methodologies, and working in collaboration with a diverse group of colleagues. The field values—and needs—both careful data collection and broad, synthetic thinking by scholars who are practicing on Tuesday what they were studying on Monday, and whose conclusions can very quickly ripple outward into large populations of composition scholars, teachers, and students.

GAINING MOMENTUM: THE FUTURES OF WPE SCHOLARSHIP

Like many WPE practitioners, we have benefited from recent scholarship that defines, discusses, and raises questions about the work of WPE. The field has in the past decades gained momentum and influence in both its practices and its published scholarship. To sustain our new work, direct our practices wisely, and further extend the range of our understanding about how teachers learn to teach writing, we will need both new paradigms and additional data analysis. Looking forward, we imagine at least two areas of work that will continue to enhance how we approach the work of pedagogy education. First, WPE scholarship can and will continue to flourish with support from a sustained professional conversation, one in which we continue to articulate local issues and concerns while building toward national heuristics. What those heuristics might look like or be is beyond the scope of this chapter; however, we might be well served by looking again at the progress made within first-year composition scholarship. There, the "WPA Outcomes Statement for First-Year Composition" has become a living document. It both provides a national vision and context and lends language to those working within writing programs across the country. From it, instructors of first-year writing have developed their own outcomes that speak to the needs of their local student populations.

Similarly, some kind of framework—guiding principles, goals, and outcomes—of robustly imagined WPE programs might also be supported through our national organizations like CCCC (and its host organization, NCTE). Just as the WPA Outcomes can be used to set high standards, bring awareness of the similarities between national and local concerns, and advocate for teaching and learning conditions, a heuristic for WPE programs would help pedagogy education scholars design and reimagine sustained, systematic teaching, mentoring, and learning efforts across departments and across institutions. At the same time, this kind of professional work would provide us the opportunity to collaborate with our colleagues "down the hall" in English education as we all work to add to our shared understandings of "writing teacher education" (Tremmel, "Seeking").

Secondly, our research base in WPE can expand in thoughtful, careful ways. While disciplinary self-doubt about all that we don't know about writing seems to be pervasive right now (see, for example, Smit's *The End of Composition Studies*), there are key issues that do in fact have decades of accumulated scholarship within composition studies. For example, two recent, substantial handbooks of research on writing both detail the state of scholarship on key issues, namely, Smagorinsky's *Research on Composition* and Bazerman's *Handbook of Research on Writing*. There are, then, some things we do *know about writing* (however provisionally) that can inform our research on writers and our instruction of writers.

But what we *know* about how to best *teach and mentor those who teach writing at the college level* is not nearly as certain. Wilhoit provides a good initial list of elements of WPE about which we need more information:

- Which instructional or co-curricular approaches "have lasting value for TAs";

- The complex relationship "between TA instructional techniques and gender, race, age, and teaching styles"'

- The challenges facing those involved with TA preparation at comprehensive universities;

- Appropriate and effective strategies for preparing TAs "for increasingly diverse student populations and an increasingly technological workplace"; and

- Appropriate and effective strategies to prepare TAs to work in two-year colleges and high schools. (23–24)

To Wilhoit's list we would add several more recommended areas of future scholarship:

- The kinds of writing experiences that affect TA classroom instruction;

- The relationship between TA program of study and other elements, such as individual confidence, instructional commitment, and teaching effectiveness;
- The costs, benefits, and effectiveness of integrating and scaffolding pedagogy education experiences throughout a graduate program; and
- The roles WPE plays and should play in the increasingly diverse and professionalized discipline(s) of composition/rhetoric.

As we continue to take the work of pedagogy education seriously, we will address these kinds of issues (and undoubtedly uncover others). As Reid ("Teaching") notes, we have as yet no extended rationale for any one purpose, balance, or blend of activities, nor even a more qualified "if . . . then" set of strategies to help local educators and administrators decide what will best serve their new teachers. With both visible national frameworks and a coherent, robust research agenda, pedagogy educators and program administrators will be able to wisely adapt local resources to local students. New data and explorations can lead us to new programs—what might it look like to have an integrated, systematic WPE program stretching beyond the TA seminar?—and can lead us to further scholarship as we assess those endeavors and posit others.

WPE scholarship and practices will strengthen if we respond to recent calls within composition studies more generally for more methodologically diverse research. In his 2006 plenary address at the WPA conference, Chris Anson proposes a framework for writing program administration research that is "more robust [and] evidence-based" ("Intelligent Design" 24); he asserts that writing program administrators need research-based evidence to, among other things, teach more effectively and better respond to a wide range of publics. Within WPE, a robust research agenda will have similar important effects. First, such an agenda allows WPE practitioner-scholars the opportunity to make sound pedagogical and programmatic decisions that are context sensitive; second, it helps us speak with authority to those beyond our field and within it. At least three crucial genres of research are as of yet lacking in WPE and therefore lie ahead of us here:

- Large-scale, longer-term research on the effects of WPE on TAs;
- Data-based analysis of the ways in which preservice, in-service,

and continuing-service WPE interact and reinforce one another and/or support different, complementary aspects of faculty education and development; and

- Comparative studies of WPE programs (e.g., with other programs; with parallel teacher-education programs in other contexts).

In our calls for both continued national conversations among all compositionists and an intensified research agenda among WPE specialists, we do not mean to supplant the narrative-based accounts in the literature of WPE that provide useful and compelling information on how new teachers of writing work and what writing pedagogy education programs are enacted. We are also not proposing any kind of narrow national model for WPE; local iterations are too context specific for a single strict model to be useful. But research-based principles for action will emerge over time, and these kinds of principles will marshal evidence so that we can speak more effectively to a variety of constituencies about the resources, complexities, and time needed for productive, sustained writing pedagogy education.

It is clear to us that writing pedagogy education's roots—like those of practice and scholarship in first-year writing, writing across the curriculum, and writing center studies—developed in reaction to local exigencies. As "composition" became a large but low-value enterprise within higher education, teachers were recruited en masse to meet those needs and then were educated as well as could be done within the constraints of institutional resources and priorities. Writing pedagogy educators are still often working in primarily *reactive* modes, claiming a little ground here and there where possible, but frequently under pressure to follow others' leads. Changes in local institutional policies or resources; new developments in scholarship about writing-learning or in available technologies; changes in the very ways in which people write—any of these can require a pedagogy educator to respond with new information and strategies, often in an improvised fashion with very little notice or time for preparation. The future of this field, however, depends on our ability to move more regularly and confidently under our own power: to set goals and standards; to identify key questions and collect data about them; to assess and share our best practices with others and draw on their successes. Despite—or perhaps because of—the large territory open in front of WPE scholars, we see a field today that is ready to make significant strides away from reactive and toward generative practices in teaching and in scholarship. We are excited about the progress made so far and look forward to the next decades of lively, wide-ranging work in the education and mentoring of writing teachers.

AFTERWORD
REDEFINING THE INEFFABLE—OR,
CREATING SCHOLARLY PRESENCE AND
A USABLE FUTURE

An Editor's Perspective

Deborah H. Holdstein

Most editors of professional journals, likely all, provide guidelines for evaluating manuscripts submitted for possible publication. A key question within these guidelines is as follows, and this will come as no surprise: Does the article contribute something new to the field? Are we as readers and fellow travelers in scholarship somehow enriched, renewed, potentially forced to think in new ways, if this article is published? Has the author or authors done his or her homework—that is, is the author accountable, having acknowledged and built upon previous work (or acknowledged the absence of that work) in the field or fields?

Well, Dear Reader, in the case of this volume, the answer to all questions is "yes." But as with any robust collection of scholarly work, the eventual implementation of and accountability for *Exploring Composition Studies*—in this century or any other—is with those of us out here who are continuing the work of teacher-scholars by both thinking about writing and teaching writing. No matter the transgenre-d mixing of our media—visual rhetorics, Web texts, and social media notwithstanding—the core of our work is, nonetheless and ultimately, the act of writing in and of itself. And through its multiplicity of voices (both in concert and in careful but pronounced cacophony), and by crafting this volume, as Andrea Lunsford affirms in her foreword, "Ritter and Matsuda are in intertextual conversation with . . . earlier mapping expeditions," with authors here aiming to "map a scholarly agenda for writing studies in the coming years."

But is it clear that this volume truly aims to "map" a scholarly agenda—and would such a map, taken strictly, be desirable? Why have the authors chosen to "explore," rather than "define?" I'm taken by the appropriate and inherent vigor and useful "messiness" of the intellectual mix here—all to the good, I might add—one that forces us as scholar-teachers to consider this eclectic work within the larger contexts of the profession and within our own institutional and pedagogical contexts and constraints. The global and the local must both, it appears, continue to guide us. How do the editors of this volume and its authors appropriately fill absences and make our scholarly assumptions more complex? And how is this complexity useful to us? As Kelly Ritter and Paul Kei Matsuda affirm in their smart, cogent, and appropriately nuanced introduction to this volume, "[R]eaders can see how even in retelling its history, composition studies becomes a tricky entity to narrate in any agreed-upon way." And such is the strength, indeed, the hallmark, of a vigorous and significant discipline, as the essays within this volume fully attest.

During my five-year editorship of *College Composition and Communication* (February 2005–December 2009), I acquired a heightened awareness of several issues: the ongoing, ever-present need for accountable, fully contextualized scholarship, and the equally essential need to remember and acknowledge our intellectual and pedagogical histories. Within those self-imposed directives for my editorship, however, I had the privilege of the proverbial "bird's-eye view" of the profession, learning what we were achieving—and realizing what might, indeed, be missing. Having completed with my coeditor Andrea Greenbaum our volume *Judaic Perspectives in Rhetoric and Composition*, a collection that documents a politics of exclusion that, as I have written, "troubles the dominant rhetorical tradition," I knew that there were additional instances where the following questions were more relevant than ever before. I paraphrase here the questions I posed in my final "From the Editor" in the December 2009 issue of *College Composition and Communication*: What's missing from our scholarly work, and how do we bring it to light? What in previous scholarship or research must be challenged or reclaimed or more accountably read and interpreted? What are the philosophical or theoretical assumptions with which we operate that, upon brave reexamination, prove to be centers that cannot hold? How do we create a professional atmosphere that encourages rather than suppresses constructive debate?

As I wrote in the first issue of my editorship (February 2005), the field of composition studies reflects a kind of Cartesian duality in several ways; first, in the constructive, intellectual tension between a scholarship of pedagogy and more traditional forms of scholarship; and, second, in the desire to feature an expansive representation of approaches, issues, and interdisciplinarity that competes with a prudent, if sometimes misguided, desire to promote a narrow scope or focus. (406)

And as I have acknowledged elsewhere, composition studies is not alone in needing to reclaim or rethink its directions or basic tenets. For instance, historian Stephen Hahn reminds us that scholarly work often hides large elisions: what historians (in his case) don't write about—and why. In my last "From the Editor" in 2009, I first paraphrase Hahn in an attempt to encourage and extend the compelling need for wide-ranging, scholarly representation to composition and rhetoric and to the types of work we are willing to publish in major journals that often set the pace for our disciplines. Writes Hahn, "Why are there subjects we so easily avoid or disown, even when they are of genuine significance? Why are there interpretations we are reluctant to embrace? Why do some frameworks of analysis become so deeply entrenched that they resist displacement?" (). The essays in this particular volume offer further hope of that expansion and significant thinking, a means with which to identify and embrace contraries, elisions, and absences. And I am most aware as I read these essays that each in its way *reinvigorates* and extends for its audiences the myriad possibilities of the article's respective focus—with "focus" often broadly writ.

For instance, an especially pivotal moment in this collection is, for me, the conclusion to Jeanne Gunner's essay, "Scholarly Positions in Writing Program Administration." As you likely have read, the paragraph proceeds as follows:

> The limits of WPA scholarship are historical, not fated, not inherent. . . . In the line from Stanley Fish that I do find useful for WPA scholarly purposes, the writing program 'points *away* from itself to something its forms cannot capture,' and beyond the formal conventions of writing program work, much remains to be explored.

Certainly, one can argue, the notion of things scholarly that "remain to be explored" has been a hallmark phrase of the scholarly article for many, many years—that a frequent rhetorical move, even something akin to a trope, occurs when a scholar decides that he or she has exhausted the purview of his or her article and announces that "such speculation [whatever that speculation might be] goes beyond the scope of this article."

But Gunner is doing much, much more: She opens a scholarly door, as it were, affirming that for WPA research and, by implication, for many areas in composition studies, there is even more work to do than we'd realized through previous scholarship, many subjects perhaps mistakenly considered unworthy of active, publishable exploration. Gunner encourages scholar-teachers to explore beyond their respective "stations," as it were: one does not need to have been a WPA to find research in that area productive, useful, and appropriate. Through Gunner's metaphorical door lie numerous opportunities for scholarly investigation that potentially bring presence to *absences* and silences in our scholarship—with productive implications for our teaching. Similarly, as Kathleen Yancey writes in her essay on assessment, "[T]he concerns of compositionists relative to writing assessment have changed and developed—depending on the definition of writing and the purpose(s) of writing assessment; on the power of given terms at different moments in time; and on the values and ideologies represented in those terms, especially and increasingly as they interface—or not—with the interests and directions of public policy makers." Yancey skillfully and immediately captures the scholarly, pedagogical, and practical vexations of assessment, and, similar to Gunner, exhorts us by implication to awareness and careful thinking—opening still other research-based and pedagogically crucial mandates for our work.

However, Christiane Donahue encourages another, more contemporary foray toward these disciplinary "others," reviewing the literature from "education, psychology, sociology and, more recently, composition studies, on transfer," noting that "the contexts and principles identified in the education and psychology research are precisely what drive our composition teaching," encouraging exactly the kind of "boundary crossing" the field professes but often resists. Linda Adler-Kassner and Susanmarie Harrington deftly review narratives and debates regarding basic writing, urging that the field—and therefore institutions—reconfigure and through reframing newer narratives of basic writing acknowledge once again its centrality to the college experience.

I am struck by the essays' frequent *reenvisioning* of possibilities for exploration in composition and rhetoric: for instance, Elizabeth Chiseri-Strater updates and reframes ethnography, a borrowing from the social sciences that I recall from a conflicted heyday in the 1980s. She invokes Stephen North's pessimism at the time in describing composition studies' "embattled Ethnographic community" that lacked "methodological integrity." But Chiseri-Strater emphasizes the tension between the classical, more positivist strategies of ethnographers and current trends that invite adherence to the "ethical turn," where researchers become "activists, collaborators engaged in critical praxis." The possibilities for further research seem infinite, as she notes, "Ethnography, feminism, and postcolonial theory intersect in their desires to challenge textual authority and power and to experiment with issues of representation and otherness."

Additionally, this volume mixes newer, authoritative voices with those on whom we can rely for equally astute and comprehensive thinking about expansive areas within our field: for instance, Lauren Fitzgerald freshens the possibilities for exploring the complexities of the writing center, detailing the ways in which "[t]his is an exciting time to contribute research to writing center studies," and arguing that the center is a site in which we can "demystify" academic literacy practices. Similarly, Kathleen Yancey's essay on assessment; Heidi Estrem and E. Shelley Reid's article on writing pedagogy education; Gail Hawisher and Cynthia Selfe's contribution on digital literacies; Paul Kei Matsuda's ongoing work on second language writing; and Rita Malenczyk's foray into writing across the curriculum, revitalize and take forward long-held areas within composition studies that merit such thorough and smart reinvigoration. Doug Downs and Elizabeth Wardle argue for writing about writing as a tangible "recognition of our disciplinary history and an assumption that our disciplinary knowledge can and should be shared with students in meaningful ways."

The effects of such teaching-learning undoubtedly affects long-term assessments and notions about transfer of abilities from one disciplinary context to another—implying and suggesting the need for conversations with Yancey's, Estrem and Reid's, and Donahue's chapters. Arguably, should we take on their project of students writing about writing, Downs and Wardle's chapter has not only conversational and theoretical but also practical implications for every other chapter in this book. Arguing *against* Downs and Wardle would in and of itself provoke necessary discussion that articulates much of what we do (and do not) hope for composition studies in research, theory, and pedagogy. In the spirit of that very important type of inter-area conversation, Tim Peeples and Bill

Hart-Davidson in their chapter engage in important historical, contextual conversation with Patricia A. Sullivan and James E. Porter's 1993 piece on professional writing as well as the field of composition studies itself, locating "professional writing and composition studies, along with some related areas, on two continua, one extending from service status to major status and another extending from humanist orientation to professional orientation." Each well-chosen article in this volume speaks to my own perhaps obsessive concern with bringing presence to absence, to revitalizing conversations in the field—and with often controversial, unanticipated perspectives. Ritter and Matsuda, strong thinkers both, have brought forth a volume that, to its credit, does everything *but* "define" composition studies. Rather, they and their authors appropriately explore and yet question it, challenging other thinkers, writers, and teachers through this set of contrapuntal perspectives to carry forward the work of these provocative and ultimately useful pieces.

WORKS CITED

Adler-Kassner, Linda. *The Activist WPA: Changing Stories about Writing and Writers.* Logan: Utah State UP, 2008. Print.

Adler-Kassner, Linda, R. Crooks, and A. Watters, eds. *Writing the Community: Concepts and Models for Service Learning in Composition.* Washington, DC: American Association for Higher Education, 1997. Print.

Adler-Kassner, Linda, and Susanmarie Harrington. *Basic Writing as a Political Act: Public Conversations about Writing and Literacies.* Cresskill, NJ: Hampton, 2002. Print.

Alexander, Jonathan. "Ravers on the Web: Resistance, Multidimensionality, and Writing (about) Youth Culture." *Kairos* 7.3 (2002). Web. 4 May 2009.

Alexander, P. A., and P. K. Murphy. "Nurturing the Seeds of Transfer: A Domain-Specific Perspective." *International Journal of Educational Research* 31 (1999): 561–76. Print.

Allen, Nancy. *Working with Words and Images: New Steps in an Old Dance.* Stamford, CT: Ablex, 2002. Print.

Allen, Nancy, and Steven T. Benninghoff. "TPC Program Snapshots: Developing Curricula and Addressing Challenges." *Technical Communication Quarterly* 13.2 (2004): 157–85. Print.

Allen, O. Jane, and Lynn H. Deming. *Publications Management: Essays for Professional Technical Communicators.* Technical Communication. Amityville, NY: Baywood, 1994. Print.

Alsup, Janet, and Michael Bernard-Donals. "The Fantasy of the 'Seamless Transition.'" *Teaching Writing in High School and College.* Ed. Thomas Thompson. Bloomington, IN: NCTE, 2002. 115–35. Print.

Amidon, Steven, and Stuart Blythe. "Wrestling with Proteus: Tales of Communication Managers in a Changing Economy." *Journal of Business & Technical Writing* 22.1 (2008): 5–37. Print.

Anderson, Paul. "Conference on Assessment in the Humanities That Can Benefit WPAs." Online posting. WPA-L, 5 Jan. 2011. Accessed 18 February 2012. Web.

"Announcements." *WPA: Writing Program Administration* 31.3 (Spring 2008): 3. Print.

Anson, Chris. "The Intelligent Design of Writing Programs: Reliance on Belief or a Future of Evidence?" *WPA: Writing Program Administration* 32.1 (2008): 11–36. Print.

———. "Portfolios for Teachers: Writing Our Way to Reflective Practice." Black et al. 185–200.

Anson, Chris M., and L. Lee Forsberg. "Moving beyond the Academic Community: Transitional Stages in Professional Writing." *Written Communication* 7.2 (1990): 200–231. Print.

Arthurs, Jeffrey. "The Term Rhetor in Fifth- and Fourth-Century B.C.E. Greek Texts." *Rhetoric Society Quarterly* 23.3–4 (1994): 1–10. Print.

Arum, Richard, and Josipa Roksa. *Academically Adrift: Limited Learning on College Campuses.* Chicago: U of Chicago P, 2011. Print.

Ashwell, Tim. "Patterns of Teacher Response to Student Writing in a Multiple-Draft Composition Classroom: Is Content Feedback Followed by Form Feedback the Best Method?" *Journal of Second Language Writing* 9.3 (2000): 227–57. Print.

"Author's Guide." *WPA: Writing Program Administration.* 3.1 (1979): 2. Print.

"Author's Guide." *WPA: Writing Program Administration* 13.3 (1990): 3. Print.

"Author's Guide." *WPA: Writing Program Administration* 17.3 (1994): 3. Print.

"Author's Guide." *WPA: Writing Program Administration* 31.3 (2008): 5. Print.

Bakhtin, M. M. *Speech Genres and Other Late Essays*. Austin: U of Texas P, 1986. Print.

Banks, Adam. *Race, Rhetoric, and Technology: Searching for Higher Ground*. Urbana, IL: NCTE, 2005. Print.

Barnett, Robert W., and Jacob S. Blumner. *The Allyn & Bacon Guide to Writing Center Theory and Practice*. Boston: Allyn & Bacon, 2001. Print.

Barnum, Carol M. *Usability Testing and Research*. New York: Longman, 2002. Print.

Barr Ebest, Sally. *Changing the Way We Teach: Writing and Resistance in the Training of Teaching Assistants*. Carbondale: Southern Illinois UP, 2005. Print.

———. "Gender Differences in Writing Program Administration." *WPA: Writing Program Administration* 18.3 (1995): 53-73. Print.

Bartholomae, David. "Inventing the University." *Journal of Basic Writing* 5.1 (1986): 4- 23.

Bartholomae, David. "The Tidy House: Basic Writing in the American Curriculum." *Journal of Basic Writing* 12 (1993): 4–21. Rpt. in *Writing on the Margins: Essays on Composition and Teaching*. Boston: Bedford/St. Martin's, 2005: 312–26. Print.

Bartholomae, David, and Anthony Petrosky. Eds. *Ways of Reading: An Anthology for Writers*. New York: Bedford/St. Martin's, 2004. Print.

Barton, David. "Understanding Textual Practices in a Changing World." *The Future of Literacy Studies*. Eds. M. Baynham & M. Prinsloo. Basingstoke: Palgrave Macmillan, 2009. 38-53. Print.

Basmadjian, Kevin G. "Watching What We Say: Using Video to Learn about Discussions." *English Education* 41.1 (2008): 13–38. Print.

Bautier, Elisabeth. "Formes et activités scolaires: Secondarisation, reconfiguration et différenciation sociale." *Le français hier et aujourd'hui: Politiques de la langue et apprentissages scolaires*. Ed. N. Ramognino and P. K. Vergès. Aix en Provence: Presses de l'Université de Provence, 2004. Print.

Bawarshi, Anis. *Accessing Academic Discourse: The Influence of First-Year Composition Students' Prior Genre Knowledge*. Presentation given at 2007 Council of Writing Program Administrators Conference. 2007. Print.

Bawarshi, Anis, and Stephanie Pelkowski. "Postcolonialism and the Idea of a Writing Center." *Writing Center Journal* 19.2 (1999): 41–58. Print.

Bazerman, Charles. *Handbook of Research on Writing: History, Society, School, Individual, Text*. Mahwah, NJ: Erlbaum, 2007. Print.

———. "Systems of Genre and the Enactment of Social Intentions." In Freedman, Aviva; Peter Medway (Eds.), *Genre and the New Rhetoric*. London; Bristol, PA: Taylor & Francis, 1994: 79-101. Print.

Bazerman, Charles, and James Paradis. *Textual Dynamics of the Professions: Historical and Contemporary Studies of Writing in Professional Communities*. Madison: U of Wisconsin P, 1991. Print.

Beach, King. "Consequential Transitions: A Developmental View of Knowledge Propagation Through Social Organizations." *Between School and Work: New Perspectives on Transfer and Boundary-Crossing*. Eds. Tuomi-Groehn and Engestroem. New York: Pergamon, 2003. 39-61. Print.

Bean, John C. *Engaging Ideas: The Professor's Guide to Integrating Writing, Critical Thinking, and Active Learning in the Classroom*. San Francisco: Jossey-Bass, 1996. Print.

Beaufort, Anne. *College Writing and Beyond: A New Framework for University Writing Instruction*. Logan: Utah State UP, 2007. Print.

———. *Writing in the Real World: Making the Transition from School to Work*. New York: Teachers College Press, 1999. Print.

Behar, Ruth. *Translated Woman: Crossing the Border with Esperanza's Story*. Boston: Beacon, 1993. Print.

Behar, Ruth, and Deborah Gordon, eds. *Women Writing Culture*. Berkeley: U of California P, 1995. Print.

Belanoff, Pat. "Forward." *The Theory and Practice of Grading Writing: Problems and Possibilities.* Ed. Frances Zak and Christopher Weaver. Albany: State U of New York P, 1998. ix–xiii. Print.

Belanoff, Pat, and Marcia Dickson, eds. *Portfolio Grading: Process and Product.* Portsmouth, NH: Boynton/Cook, 1991. Print.

Belanoff, Pat, and Peter Elbow. "Using Portfolios to Increase Collaboration and Community in a Writing Program." *WPA: Writing Program Administration* 9 (Spring 1986): 27–39. Print.

Bell, Diana, and Madeline Youmans. "Politeness and Praise: Rhetorical Issues in ESL (L2) Writing Center Conferences." *Writing Center Journal* 26.2 (2006): 31–47. Print.

Belmont, J. M., E. C. Butterfield, and R. P. Ferretti. "To Secure Transfer of Training Instruct Self-Management Skills." *How and How Much Can Intelligence Be Increased?* Ed. Douglas Detterman and Robert Sternberg. Norwood, NJ: Ablex, 1982. 147–54. Print.

Bereiter, Carl. "Situated Cognition and How to Overcome It." *Situated Cognition: Social, Semiotic, and Psychological Perspectives.* Ed. D. Kirshner and J. A. Whitson. Hillsdale, NJ: Erlbaum, 1997. 281–300. Print.

Bergmann, Linda S. "Re: Writing Intensive Course Criteria." Online posting. WPA-L, 11 Oct. 2010. Web. 14 Feb. 2011.

Bergmann, Linda S., and Janet S. Zepernick. "Disciplinarity and Transfer: Students' Perceptions of Learning to Write." *WPA: Writing Program Administration* 31.1–2 (2007): 124–49. Web. 3 Apr. 2009.

Berkenkotter, Carol. "Decisions and Revisions: The Planning Strategies of a Publishing Writer." *College Composition and Communication* 34.2 (1983): 159-69.

Berlin, James. "Rhetoric and Ideology in the Writing Class." *College English* 50 (1988): 477-94.

———. *Rhetoric and Reality: Writing Instruction in American Colleges, 1900–1985.* Studies in Writing and Rhetoric. Carbondale, IL: Southern Illinois UP, 1987. Print.

———. *Writing Instruction in Nineteenth-Century American Colleges.* Studies in Writing and Rhetoric. Carbondale: Southern Illinois UP, 1984. Print.

Berlin, James. "Contemporary Composition: The Major Pedagogical Theories." *College English* 44 (1982): 765-77.

Bialystok, Ellen. *Bilingualism in Development: Language, Literacy, and Cognition.* New York: Cambridge UP, 2001. Print.

Bird, Barbara. "Re: Writing Intensive Course Criteria." Online posting. WPA-L, 11 Oct. 2010. Web. 14 Feb. 2011.

Bird, Barbara. "Writing about Writing as the Heart of a Writing Studies Approach to FYC: Response to Douglas Downs and Elizabeth Wardle, 'Teaching about Writing, Righting Misconceptions' and to Libby Miles et al., ' Thinking Vertically'" *College Composition and Communication* 60.1 (2008): 165-181.

Birkenstein, Cathy, and Gerald Graff. "In Teaching Composition, 'Formulaic' Is Not a 4-Letter Word." *Chronicle of Higher Education* 4 Apr. 2008. Accessed 1 October 2008. Web.

Bishop, Wendy. *Ethnographic Writing Research: Writing It Down, Writing It Up, and Reading It.* Portsmouth, NH: Boynton/Cook, 1999. Print.

———. *On Writing: A Process Reader.* New York: McGraw-Hill, 2003. Print.

———. *Something Old, Something New: College Writing Teachers and Classroom Change.* Carbondale: Southern Illinois UP, 1990. Print.

Bishop, Wendy, and Gay Lynn Crossley. "How to Tell a Story of Stopping: The Complexities of Narrating a WPA's Experience." *WPA: Writing Program Administration* 193. (1996): 70-79, Print.

Bizzell, Patricia, and Bruce Herzberg, eds. *The Rhetorical Tradition: Readings from Classical Times to the Present.* Boston: Bedford, 1990. Print.

Bjork, R. A., and A. Richardson-Klavhen. "On the Puzzling Relationship between Environment Context and Human Memory." *Current Issues in Cognitive Processes.* Ed. C. Izawa. Hillsdale, NJ: Erlbaum, 1989. Print.

Black, Laurel, Donald A. Daiker, Jeffrey Sommers, and Gail Stygall, eds. *New Directions in Portfolio Assessment.* Portsmouth, NH: Heinemann, 1994. Print.

Blakesley, David. "Directed Self-Placement in the University." *WPA: Writing Program Administration* 25.3 (2002): 9–39. Print.

Blakesley, David, E. Harvey, and E. Reynolds. "Southern Illinois Carbondale as an Institutional Model: The English 100/101 Stretch and Directed Self Placement Program." *Directed Self Placement: Principles and Practices.* Ed. Roger Giles and David Royer. Cresskill, NJ: Hampton, 2003. 207–43. Print.

Blakesley, David, and Karl Stolley. *Kairosnews,* 2004. Web. 2 May 2009.

Blanton, Linda Lonon, and Barbara Kroll with Alister Cumming, Melinda Erickson, Ann M. Johns, Ilona Leki, Joy Reid, and Tony Silva. *ESL Composition Tales: Reflections on Teaching.* Ann Arbor: U of Michigan P, 2002. Print.

Blau, Susan, John Hall, and Sarah Sparks. "Guilt-Free Tutoring: Rethinking How We Tutor Non-Native-English-Speaking Students." *Writing Center Journal* 23.1 (2002): 23–44. Print.

Blau, Susan R., John Hall, and Tracy Strauss. "Exploring the Tutor/Client Conversation: A Linguistic Analysis." *Writing Center Journal* 19.1 (1998): 19–48. Print.

Bloom, Lynn Z., Donald A. Daiker, and Edward M. White, eds. *Composition in the Twenty-first Century: Crisis and Change.* Carbondale: Southern Illinois UP, 1996. Print.

Blyler, Nancy Roundy, and Charlotte Thralls. *Professional Communication: The Social Perspective.* Newbury Park, CA: Sage, 1993. Print.

Boquet, Elizabeth H. "Disciplinary Action: Writing Center Work and the Making of a Researcher." Gillespie et al. 23–37.

———. *Noise from the Writing Center.* Logan: Utah State UP, 2002. Print.

———. "'Our Little Secret': A History of Writing Centers, Pre– to Post–Open Admissions." *College Composition and Communication* 50.3 (1999): 463–82. Print.

Boquet, Elizabeth H., and Neal Lerner. "After 'The Idea of a Writing Center.'" *College English* 71.2 (2008): 170–89. Print.

Bordelon, Suzanne. "George Pierce Baker's Principles of Argumentation: 'Completely Logical'?" *College Composition and Communication.* 57.3 (2006): 416–41. Print.

Bousquet, Marc. "Composition as Management Science: Toward a University without a WPA." *JAC* 22 (2002): 493–526. Print.

Bousquet, Marc, Tony Scott, and Leo Parascondola, eds. *Tenured Bosses and Disposable Teachers: Writing Instruction in the Managed University.* Carbondale: Southern Illinois UP, 2004. Print.

Braine, G. "ESL Students in First Year Writing Courses: ESL versus Mainstream Classes." *Journal of Second Language Writing* 5 (1996): 91–107. Print.

Brandt, Deborah. "Accumulating Literacy." *College English* 57 (1995): 649–68. Print.

Brannon, Lil, and Stephen M. North. "The Uses of the Margins." *Writing Center Journal* 20.2 (2000): 7–12. Print.

Bransford, J. D., Brown, A. L., & Cocking, R. R. (Eds.). "Learning and Transfer." *How People Learn: Brain, Mind, Experience, and School.* Washington, DC: National Academy Press, 2000. 51-78. Print.

Bransford, J. D., & Schwartz, D. L. Rethinking transfer: A simple proposal with multiple implications. *Review of Research in Education.* Eds. A. Iran-Nejad & P. D. Pearson. Washington, DC: American Educational Research Association, 1999. 61-100. Print.

Brereton, John C., ed. *The Origins of Composition Studies in the American College, 1875–1925: A Documentary History.* Pittsburgh: U of Pittsburgh P, 1996. Print.

Briggs, Lynn Craigue, and Meg Woolbright, eds. *Stories from the Center: Connecting Narrative and Theory in the Writing Center.* Urbana, IL: NCTE, 2000. Print.

Broad, Bob, Linda Adler-Kassner, Barry Alford, Jane Detweiler, Heidi Estrem, Susanmarie Harrington, Maureen McBride, Eric Stalions, and Scott Weeden. *Organic Writing Assessment: Dynamic Criteria Mapping in Action.* Logan: Utah State UP, 2009. Print.

Broadhead, Glenn J., and Richard C. Freed. *The Variables of Composition: Process and Product in a Business Setting.* Carbondale, IL: NCTE, 1986.

Brodkey, Linda. "Writing Critical Ethnographic Narratives."*Anthropology and Education Quarterly* 18.2 (2009): 67–76. Print.

———. "Writing Ethnographic Narratives" *Written Communication* 9 (1992): 25–50. Print.

Brown, Michael E., Linda K. Trevino, and David Harrison. "Ethical Leadership: A Social Learning Perspective for Construct Development and Testing." *Organizational Behavior and Human Decision Processes* 97 (2005): 117-134. Print.

Brown, Renee, Brian Fallon, Jessica Lott, Elizabeth Matthews, and Elizabeth Mintie. "Taking on Turnitin: Tutors Advocating Change." *Writing Center Journal* 27.1 (2007): 7–28. Print.

Brown, Robert. "Representing Audiences in Writing Center Consultation: A Discourse Analysis." *Writing Center Journal* 30 (2010): 72–99. Print.

Brown, Stephen, and Sidney Dobrin, eds. *Ethnography Unbound: From Theory Shock to Critical Praxis.* Albany: State U of New York P, 2004. Print.

Brown, Stuart C., and Theresa Enos, eds. *The Writing Program Administrator's Resource: A Guide to Reflective Institutional Practice.* Mahwah, NJ: Erlbaum, 2002. Print.

Bruffee, Kenneth A. "Collaborative Learning and the 'Conversation of Mankind.'" *College English* 46.7 (1984): 635–52. Print.

———. "Peer Tutoring and the 'Conversation of Mankind.'" *Writing Centers: Theory and Administration.* Ed. Gary A. Olson. Urbana, IL: NCTE, 1984. 3–15. Print.

Buranen, Lise, and Alice M. Roy, eds. *Perspectives on Plagiarism and Intellectual Property in a Postmodern World.* Albany: State U of New York P, 1999. Print.

Burns, Hugh. "Stimulating Rhetorical Invention in English Composition through Computer-Assisted Instruction." Diss. U of Texas, 1979. ERIC Document Reproduction Service ED 188 245. Accessed 1 May 2009. Web.

Campbell, Elizabeth. "Being and Writing with Others: On the Possibilities of an Ethnographic Composition Pedagogy." Diss. Indiana U of Pennsylvania, 2009. Print.

Campbell, Jennifer. Final Report. Presentation at Meeting of the Inter/National Coalition for Electronic Portfolio Research. Feb. 4, 2011.

Campbell, Jennifer, Richard Colby, David Daniels, Doug Hesse, Matt Hill, Jeff Ludwig, Heather Martin, Jennifer Novak Ladd, and Rebekah Shultz-Colby. "The Value of a First Year Portfolio Assessment for Faculty and Student Learning." Inter/National Coalition for Electronic Portfolio Research, 2011. Web. 21 Jan. 2011.

Campbell, JoAnn. "Controlling Voices: The Legacy of English A at Radcliffe College, 1883–1917." *College Composition and Communication.* 43.4 (1992): 472–85. Print.

———, ed. *Toward a Feminist Rhetoric: The Writing of Gertrude Buck.* Pittsburgh: U of Pittsburgh P, 1996. Print.

Campus Writing Program. U of Missouri, n.d. Web. 14 Feb. 2011.

Canagarajah, A. Suresh. *Critical Academic Writing and Multilingual Students.* Ann Arbor: U of Michigan P, 2002. Print.

Carino, Peter. "Early Writing Centers: Toward a History." *Writing Center Journal* 15.2 (1995): 103–15. Print.

———. "Open Admissions and the Construction of Writing Center History: A Tale of Three Models." *Writing Center Journal* 17.1 (1996): 30–48. Print.

———."Theorizing the Writing Center: No Easy Task." *Dialogue: A Journal for Writing Specialists* 2.1 (1995). Rpt. in *The Longman Guide to Writing Center Theory and Practice.* Ed. Robert W. Barnett and Jacob S. Blumner. New York: Longman, 2008. 124–38. Print.

———."Writing Centers and Writing Programs: Local and Communal Politics." *The Politics of Writing Centers*. Ed. Jane Nelson and Kathy Evertz. Portsmouth, NH: Boynton/Cook, 2001. 1–14. Print.

Carpenter, William J. "Professional Development for Writing Program Staff." Ward and Carpenter 156–65.

Carrick, Tracy Hamler. "Where There's Smoke, Is There Fire? Understanding Coathorship in the Writing Center." *Pluralizing Plagiarism: Identities, Contexts, Pedagogies*. Ed. Rebecca Moore Howard and Amy E. Robillard. Portsmouth, NH: Boynton/Cook Heinemann, 2008. 62–76. Print.

Carroll, Lee Ann. *Rehearsing New Roles: How College Students Develop as Writers*. Carbondale: Southern Illinois UP, 2002. Print.

Carter, Michael. "The Idea of Expertise: An Exploration of Cognitive and Social Dimensions of Writing." *College Composition and Communication* 41 (1990): 265–86. Print.

Casanave, Christine Pearson. *Writing Games: Multicultural Case Studies of Academic Literacy Practices in Higher Education*. Mahwah, NJ: Erlbaum, 2002. Print.

Casanave, Christine Pearson, and Stephanie Vandrick, eds. *Writing for Publication: Behind the Scenes in Language Education*. Mahwah, NJ: Erlbaum, 2003. Print.

CCCC Committee on the Writing Major. "Writing Majors at a Glance (Spring 2007)," 31 Dec. 2007. Web. Accessed 1 February 2012.

"CCCC Statement on Ebonics." *College Composition and Communication* 50.3 (1999): 524. Print.

"CCCC Statement on Second Language Writing and Writers." *College Composition and Communication* 52.4 (2001): 669–74. Print.

Charney, Davida. "Empiricism is not a Four-Letter Word." *College Composition and Communication* 47 (1996), 567-93. Print.

Chiseri-Strater, Elizabeth. *Academic Literacies: The Public and Private Discourse of University Students*. Portsmouth, NH: Boynton/Cook, 1991. Print.

———. "Turning in upon Ourselves: Positionality, Subjectivity, and Reflexivity in Case Study and Ethnographic Research." Mortensen and Kirsch 115–33.

Chiseri-Strater, Elizabeth, and Bonnie S. Sunstein. *Fieldworking: Reading and Writing Research*. 3rd ed. New York: Bedford/St. Martin's, 2007. Print.

Cintron. Ralph. *Angel's Town: Chero Ways, Gang Life, and the Rhetorics of Everyday*. Boston: Beacon, 1997. Print.

Clark, Irene. *Concepts in Composition: Theory and Practice in the Teaching of Writing*. Mahwah, NJ: Lawrence Erlbaum Associates, 2003.

———. "Writing Centers and Plagiarism." Buranen and Roy 155–67.

Clark, Irene L., and Dave Healy. "Are Writing Centers Ethical?" *WPA: Writing Program Administration* 20.1–2 (1996): 32–38. Print.

Clifford, James, and George Marcus, eds. *Writing Culture: The Poetics and Politics of Ethnography*. Berkeley: U of California P, 1986. Print.

Cogie, Jane. "ESL Student Participation in Writing Center Sessions." *Writing Center Journal* 26.2 (2006): 48–66. Print.

Coles, Robert. *The Call of Stories*. New York: Houghton Mifflin, 1989. Print.

Collins, Terence G. "A Response to Ira Shor's 'Our Apartheid: Writing Instruction and Inequality.'" *Journal of Basic Writing* 16 (1997): 95–100. Print.

Collins, Terry, and Paul Hunter. "'Waiting for an Aristotle': A Moment in the History of the Basic Writing Movement." *College English* 54 (1992): 914–27. Print.

Composition Studies/Freshman English News. Special Issue on Doctoral Training in Rhetoric and Composition. 23.1 (1995). 1-132. Print.

Computers and Composition: An International Journal. Web.

Computers and Composition Digital Press. An Imprint of Utah State UP. Web.

Computers and Composition Online. Web.

Condon, William, and Diane Kelly-Riley. "Assessing and Teaching What We Value: The Relationship between College-level Writing and Critical Thinking Abilities." *Assessing Writing* 9.1 (2004): 56–75. Print.

Connors, Robert. *Composition-Rhetoric: Backgrounds, Theory, and Pedagogy.* Pittsburgh: U of Pittsburgh P, 1997. Print.

———. "Octalog: The Politics of Historiography." *Rhetoric Review* 7.1 (1988): 5–49. Print.

———. "The Rise of Technical Writing Instruction in America." *Journal of Technical Writing and Communication* 12.4 (1982): 329–52. Print.

Cook, Vivian J., ed. *Effects of the Second Language on the First.* Clevedon, United Kingdom: Multilingual Matters, 2003. Print.

Cope, Bill, and Mary Kalantzis, eds. *Multiliteracies: Literacy Learning and the Design of Social Futures.* London: Routledge, 2000. Print.

Costino, Kimberly A., and Sunny Hyon. "'A Class for Students Like Me': Reconsidering Relationships among Identity Labels, Residency Status, and Students' Preferences for Mainstream or Multilingual Composition." *Journal of Second Language Writing* 16.2 (2007): 63–81. Print.

Council of Writing Program Administrators. "WPA Outcomes Statement for First Year Composition." *WPA: Writing Program Administration* 23 (2000): 59–66. Print.

Crapanzano, Vincent. *Tuhami: Portrait of a Moroccan.* Chicago: U of Chicago P, 1980. Print.

Crowley, Sharon. *Composition in the University: Historical and Polemical Essays.* Pittsburgh: U of Pittsburgh P, 1998. Print.

———. "Composition Is Not Rhetoric." *Enculturation* 5.1 (Fall 2003). 1-5. Print.

———. "Let Me Get This Straight." *Writing Histories of Rhetoric.* Ed. Victor Vitanza. Carbondale: Southern Illinois UP, 1994. 1–19. Print.

Crusan, Deborah. "An Assessment of ESL Writing Placement Assessment." *Assessing Writing* 8.1 (2002): 17–30. Print.

Cummins, Gail, and Elizabeth Spalding. "It Was the Best of Times, It Was a Waste of Time: University of Kentucky Students' Views of Writing under KERA." *Assessing Writing* 5 (1998): 167–99. Print.

Cushman, Ellen. *The Struggle and the Tools: Oral and Literate Strategies in an Inner City Community.* Albany: State U of New York P, 1998. Print.

"CWPA Call for Research Proposals." http://wpacouncil.org/grants/index.html. Accessed 15 March 2009. Web.

Danielewicz, Jane. *Teaching Selves: Identity, Pedagogy, and Teacher Education.* Albany: State U of New York P, 2001. Print.

"Dartmouth Has Writing Clinic." *New York Times* 15 October 1939: 57. Print.

Dautermann, Jennie. *Writing at Good Hope: A Study of Negotiated Composition in a Community of Nurses.* ATTW Contemporary Studies in Technical Communication. Greenwich, CN: Ablex, 1997. Print.

Davydov, V.V. *Types of Generalization in Instruction: Logical and psychological problems in the structuring of school curricula.* Reston, National Council of Teachers of Mathematics, 1990. Print.

Deans, Thomas. *Writing Partnerships: Service Learning in Composition.* Urbana, IL: NCTE, 2000. Print.

DeCiccio, Al, Lisa Ede, Neal Lerner, Beth Boquet, and Muriel Harris. "Work in Progress: Publishing Writing Center Scholarship." *Writing Lab Newsletter* 31.7 (2007): 1–6. Print.

De Corte, Eric. "On the Road to Transfer: An Introduction." *International Journal of Educational Research* 31 (1999): 555–59. Print.

Delli Carpini, Dominic. *Composing a Life's Work: Writing, Citizenship, and Your Occupation.* New York: Allyn & Bacon, 2004. Print.

Denny, Harry C. *Facing the Center: Toward an Identity Politics of One-to-One Mentoring.* Logan: Utah State UP, 2010. Print.

Derry, Sharon, Nagarajan Anandi, Cindy Hmelo-Silver, Ellina Chernobilsky, and Brian Beitzel. "Cognitive Transfer Revisited: Can We Exploit New Media to Solve Old Problems on a Large Scale?" *Journal of Educational Computing Research* 35.2 (2006): 145-62. Print.

Detterman, Douglas, and Robert Sternberg. eds. *How and How Much Can Intelligence Be Increased?* Norwood, NJ: Ablex, 1982. Print.

Devitt, Amy. *Writing Genres.* Carbondale: Southern Illinois University Press, 2004.

DeVoss, Danielle, Heidi McKee, and Richard Selfe, eds. *Technological Ecologies and Sustainability.* Logan: CCDP/Utah State UP, 2009. Accessed 1 May 2009. Web.

Dew, Debra Frank. "Language Matters: Rhetoric and Writing I as Content Course." *WPA: Writing Program Administration* 26.3 (2003): 87–104. Print.

———. *Rhetoric and Writing I: Academic Reading and Analytical Writing.* UCCS Writing Program. In-house publication. Print.

DeWitt, Donald L. *Articles Describing Archives and Manuscript Collections in the United States: An Annotated Bibliography.* Westport, CT: Greenwood, 1997. Print.

Dias, Patrick, Aviva Freedman, Peter Medway, and Anthony Paré. *Worlds Apart: Acting and Writing in Academic and Workplace Contexts.* Mahwah, NJ: Erlbaum, 1999. Print.

Dias, Patrick, and Anthony Paré. *Transitions: Writing in Academic and Workplace Settings.* Cresskill, NJ: Hampton, 2000. Print.

Dobrin, Sidney I., ed. *Don't Call It That: The Composition Practicum.* Urbana, IL: NCTE, 2005. Print.

———."Introduction: Finding Space for the Composition Practicum." Dobrin, *Don't Call It That,* 1–34.

Doheny-Farina, Stephen. "Creating a Text/Creating a Company: The Role of a Text in the Rise and Decline of a New Organization." *Textual Dynamics of the Professions: Historical and Contemporary Studies of Writing in Professional Communities.* Ed. Charles Bazerman and James Paradis. Madison: U of Wisconsin P, 1991. Print.

———. "Writing in an Emerging Organization: An Ethnographic Study." *Written Communication* 3 (1986): 158–85. Print.

Dombrowski, Paul. *Ethics in Technical Communication.* Allyn & Bacon Series in Technical Communication. Boston: Allyn & Bacon, 2000. Print.

Donahue, Christiane. "Évolution des Pratiques et des Discours sur l'Ecrit à l'Université: Etude de Cas." *LIDIL* 41 (2010). Print.

Donahue, Patricia, and Gretchen Flesher Moon, eds. *Local Histories: Reading the Archives of Composition.* Pittsburgh: U of Pittsburgh P, 2007. Print.

Downs, Douglas, and Elizabeth Wardle. "Teaching about Writing, Righting Misconceptions: (Re)Envisioning 'First-Year Composition' as 'Introduction to English Studies.'" *College Composition and Communication* 58 (2007): 552–84. Print.

Dragga, Sam, and Gwendolyn Gong. *Editing: The Design of Rhetoric.* Technical Communication. Farmingdale, NY: Baywood, 1989. Print.

Dressman, Mark. "Theory *into* Practice? Reading against the Grain of Good Practice Narratives." *Language Arts* 78.1 (2000): 50–59. Print.

Durst, Russell. *Collision Course: Conflict, Negotiation, and the Teaching of Composition.* Urbana, IL: NCTE, 1999. Print.

Eckerle, Julie, Karen Rowan, and Shevaun Watson. "IWCA Graduate Student Position Statement." *Writing Center Journal* 23.1 (2002): 59–61. Print.

Ede, Lisa. *On Writing Research: The Braddock Essays, 1975–1998.* Boston: Bedford/St. Martin's, 1999. Print.

———. *Situating Composition: Composition Studies and the Politics of Location.* Carbondale: Southern Illinois UP, 2004. Print.

Eich, E. "Context, Memory, and Integrated Item/Context Imagery." *Journal of Experimental Psychology* 11 (1985): 764–70. Print.

Elbow, Peter. *Writing Without Teachers.* New York: Oxford UP, 1973.

Elliot, Norbert. *On a Scale: A Social History of Writing Assessment in America.* New York: Peter Lang, 2005. Print.

Emig, Janet. *The Composing Process of Twelfth Graders.* Urbana, IL: NCTE, 1971. Print.

———. "Writing as a Mode of Learning." *College Composition and Communication* 28 (1977): 122–28. Print.

Engestrom, Yrjo. "Expansive Learning at Work: toward an activity theoretical reconceptualization." *Journal of Education and Work*, 14.1 (2001): 133-56.

Enos, Theresa, and Shane Borrowman, eds. *The Promise and Perils of Writing Program Administration.* West Lafayette, IN: Parlor, 2008. Print.

Ervin, Elizabeth. *Public Literacy.* New York: Longman, 2000. Print.

Faber, Brenton. *Community Action and Organizational Change.* Carbondale: Southern Illinois UP, 2002. Print.

Faigley, Lester. "Nonacademic Writing: The Social Perspective." *Writing in Nonacademic Settings.* Ed. Lee Odell and Dixie Goswami. New York: Guilford, 1985. Print.

Farris, Christine. *Subject to Change: New Composition Instructors' Theory and Practice.* Cresskill, NJ: Hampton, 1996. Print.

Ferreira-Buckley, Linda. Octalog II: The (Continuing) Politics of Historiography." *Rhetoric Review* 16.1 (1998): 22–44. Print.

Ferris, Dana R. "The 'Grammar Correction' Debate in L2 Writing: Where Are We, and Where Do We Go from Here? (and What Do We Do in the Meantime . . .?)." *Journal of Second Language Writing* 13.1 (2004): 49–62. Print.

———. *Teaching College Writing to Diverse Student Populations.* Ann Arbor: U of Michigan P, 2009. Print.

———. *Treatment of Error in Second Language Student Writing.* Ann Arbor: U of Michigan P, 2002. Print.

Fish, Stanley. *Save the World on Your Own Time.* New York, Oxford UP, 2008. Print.

Fish, Stanley E. *Self-Consuming Artifacts: The Experience of Seventeenth Century Literature.* 1972. Pittsburgh: Duquesne UP, 1994. Print.

Fisher, Ruth Overman. "Theory in a TA Composition Pedagogy Course: Not if, but How." Dobrin, *Don't Call It That* 200–14.

Fisher, Steven, ed. *Archival Information: How to Find It, How to Use It.* Westport, CT: Greenwood, 2004. Print.

Fishman, Andrea. *Amish Literacy: What and How It Means.* Portsmouth, NH: Heinemann, 1988. Print.

Fishman, Stephen, and Lucille McCarthy. "Teaching for Student Change: A Deweyan Alternative to Radical Pedagogy." *College Composition and Communication* 47 (1996): 342–66. Print.

Fitzgerald, Lauren, and Denise Stephenson. "Directors at the Center: Relationships across Campus." *The Writing Center Director's Resource Book.* Ed. Christina Murphy and Byron L. Stay. Mahwah, NJ: Erlbaum, 2006. Print.

Fleckenstein, Kristie. "A Matter of Perspective: Cartesian Perspectivalism and the Testing of English Studies." *JAC* 28 (2008): 85–121. Print.

Fleischer, Cathy. *Teachers Organizing for Change: Making Literacy Everybody's Business.* Urbana, IL: NCTE, 2000. Print.

Fleming, David. "Rhetoric as a Course of Study." *College English* 61.2 (1998): 109-129. Print.

Flower, Linda. "Cognition, Context, and Theory Building." *College Composition and Communication* 40 (1979): 282–311. Print.

Flowerdew, John. "Problems in Writing for Scholarly Publication in English: The Case of Hong Kong." *Journal of Second Language Writing* 8.3 (1999): 243–64. Print.

Flowerdew, John, and Yongyan Li. "English or Chinese? The Trade-off between Local and International Publication among Chinese Academics in the Humanities and Social Sciences." *Journal of Second Language Writing* 18.1 (2009): 1–16. Print.

Foertsch, Julie. "Where Cognitive Psychology Applies." *Written Communication* 12.3 (1995): 360–83. Print.

Ford, Julie Dyke. "Knowledge Transfer across Disciplines: Tracking Rhetorical Strategies from a Technical Communications Classroom to an Engineering Classroom." *IEEE* 47.4 (2004): 301–45. Print.

———. "Knowledge Transfer across Disciplines: Tracking Rhetorical Strategies from Technical Communication to Engineering Contexts." Diss. New Mexico State U, 1995. Print.

Fowler, Charlotte. "Archive." Glossary of Library and Internet Terms. U of South Dakota, 9 Jan. 2001. Web. 12 Aug. 2009.

Fox, Tom. *Defending Access: A Critique of Standards in Higher Education.* Portsmouth, NH: Heinemann Boynton/Cook, 1999. Print.

François, Frédéric. "Le fonctionalisme en syntaxe." *Langue française* 35 (1977): 6–25. Print.

Frazier, Dan. "First Steps beyond First Year: Coaching Transfer After FYC." *WPA: Writing Program Administration* 33.3 (2010): 34–57. Print.

Fulkerson, Richard. "Composition at the Turn of the Twenty-first Century." *College Composition and Communication* 56 (2005): 654–87. Print.

———. "Composition Theory in the Eighties: Axiological Consensus and Paradigmatic Diversity." *College Composition and Communication* 41 (1990): 409–29. Print.

———. "Four Philosophies of Composition." *College Composition and Communication* 30 (1979): 343–48. Print.

Gage, John T. "On 'Rhetoric' and 'Composition.'" *An Introduction to Composition Studies.* John T. Gage and Erika Lindemann, Eds. New York: Oxford UP, 1991. 15-32. Print.

Gagné, E. D. *The Cognitive Psychology of School Learning.* Boston: Little, Brown, 1985. Print.

Gaillet, Lynée Lewis. "Archival Survival: Navigating Historical Research." Ramsey et al. 28–39.

Gallagher, Chris. "Being There: (Re)Making the Assessment Scene." *College Composition and Communication* 62.3 (2011): 450–77. Print.

Gebhardt, Richard C. "Balancing Theory with Practice in the Training of Writing Teachers." *College Composition and Communication* 28.2 (1977): 134–40. Print.

———. "Unifying Diversity in the Training of Writing Teachers." *Training the New Teacher of College Composition.* Ed. Charles Bridges. Urbana, IL: NCTE, 1986. 1–12. Print.

Gee, James Paul. "Literacy, Discourse, and Linguistics: Introduction." *Journal of Education* 171.1 (1989): 5–17. Print.

Geertz, Clifford. *Works and Lives: The Anthropologist as Author.* Stanford, CA: Stanford UP, 1988. Print.

Geller, Anne Ellen, Michele Eodice, Frankie Condon, Meg Carroll, and Elizabeth H. Boquet. *The Everyday Writing Center: A Community of Practice.* Logan: Utah State UP, 2007. Print.

Gentner, D., & Toupin, C. Systematicity and Surface Similarity in the Development of Analogy. *Cognitive Science* 10.3 (1986). 277-300. Print.

George, Diana. "From Analysis to Design: Visual Communication in the Teaching of Writing." *College Composition and Communication* 54.1 (2002): 11–39. Print.

———, ed. *Kitchen Cooks, Plate Twirlers and Troubadours: Writing Program Administrators Tell Their Stories.* Portsmouth, NH: Boynton/Cook, 1999. Print.

Gere, Anne Ruggles, Laura Aull, Timothy Green, and Anne Porter. "Assessing the Validity of Directed Self-Placement at a Large University. *Assessing Writing* 15.3 (2010): 154–76. Print.

Giberson, Greg A., and Thomas A. Moriarty. *What We Are Becoming: Developments in Undergraduate Writing Majors.* Logan: Utah State UP. 2010. Print.

Gick, Mary, and K. J. Holyoak. "Schema Induction and Analogical Transfer." *Cognitive Psychology* 15 (1983): 1–38. Print.

Gillam, Alice. "The Call to Research: Early Representations of Writing Center Research." Gillespie et al. 3–21.

———. Introduction. Gillespie et al. xv–xxiv.

Gillespie, Paula, Alice Gillam, Lady Falls Brown, and Byron Stay, eds. *Writing Center Research: Extending the Conversation*, Mahwah, NJ: Erlbaum, 2002. Print.

Glau, Gregory R. "Stretch at 10: A Progress Report on Arizona State University's Stretch Program." *Journal of Basic Writing* 26 (2007): 30–48. Print.

———. "The 'Stretch Program': Arizona State University's New Model of University-Level Basic Writing Instruction." *WPA: Writing Program Administration* 20.1–2 (1996): 79–91. Print.

Glenn, Cheryl. *Unspoken: A Rhetoric of Silence.* Carbondale: Southern Illinois UP, 2004. Print.

Goffman, Erving. "Footing." *Terms of Talk.* Philadelphia: U of Pennsylvania P, 1981. 124–151. Print.

Goffman, Erving. *Interaction Ritual.* New York: Pantheon, 1967. Print.

Goffman, Erving. "On Face-Work: An Analysis of Ritual Elements in Social Interaction." *Psychiatry* 18 (1955): 213-31. Print.

Goldblatt, Eli. *Because We Live Here: Sponsoring Literacy beyond the College Curriculum.* Cresskill, NJ: Hampton, 2007. Print.

Goleman, Judith. "Educating Literacy Instructors: Practice versus Expression." Pytlik and Liggett 86–96.

Goody, Jack. *The Domestication of the Savage Mind.* Cambridge: Cambridge UP, 1977. Print.

Gottschalk, Katherine K. "Preparing Graduate Students across the Curriculum to Teach Writing." Pytlik and Liggett 135–46.

Gottschalk, Katherine, and Keith Hjortshoj. *The Elements of Teaching Writing: A Resource for Instructors in All Disciplines.* Bedford/St. Martin's Professional Resources. Boston: Bedford/St. Martin's, 2004. Print.

Graves, Donald H., and Bonnie S. Sunstein, eds. *Portfolio Portraits.* Portsmouth, NH: Heinemann, 1992. Print.

Graves, Richard L. *Rhetoric and Composition: A Sourcebook for Teachers and Writers.* Montclair, NJ: Boynton/Cook, 1984. Print.

Gray-Rosendale, Laura. *Rethinking Basic Writing: Exploring Identity, Politics and Community in Interaction.* Mahwah, NH: Erlbaum, 2001. Print.

Greenberg, Karen. "Reply to Ira Shor." *Journal of Basic Writing* 16 (1997): 90–94. Print.

Grego, Rhonda, and Nancy Thompson. "Repositioning Remediation: Renegotiating Composition's Work in the Academy." *College Composition and Communication* 47 (1996): 62–84. Print.

Griffin, Jo Ann, Daniel Keller, Iswari P. Pandey, Anne-Marie Pedersen, and Carolyn Skinner. "Local Practices, National Consequences: Surveying and (Re)Constructing Writing Center Identities." *Writing Center Journal* 26.2 (2006): 3–21. Print.

Grimm, Nancy Maloney. *Good Intentions: Writing Center Work for Postmodern Times.* Portsmouth, NH: Boynton/Cook, 1999. Print.

———. "In the Spirit of Service: Making Writing Center Research a 'Featured Character.'" Pemberton and Kinkead 41–57.

Guile, David, and Michael Young. "Transfer and Transition from Vocational Education: Some Theoretical Considerations." *Between School and Work: New Perspectives on Transfer and Boundary-crossing.* Ed. T. Tuomi-Grohn and Yrge Engestrom. New York: Pergamon, 2003. 63–81. Print.

Gunner, Jeanne. "Doomed to Repeat It? A Needed Space for Critique in Historical Recovery." *Historical Studies of Writing Program Administration: Individuals, Communities, and the Formation of a Discipline.* Ed. Barbara L'Eplattenier and Lisa Mastrangelo. West Lafayette, IN: Parlor, 2004. 263–77. Print.

———. "Iconic Discourse: The Troubling Legacy of Mina Shaughnessy." *Journal of Basic Writing* 17 (1998): 25–43. Print.

———. "Identity and Location: A Study of WPA Models, Memberships, and Agendas." *WPA: Writing Program Administration* 22 (Spring 1999): 31–54. Print.

Gutierrez, K., B. Rymes, and J. A. Larson. "Script, Counterscript, and Underlife in the Classroom: James Brown versus *Brown v. Board of Education*." *Harvard Educational Review* 65 (1995): 445–71. Print.

Hackos, JoAnn T. *Managing Your Documentation Projects*. Wiley Technical Communication Library. New York: John Wiley & Sons, 1994. Print.

Hahn, Stephen. "On History: A Rebellious Take on African-American History." *Chronicle Review* 3 August 2009. Web. Accessed 4 August 2009.

Hairston, Maxine. "The Winds of Change: Thomas Kuhn and the Revolution in the Teaching of Writing." *College Composition and Communication* 33 (1982): 76–88. Print.

Halbritter, Bump, and Julie Lindquist. "LiteracyCorps Michigan: Documenting Living Stories of Community and Access." Abstract. *The WAC Clearinghouse*. The Research Exchange, 3 Apr. 2009. Date Accessed 2 March 2011. Web.

Hamer, Philip M., ed. *A Guide to Archives and Manuscripts in the United States*. New Haven: Yale UP, 1961. Print.

Handa, Carolyn, ed. *Digital Rhetoric, Digital Literacy, Computers, and Composition*. Spec. issues of *Computers and Composition* 18.1 and 18.2 (2001). Print.

———. *Visual Rhetoric in a Digital World: A Critical Sourcebook*. New York: Bedford/St. Martin's, 2004. Print.

Hanson, Susan. "Critical Auto/Ethnography: A Constructive Approach to Research in the Composition Classroom." Stephen Brown and Dobrin 183–201.

Haraway, Donna J. *Simians, Cyborgs, and Women: The Reinvention of Nature*. New York: Routledge, 1991. Print.

Haring-Smith, Tori. "The Importance of Theory in the Training of Teaching Assistants." *ADE Bulletin* 82 (1995): 33–39. Print.

Harklau, Linda, Kay M. Losey, and Meryl Siegal, eds. *Generation 1.5 Meets College Composition: Issues in the Teaching of Writing to U.S.–Educated Learners of ESL*. Mahwah, NJ: Erlbaum, 1999. Print.

Harrington, Susanmarie. "Re: Professional Question for You." Message to Rita Malenczyk. 24 Jan. 2011. E-mail.

Harrington, Susanmarie, and Linda Adler-Kassner. "The Dilemma That Still Counts: Basic Writing at a Political Crossroads." *Journal of Basic Writing* 17 (1998): 3–24. Print.

Harris, Jeannette. "Review: Reaffirming, Reflecting, Reforming: Writing Center Scholarship Comes of Age." *College English* 63.5 (2001): 662–68. Print.

Harris, Joseph. *A Teaching Subject: Composition since 1966*. Upper Saddle River, NJ: Prentice-Hall, 1997. Print.

Harris, Muriel. "Diverse Research Methodologies at Work for Diverse Audiences: Shaping the Writing Center to the Institution." *The Writing Program Administrator as Researcher: Inquiry in Action and Reflection*. Ed. Shirley K. Rose and Irwin Weiser. Portsmouth, NH: Boynton/Cook. 1999. 1–17. Print.

———. "Writing Center Administration: Making Local, Institutional Knowledge in Our Writing Centers." Gillespie et al. 75–89.

Haskell, Robert. *Transfer of Learning: Cognition, Instruction, and Reasoning*. San Diego: Academic, 2001. Print.

Haswell, Rich. "NCTE/CCCC's Recent War on Scholarship." *Written Communication* 22.2 (2005). 198-223. Print.

Haswell, Richard H. *Gaining Ground in College Writing: Tales of Development and Interpretation*. Dallas: Southern Methodist UP, 1991. Print.

Haswell, Rich, and Glenn Blalock. *CompPile*, 28 Sept. 2009. Accessed 25 September 2009. Web.

Hatano, Giyoo, and James Greeno. "Commentary: Alternative Perspectives on Transfer and Transfer Studies." *International Journal of Educational Research* 31 (1999): 645–54. Print.

Hawisher, Gail E., and Cynthia L. Selfe, eds. *CCCC Bibliography on Composition and Rhetoric, 1991.* Carbondale: Southern Illinois UP, 1993. Print.

———. *CCCC Bibliography on Composition and Rhetoric, 1992.* Carbondale: Southern Illinois UP, 1994. Print.

———. *CCCC Bibliography on Composition and Rhetoric, 1993.* Carbondale: Southern Illinois UP, 1995. Print.

———. *CCCC Bibliography on Composition and Rhetoric, 1994.* Carbondale: Southern Illinois UP, 1996. Print.

———. *Global Literacies and the World Wide Web.* New York: Routledge, 2000. Print.

———, series eds. New Dimensions in Computers and Composition. Cresskill, NJ: Hampton. Print.

Hawisher, Gail E., and Cynthia L. Selfe with Yi-Huey Guo, and Lu Liu. "Globalization and Agency: Designing and Redesigning the Literacies of Cyberspace." *College English* 68 (July 2006): 619–36. Print.

Hawisher, Gail E., and Patricia Sullivan, eds. *Eloquent Images: Word and Image in the Age of New Media.* Cambridge, MA: MIT Press, 2003. Print.

Heath, Shirley Brice. *Ways With Words: Language, Life, and Work in Communities and Classrooms.* New York: Cambridge UP, 1983. Print.

Herndl, Carl G., and Adela C. Licona. "Shifting Agency: Agency, Kairos, and the Possibilities of Social Action." *Communicative Practices in Workplaces and the Professions.* Ed. Mark Zachry and Charlotte Thralls. Amityville, NY: Baywood, 2007. 133–53. Print.

Herrington, Anne. *Persons in Process.* Bloomington, IN: NCTE, 2000. Print.

Hesse, Doug. "Re: Writing Intensive Course Criteria." Online posting. WPA-L, 11 Oct. 2010. Web. 15 Feb. 2011.

Hesse, Doug. "The Place of Creative Writing in Composition Studies." *CCC* 62.1 (2010): 31-52. Print.

———. "Teachers as Students, Reflecting Resistance." *College Composition and Communication* 44.2 (1993): 224-231. Print.

Hillocks, George. *Teaching Writing as Reflective Practice.* New York: Teachers College Press, 1995. Print.

Hochstetler, Sarah. "The Preparation of Preservice Secondary English Teachers in Writing Instruction: A Case Study of Three California Colleges' Education Programs." *Action in Teacher Education* 29.2 (2007): 70–79. Print.

Hogg, Charlotte. *From the Garden Club: Rural Women Writing Community.* Lincoln: U of Nebraska P, 2006. Print.

Holdstein, Deborah. *College Composition and Communication* 56.3 (2005): 405-409. Print.

Holdstein, Deborah, and Andrea Greenbaum, eds. *Judaic Perspectives in Rhetoric and Composition.* Cresskill, NJ: Hampton, 2008. Print.

Horner, Bruce. *Terms of Work in Composition: A Materialist Critique.* Albany, NY: State University of New York P, 2000. Print.

Hughes, Bradley, Paula Gillespie, and Harvey Kail. "What They Take with Them: Findings from the Peer Tutor Alumni Research Project." *Writing Center Journal* 30.2 (2010): 12–46. Print.

Hult, Christine. "The Scholarship of Administration." *Resituating Writing: Constructing and Administering Writing Programs.* Joseph Janangelo and Kristine Hansen, Eds. Portsmouth, NH: Boynton/Cook, 1995. 119-131. Print.

Hunt, Doug. *Misunderstanding the Assignment: Teenage Students, College Writing and the Pains of Growth.* Portsmouth, NH: Boynton/Cook, 2002. Print.

Huot, Brian. Opinion: "Consistently Inconsistent: Business and the Spellings Commission Report on Higher Education." *College English* 69 (2007): 512–25. Print.

———. *(Re)Articulating Writing Assessment for Teaching and Learning.* Logan: Utah State UP, 2002. Print.

Huot, Brian, and Peggy O'Neill, eds. *Assessing Writing: A Critical Sourcebook.* Boston: Bedford/St. Martin's; Urbana, IL: NCTE, 2009. Print.

Ianetta, Melissa. "If Aristotle Ran the Writing Center: Classical Rhetoric and Writing Center Administration." *Writing Center Journal* 24.2 (2004): 37–59. Print.

Ianetta, Melissa, Linda Bergmann, Lauren Fitzgerald, Carol Peterson Havilland, Lisa Lebduska, and Mary Wislocki. "Polylog: Are Writing Center Directors Writing Program Administrators?" *Composition Studies* 34.2 (2006): 11–42. Print.

Inoue, Asao. Handout. 2005. Print.

Jackson, Rebecca, Carrie Leverenz, and Joe Law. "(Re)Shaping the Profession: Graduate Courses in Writing Center Theory, Practice, and Administration." Pemberton and Kinkead 130–50.

Janangelo, Joseph, and Kristine Hansen, eds. *Resituating Writing: Constructing and Administering Writing Programs.* Portsmouth, NH: Boynton/Cook, 1995. Print.

Jarratt, Susan, K. Mack, A. Sartor, and S. E. Watson. *Pedagogical Memory and the Transferability of Writing Knowledge: An Interview-based Study of UCI Juniors and Seniors.* 27 April 2008. Web. 27 Accessed 9 October 2009.

Jaxon, Kim. "And Now a Word from the Sponsors: The University, High School, and Student Identity." CCCC conference presentation, 2003.

Jewitt, Carey, and Gunther Kress. *Multimodal Literacy.* New York: Peter Lang, 2003. Print.

Johanek, Cindy. *Composing Research: A Contextualist Paradigm for Rhetoric and Composition.* Logan: Utah State UP, 2000. Print.

Johns, Ann M. "Interpreting an English Competency Examination: The Frustration of an ESL Science Student." *Written Communication* 8.1 (1991): 379–401. Print.

———. "Too Much on Our Plates: A Response to Terry Santos' 'Ideology in Composition: L1 and ESL.'" *Journal of Second Language Writing* 2.1 (1993): 83–88. Print.

Johnson, Nan. "Autobiography of an Archivist." Ramsey et al. 290–300.

Johnson-Eilola, Johndan, and Stuart Selber. *Central Works in Technical Communication.* New York: Oxford UP, 2004. Print.

Judd, C. H. "The Relation of Special Training to General Intelligence." *Educational Review* 36 (1908): 28–42. Print.

Kahn, Seth. "Ethnographic Writing as Grassroots Democratic Action." *Composition Studies* 31.1 (2003): 63–81. Print.

Kail, Harvey, ed. *Kenneth Bruffee and the Brooklyn Plan.* Spec. issue of *Writing Center Journal* 28.2 (2008): 1–116. Print.

Kairos: A Journal of Rhetoric, Technology, and Pedagogy. Web.

Katz, Susan M. *The Dynamics of Writing Review: Opportunities for Growth and Change in the Workplace.* ATTW Contemporary Studies in Technical Communication. Stamford, CN: Ablex, 1998. Print.

Kaufman, Janet E. "Language, Inquiry, and the Heart of Learning: Reflection in an English Methods Course." *English Education* 36.3 (2004): 174–91. Print.

Kendall, Connie, Darci Thoune, and Deborah Kirkman. Kentucky Assessment Narrative. WPA Assessment Gallery Models, 2010. Web. Accessed 18 February 2011.

Kennedy, Mary M. *Learning to Teach Writing: Does Teacher Education Make a Difference?* New York: Teachers College Press, 1998. Print.

Kent, Thomas. "The 'Remapping' of Professional Writing." *Journal of Business and Technical Communication* 21.1 (2007): 12–14. Print.

Kiefer, Kate, and Aaron Leff. "Client-Based Writing about Science: Immersing Science Students in Real Writing Contexts." *Across the Disciplines* 5 (2008). Web. 3 Apr. 2009.

King, Kendall, and Alison Mackey. *The Bilingual Edge: Why, When and How to Teach Your Child a Second Language.* New York: HarperCollins, 2007. Print.

Kinkead, Joyce, and Jeanette Harris. "What's Next for Writing Centers?" *Writing Center Journal* 20.2 (2000): 23–24. Print.

Kirsch, Gesa, and Liz Rohen, eds. *Beyond the Archives.* Bloomington: Southern Illinois UP, 2008. Print.

Kitzhaber, Albert R. *Rhetoric in American Colleges, 1850–1900.* Dallas: Southern Methodist UP, 1990. Print.

Kobayashi, Hiroe, and Carol Rinnert. "Effects of First Language on Second Language Writing: Translation versus Direct Composition." *Language Learning* 42.2 (1992): 157–313. Print.

Konkola, R. "Boundary-zone Activity as a Model for Collaboration and Developmental Transfer between School and Work." *Transferability, Flexibility and Mobility as Targets of Vocational Education and Training.* Eds. F. Achtenhagen & P-O. Thång. Proceeding of the Final Conference of the COST Action A11, Gothenburg, June, 13th -16th, 2002. 4.

Kostelnick, Charles, and David D. Roberts. *Designing Visual Language: Strategies for Professional Communicators.* Allyn & Bacon Series in Technical Communication. Boston: Allyn & Bacon, 1998. Print.

Kress, Gunther. "'English at the Crossroads': Rethinking Curricula of Communication in the Context of the Turn to the Visual." *Passions, Pedagogies, and 21st Century Technologies.* Ed. Gail E. Hawisher and Cynthia L. Selfe. Logan: Utah State UP, 1999. 66–88. Print.

———. *Literacy in the New Media Age.* London: Routledge, 2003. Print.

Kroll, Barbara. "The Composition of a Life in Composition." *On Second Language Writing.* Ed. Tony Silva and Paul Kei Matsuda. Mahwah, NJ: Erlbaum, 2001. 1–16. Print.

———, ed. *Second Language Writing: Research Insights for the Classroom.* New York: Cambridge UP, 1990. Print.

Kutney, Joshua. "Will Writing Awareness Transfer to Writing Performance?" *College Composition and Communication* 59.2 (2007): 276–79. Print.

Lalicker, William. "A Basic Introduction to Basic Writing Program Structures: A Baseline and Five Alternatives." *BWe: Basic Writing E-journal.* Accessed 10 June 2009. Web.

Langer, E. J. *Mindfulness.* Reading, MA: Addison-Wesley, 1989. Print.

Lassiter, Luke Eric. *The Chicago Guide to Collaborative Ethnography.* Chicago: U of Chicago P, 2005. Print.

Lassiter, Luke Eric, Hurley Goodall, Elizabeth Campbell, and Michelle Natasya Johnson. *The Other Side of Middletown: Exploring Muncie's African American Community.* Walnut Creek, CA: AltaMira, 2004. Print.

Latterell, Catherine. "Training the Workforce: An Overview of GTA Education Curricula." *Writing Program Administration* 19.3 (1996): 7–23. Print.

Laurence, Patricia, et al. "Symposium on Basic Writing, Conflict and Struggle, and the Legacy of Mina Shaughnessy." *College English* 55 (1993): 879–903. Print.

Lave, Jean. "Situated Learning in Communities of Practice." *Perspectives on Socially Shared Cognition.* Ed. L. Resnick, J. Levine, and S. E. Teasley. Washington, DC: APA, 1991. 63–82. Print.

Lawless, Elaine J. *Women Escaping Violence: Empowerment Through Narrative.* Columbia, MO: University of Missouri P, 2001. Print.

Lay, Mary M., and William M. Karis. *Collaborative Writing in Industry: Investigations in Theory and Practice.* Technical Communication. Farmingdale, NY: Baywood, 1991. Print.

Leaker, Cathy and Heather Ostman. "Composing Knowledge: Writing, Rhetoric and Reflection in Prior Learning Assessment." *College Composition and Communication* 61.4 (June 2010): 691-717. Print.

L'Eplattenier, Barbara E. "An Argument for Archival Research Methods: Thinking Beyond Methodology." *College English* 72.1 (2009) 67–79. Print.

L'Eplattenier, Barbara, and Lisa Mastrangelo, eds. *Historical Studies of Writing Program Administration: Individuals, Communities, and the Formation of a Discipline*. West Lafayette, IN: Parlor, 2004. Print.

Lerner, Neal. *The Idea of a Writing Laboratory*. Carbondale: Southern Illinois UP, 2009. Print.

———. "Introduction to a List of Dissertations and Theses on Writing Centers, 1924–2008." *Writing Lab Newsletter* 33.7 (2009): 6–9. Print.

———. "Rejecting the Remedial Brand: The Rise and Fall of the Dartmouth Writing Clinic. " *College Composition and Communication* 59 (2007): 13–35. Print.

———. "Seeking Knowledge about Writing Centers in Numbers, Talk, and Archives." *Writing at the Center: Proceedings of the 2004 Thomas R. Watson Conference*. Ed. JoAnn Griffin, Carol Mattingly, and Michele Eodice. Emmetsburg, MD: International Writing Centers Association Press, 2007. 55–90. Print.

———. "Situated Learning in the Writing Center." Macauley and Mauriello 53–73.

———. "Writing Center Assessment: Searching for the 'Proof' of Our Effectiveness." Pemberton and Kinkead 58–73.

Lettner-Rust, Heather G., et al. "Writing beyond the Curriculum: Transition, Transfer, and Transformation." *Across the Disciplines* 4 (2007). Web. 3 Apr. 2009.

Li, Yongyan, and John Flowerdew. "Shaping Chinese Novice Scientists' Manuscripts for Publication." *Journal of Second Language Writing* 16.2 (2007): 100–17. Print.

Liggett, Sarah, Kerri Jordan, and Steve Price. "Mapping Knowledge-Making in Writing Center Research: A Taxonomy of Methodologies." *Writing Center Journal* 31.2 (2011): 50-88. Print.

Lindemann, Erika, ed. *CCCC Bibliography of Composition and Rhetoric, 1987*. Carbondale: Southern Illinois UP, 1990. Print.

———. *CCCC Bibliography of Composition and Rhetoric, 1988*. Carbondale: Southern Illinois UP, 1991. Print.

———. *CCCC Bibliography of Composition and Rhetoric, 1989*. Carbondale: Southern Illinois UP, 1991. Print.

———. *CCCC Bibliography of Composition and Rhetoric, 1990*. Carbondale: Southern Illinois UP, 1992. Print.

———. *The Longman Bibliography of Composition and Rhetoric, 1984–85*. Longman Series in College Composition and Communication. White Plains, NY: Longman, 1987. Print.

———. *The Longman Bibliography of Composition and Rhetoric, 1986*. Longman Series in College Composition and Communication. White Plains, NY: Longman, 1988. Print.

Lindquist, Julie. *A Place to Stand: Politics and Persuasion in a Working Class Bar*. Oxford: Oxford UP, 2002. Print.

Lobato, Joanne. "Alternative Perspectives on the Transfer of Learning: History, Issues, and Challenges for Future Research." *Journal of Learning Sciences* 15.4 (2006): 431–49. Print.

———. "How Design Experiments can Inform a Rethinking of Transfer and Vice Versa." *Educational Researcher* 32.1 (2003). 17-20. Print.

Lofty, John. *Time to Write: The Influence of Time and Culture on Learning to Write*. Albany: State U of New York P, 1992. Print.

Long, Mark C., Jennifer H. Holberg, and Marcy M. Taylor. "Beyond Apprenticeship: Graduate Students, Professional Development Programs and the Future(s) of English Studies." *WPA: Writing Program Administration* 20.1-2 (1996): 66–78. Print.

Lu, Min-Zhan. "Conflict and Struggle: The Enemies or Preconditions of Basic Writing?" *College English* 54 (1992): 887–913. Print.

———. "The Ethics of Reading Critical Ethnography." Stephen Brown and Dobrin, 285-298. Print.

———. "Redefining the Legacy of Mina Shaughnessy: A Critique of the Politics of Linguistic Innocence." *Journal of Basic Writing* 10 (1991): 26–39. Print.

Lunsford, Andrea, and Lahoucine Ouzgane, eds. *Crossing Borderlands: Composition and Postcolonial Studies*. Pittsburgh: U of Pittsburgh P, 2004. Print.

Lunsford, Andrea. "Composing Ourselves: Politics, Commitment, and the Teaching of Writing." *College Composition and Communication* 41.1 (1990): 71-82. Print.

Lunsford, Karen, ed. *Writing Technologies and Writing across the Curriculum: Current Lessons and Future Trends*. Spec. issue of *Across the Disciplines* 6 (2009). Web. 3 Apr. 2009.

Lutz, Jean A., and C. Gilbert Storms. *The Practice of Technical and Scientific Communication: Writing in Professional Contexts*. Stamford, CT: Ablex, 1998. Print.

Lynne, Patricia. *Coming to Terms: A Theory of Writing Assessment*. Logan: Utah State UP, 2004. Print.

Macauley, William J., Jr., and Nicholas Mauriello, eds. *Marginal Words, Marginal Work? Tutoring the Academy in the Work of Writing Centers*. Creskill, NJ: Hampton, 2007. Print.

Mack, Nancy, and James Zebroski. "Ethnographic Writing for Critical Consciousness." *Social Issues in the English Classroom: Theory and Practice*. Ed. C. Mark Hurlbert and Samuel Totten. Urbana, IL: NCTE, 1992. Print.

Maimon, Elaine P. "It Takes a Campus to Teach a Writer: WAC and the Reform of Undergraduate Education." McLeod and Soven 16–31.

Marcus, George, and Michael Fischer. *Anthropology as Cultural Critique: An Experimental Moment in the Human Sciences*. Chicago: U of Chicago P, 1986. Print.

Marshall, Margaret J. *Response to Reform: Composition and the Professionalization of Teaching*. Carbondale: Southern Illinois UP, 2004. Print.

Martin, Wanda, and Charles Paine. "Mentors, Models, and Agents of Change: Veteran TAs Preparing Teachers of Writing." Pytlik and Liggett 222–32.

Martino, Marta. "Issues in ESL: Give Credit Where Credit Is Due." *College ESL* 2.1 (1992): 20–22. Print.

Massey, Lance. "Just What Are We Talking About? Disciplinary Struggle and the Ethnographic Imaginary." Stephen Brown and Dobrin 259–81.

Matalene, Carolyn. *Worlds of Writing: Teaching and Learning in Discourse Communities of Work*. New York: McGraw-Hill College, 1989. Print.

Matsuda, Paul Kei. "Basic Writing and Second Language Writers: Toward an Inclusive Definition." *Journal of Basic Writing* 22.2 (2003): 67–89. Print.

———. "Composition Studies and ESL Writing: A Disciplinary Division of Labor." *College Composition and Communication* 50.4 (1999): 699–721. Print.

———. "Embracing Linguistic Diversity in the Intellectual Work of WPAs." *WPA: Writing Program Administration* 33.1–2 (2009): 168–71. Print.

———. "The Myth of Linguistic Homogeneity in U.S. College Composition." *College English* 68.6 (2006): 637–51. Print.

———. "Proud to Be a Nonnative English Speaker." *TESOL Matters* 13.4 (2003): 15. Print.

———. "Situating ESL Writing in a Cross-Disciplinary Context." *Written Communication* 15.1 (1998): 99–121. Print.

Matsuda, Paul Kei, and Jeffrey Jablonski. "Beyond the L2 Metaphor: Towards a Mutually Transformative Model of ESL/WAC Collaboration." *Academic Writing* 1 (2000). Web. 30 Sept. 2009.

Matsuda, Paul Kei, and Aya Matsuda. "The Erasure of Resident ESL Writers." *Generation 1.5 in College Composition: Teaching Academic Writing to US–Educated Learners of ESL*. Ed. Mark Roberge, Meryl Siegal and Linda Harklau. London: Routledge, 2009. 50–64. Print.

———. "Globalizing Writing Studies: The Case of U.S. Technical Communication Textbooks. *Written Communication* 28.2 (2011): 172–92. Print.

Matsuda, Paul Kei, and Tony Silva. "Cross-Cultural Composition: Mediated Integration of US and International Students." *Composition Studies* 27.1 (1999): 15–30. Print.

Mattingly, Carol. *Water Drops from Women Writers: A Temperance Reader*. Carbondale: Southern Illinois UP, 2001. Print.

———. *Well-Tempered Women: Nineteenth-Century Temperance Rhetoric.* Carbondale: Southern Illinois UP, 2000. Print.

Mayers Tim. " Institutional Context." Blog Response to Scott Jascik, "What Direction for Rhet-Comp?" *Inside Higher Ed.* December 30, 2009. Web. Accessed 1 June 2011.

McCann, Thomas M., Larry R. Johannessen, and Bernard P. Ricca. *Supporting Beginning English Teachers: Research and Implications for Teacher Induction.* Urbana, IL: NCTE, 2005. Print.

McCarthy, Lucile. "A Stranger in Strange Lands: A College Student Writing across the Curriculum." *Research in the Teaching of English* 21.3 (1987): 233–65. Print.

McCutchen, Deborah, Paul Teske, and Catherine Bankston. "Writing and Cognition: Implications of the Cognitive Architecture for Learning to Write and Writing to Learn." *Handbook of Research on Writing: History, Society, School, Individual, Text.* Charles Bazerman, Ed. New York: Routledge, 2007. 451–70. Print.

McGee, Sharon James, and Carolyn Handa, eds. *Discord and Direction: The Postmodern Writing Program Administrator.* Logan: Utah State UP, 2005. Print.

McKay, Sandra. "ESL/Remedial English: Are They Different?" *English Language Teaching Journal* 35.3 (1981): 310–15. Print.

McKee, Heidi, and Danielle DeVoss. *Digital Writing Research: Technologies, Methodologies, and Ethical Issues.* Cresskill, NJ: Hampton, 2007. Print.

McKinney, Jackie Grutsch. "New Media Matters: Tutoring in the Late Age of Print." *Writing Center Journal* 29.2 (2009): 28-51. Print.

McLeod, Susan H. "The Future of WAC: Plenary Address, Ninth International Writing across the Curriculum Conference, May 2008 (Austin, Texas)." *Across the Disciplines* 5 (2008). Web. 3 Apr. 2009.

———. "WAC at Century's End: Haunted by the Ghost of Fred Newton Scott." *WPA: Writing Program Administration* 21.1 (1997): 67–73. Print.

McLeod, Susan H., Eric Miraglia, Margot Soven, and Christopher Thaiss, eds. *WAC for the New Millenium: Strategies for Continuing Writing-Across-the-Curriculum Programs.* Urbana: NCTE, 2001. Print.

McLeod, Susan H., and Margot Iris Soven, eds. *Composing a Community: A History of Writing across the Curriculum.* Lauer Series in Rhetoric and Composition. West Lafayette, IN: Parlor, 2006. Print.

McNenny, Gerri, and Sallyanne Fitzgerald. *Mainstreaming Basic Writers: Politics and Pedagogies of Access.* Mahwah, NJ: Erlbaum, 2001. Print.

Messick, S. "Validity." *Educational Measurement.* 3rd. ed. Ed. R. L. Linn. New York: American Council on Education and Macmillan, 1989. 13–104. Print.

Micciche, Laura. "More Than a Feeling: Disappointment and WPA Work." *College English* 64.4 (2002): 432-458. Print.

Michel, Anthony J. "From Theory to Theorizing: Rethinking the Graduate Introduction to Composition Course." Dobrin, *Don't Call It That* 183–99.

Miller, Hildy. "Postmasculinist Direction in Writing Program Administration." *WPA: Writing Program Administration* 20.1–2 (1996): 49–61. Print.

Miller, Richard E. "'Let's Do the Numbers': Comp Droids and the Prophets of Doom." *Profession* (1999): 96–105. Print.

Miller, Susan. *Textual Carnivals: The Politics of Composition.* Carbondale: Southern Illinois UP, 1993. Print.

Miller, Susan Kay, et al. "The Composition Practicum as Professional Development." Dobrin, *Don't Call It That* 67–81.

Miller, Thomas. *The Evolution of College English: Literacy Studies from the Puritans to the Postmoderns.* Pittsburgh: U of Pittsburgh P, 2010. Print.

———. *The Formation of College English: Rhetoric and Belles Lettres in the British Cultural Provinces.* Pittsburgh: U of Pittsburgh P, 1997. Print.

MLA Task Force. *Evaluating Scholarship for Tenure and Promotion.* Modern Language Association, 2007. Web. 21 Jan. 2007.

Moje, Elizabeth Birr. "A Call for New Research on New and Multi-Literacies." *Research in the Teaching of English* 43.4 (2009). 348-62. Print.

Monroe, Jonathan. *Local Knowledges, Local Practices: Writing in the Disciplines at Cornell.* Pittsburgh Series in Composition, Literacy and Culture. Pittsburgh: U of Pittsburgh P, 2006. Print.

Morgaine, Wendy. Personal communication to Kathleen Blake Yancey. 20 Sept. 2010.

Morgan, Meg. "The GTA Experience: Grounding, Practicing, Evaluating, and Reflecting." *The Writing Program Administrator's Resource: A Guide to Reflective Institutional Practice.* Ed. Stuart C. Brown and Theresa Enos. Mahwah, NJ: Erlbaum, 2002. 393–410. Print.

Morris, Sammie L., and Shirley K. Rose. "Invisible Hands: Recognizing Archivists' Work to Make Records Accessible." Ramsey et al. 51–78.

Mortensen, Peter, and Gesa Kirsch, eds. *Ethics and Representation in Qualitative Studies of Literacy.* Urbana, IL: NCTE, 1996. Print.

Moss, Beverly. *A Community Test Arises: A Literate Text and a Literacy Tradition in African American Churches.* Cresskill, NJ: Hampton, 2003. Print.

Mullin, Joan A. "Writing Centers and WAC." *WAC for the New Millennium: Strategies for Continuing Writing-across-the-Curriculum Programs.* McLeod et al. 179–99.

Murphy, Sandra. At Last: "Culture and Consequences: The Canaries in the Coal Mine." *Research in the Teaching of English* 42.2 (2007): 228–44. Print.

Murphy, Sandra, and Kathleen Blake Yancey. "Construct and Consequence: Validity in Writing Assessment." *A Handbook of Research on Writing: History, Society, School, Individual, Text.* Ed. Charles Bazerman. Mahwah, NJ: Erlbaum, 2007: 365–87. Print.

Murphy, Susan Wolff. "'Just Chuck It: I Mean, Don't Get Fixed on It': Self-Presentation in Writing Center Discourse." *Writing Center Journal* 26.1 (2006): 62–82. Print.

Murray, Donald M. "The Listening Eye: Reflections on the Writing Conference." *College English* 41.1 (1979): 13-18. Print.

Myers-Breslin, Linda, ed. *Administrative Problem-Solving for Writing Programs and Writing Centers: Scenarios in Effective Program Management.* Urbana, IL: NCTE, 1999. Print.

National Historical Publications and Records Commission. *Directory of Archives and Manuscript Repositories in the United States.* 2nd ed. New York: Oryx, 1988. Print.

Nattinger, James R. "Second Dialect and Second Language in the Composition Class." *TESOL Quarterly* 12 (1978): 77–84. Print.

NCTE. "Fostering High-Quality Formative Assessment: An NCTE Policy Research Brief." *Council Chronicle* 20.1 (2010). Accessed 18 February 2012. Web.

———. "The NCTE Definition of 21st Century Literacies." 30 Sept. 2009. Accessed 18 February 2012. Web.

NCTE and WPA. "NCTE-WPA White Paper on Writing Assessment in Colleges and Universities." 2008. Accessed 18 February 2012. Web.

Neaderhiser, Stephen, and Joanna Wolfe. "Between Technological Endorsement and Resistance: The State of Online Writing Centers." *Writing Center Journal* 29.1 (2009): 49–77. Print.

New London Group. "A Pedagogy of Multiliteracies: Designing Social Futures." *Harvard Educational Review* 66.1 (1996): 60–92. Print.

"New Writing Department Goal: Help All Students Graduate." *UCF Today.* April 29, 2010. Web. Accessed 9 June 2010.

Nicolas, Melissa, ed. *(E)Merging Identities: Graduate Students in the Writing Center.* Southlake, TX: Fountainhead, 2008. Print.

———. "Why There Is No 'Happy Ever After': A Look at the Stories and Images That Sustain Us." Macauley and Mauriello 1–17.

Noble, David. *The End of American History.* Minneapolis: U of Minnesota P, 1985. Print.

Nold, Ellen. "Fear and Trembling: A Humanist Approaches the Computer." *College Composition and Communication* 26.3 (1975): 269–73. Print.

North, Stephen M. "The Idea of a Writing Center." *College English* 46.5 (1984): 433–46. Print.

———. *The Making of Knowledge in Composition: Portrait of an Emerging Field.* Portsmouth, NH: Boynton/Cook, 1987. Print.

Novick, L. R. Analogical Transfer: Processes and Individual Differences. *Analogical Reasoning: Perspectives of Artificial Intelligence, Cognitive Science, and Philosophy.* Ed. D. H. Helman, Dordrecht, The Netherlands: Kluwer, 1988. Print.

Odell, Lee, and Dixie Goswami. *Writing in Nonacademic Settings.* New York: Guilford, 1985. Print.

Odom, Mary Lou, Michael Bernard-Donals, and Stephanie L. Kerschbaum. "Enacting Theory: The Practicum as the Site of Invention." Dobrin, *Don't Call It That* 214–37.

Oliver, Beverly. Personal communication to Kathleen Blake Yancey. 2011.

Olson, David R. "Literacy as Metalinguistic Activity." *Literacy and Orality,* Eds. David R. Olson and Nancy Torrance. Cambridge: Cambridge University Press, 1991. 251-70. Print.

Olson, Gary A. "Ideological Critique in Rhetoric and Composition." *Rhetoric and Composition as Intellectual Work.* Ed. Gary A. Olson. Carbondale: Southern Illinois UP, 2002. 81–90. Print.

O'Neill, P. *A Field of Dreams: Independent Writing Programs and the Future of Composition Studies.* Logan: Utah State UP, 2002. Print.

Ortmeier-Hooper, Christina. "English May Be My Second Language, but I'm Not 'ESL.'" *College Composition and Communication* 59.3 (2008): 389–419. Print.

Otte, George. Comments on basic writing. Online posting. WPA-L, 12 Feb. 1998. Web. Accessed 1 December 2010.

Otuya, Ebo. "The Foreign-Born Population of the 1990s: A Summary Profile." *Research Briefs* 5.6 (1994): 1–10. Print.

Paley, Karen. *I Writing: The Politics and Practice of Teaching First-Person Writing.* Carbondale: Southern Illinois UP, 2001. Print.

Paretti, Marie, and Katrina Powell, eds. *Assessing Writing.* Tallahassee: Association of Institutional Research, 2009. Print.

Parker, Robert B. "Writing Courses for Teachers: From Practice to Theory." *College Composition and Communication* 33.4 (1982): 411–19. Print.

Parks, Stephen. *Gravyland: Writing Beyond the Curriculum in the City of Brotherly Love.* Syracuse: Syracuse UP, 2010. Print.

———. Strategic Speculations on the Question of Value The Role of Community Publishing in English Studies. *College English* 71.5 (2009): 506-527. Print.

Parks, Steve, and Eli Goldblatt. "Writing beyond the Curriculum: Fostering New Collaborations in Literacy." *College English* 62.5 (2000): 584–606. Print.

Pea, Roy, and Jay Lemke. "Sharing and Reporting Video Work." *Guidelines for Video Research in Education: Recommendations from an Expert Panel.* Ed. Sharon L. Derry. Data Research and Development Center, July 2007. Web. 4 May 2009.

Peckham, Irv. "Online Challenge versus Offline ACT." *College Composition and Communication* 61.4 (2010): 718–46. Print.

Peeples, Tim. *Professional Writing and Rhetoric: Readings from the Field.* New York: Longman, 2003. Print.

Pemberton, Michael A., and Joyce Kinkead, eds. *The Center Will Hold: Critical Perspectives on Writing Center Scholarship.* Logan: Utah State UP, 2003. Print.

Perkins, Gavriel, and D. N. Salomon. *The Science and Art of Transfer.* 2007. Web. 10 Sept. 2008. Accessed 9 October 2009.

———. "Teaching for Transfer." *Educational Leadership* 46.1 (1989): 22–32. Print.

———. "Transfer of Learning." *International Encyclopedia of Education.* 2nd ed. 1992. Web. Accessed 9 October 2009.

Perl, Sondra, and Nancy Wilson. *Through Teacher's Eyes: Portraits of Writing Teachers at Work.* 2nd ed. Portland, ME: Calendar Islands, 1998. Print.

Perl, Sondra. "The Composing Processes of Unskilled College Writers." *Research in the Teaching of English* 13.4 (1979): 317-36. Print.

Petraglia, Joseph, ed. *Reconceiving Writing, Rethinking Writing Instruction.* Mahwah, NJ: Lawrence Erlbaum, 1996. Print.

Powell, Katrina M., et al. "Negotiating Resistance and Change: One Composition Program's Struggle Not to Convert." Pytlik and Liggett 121–34.

Pratt, Mary Louise. "The Arts of the Contact Zone." *Profession* 91 (1991): 33–40. Print.

Prenzel, M. and H. Mandl. "Transfer of Learning from a Constructivist Perspective." *Designing Environments for Constructive Learning.* Eds. T. M. Duffy, J. Lowyck and D. H. Jonassen. Berlin, Heidelberg: Springer, 1993. 315 – 29. Print.

Prior, Paul. *Writing/Disciplinarity: A Sociohistoric Account of Literate Activity in the Academy.* Mahwah, NJ: Erlbaum, 1998. Print.

Purcell-Gates, Victoria. *Other People's Words: The Cycle of Low Literacy.* Cambridge: Harvard UP, 1995. Print.

Pytlik, Betty P. "How Graduate Students Were Prepared to Teach Writing, 1850–1970." Pytlik and Liggett 3–16.

Pytlik, Betty P., and Sarah Liggett. *Preparing College Teachers of Writing: Histories, Theories, Programs, Practices.* New York: Oxford UP, 2002. Print.

Ramsey, Alexis E. "Viewing the Archive: The Hidden and the Digital Archive." Ramsey et al. 79–90.

Ramsey, Alexis E., Wendy B. Sharer, Barbara L'Eplattenier, and Lisa S. Mastrangelo, Eds. *Working in the Archives: Practical Research Methods for Rhetoric and Composition.* Carbondale: Southern Illinois UP, 2010. Print.

Rankin, Elizabeth. *Seeing Yourself as a Teacher: Conversations with Five New Teachers in a University Writing Program.* Urbana, IL: NCTE, 1994. Print.

Ray, Ruth. *The Practice of Theory: Teacher Research in Composition.* Urbana, IL: NCTE, 1993. Print.

Recchio, Thomas E. "Essaying TA Training." Pytlik and Liggett 254–65.

Reid, E. Shelley. "Teaching Writing Teachers Writing: Difficulty, Exploration, Reflection." *College Composition and Communication* 61.2 (2009): W197–W221. Print.

———. "Uncoverage in Composition Pedagogy." *Composition Studies* 32.1 (2004): 15–34. Print.

Reiss, Donna, Dickie Selfe, and Art Young, eds. *Electronic Communication across the Curriculum.* Urbana, IL: NCTE, 1998. Print.

———. "WAC Wired: Electronic Communication across the Curriculum." McLeod et al. 52–85.

Reuter, Yves and Dominique Lahanier-Reuter. "Presentation of a Few Concepts for Analyzing Writing in Relation to Academic Disciplines." *L1 Educational Studies in Language and Literature* 79.5 (2008): 47–57. Print.

Rhodes, Terry. Personal communication to Kathleen Blake Yancey. 20 Sept. 2008.

Rice, Jeff. "Conservative Writing Program Administrators (WPAs)." *The Writing Program Interrupted: Making Space for Critical Discourse.* Ed. Donna Strickland and Jeanne Gunner. Portsmouth, NH: Boynton/Cook Heinemann, 2009. 1–13. Print.

Rickly, Rebecca J., and Susanmarie Harrington. "Feminist Approaches to Mentoring Teaching Assistants." Pytlik and Liggett 108–20.

Ritter, Kelly. *Before Shaughnessy: Basic Writing at Yale and Harvard, 1920–1960.* Carbondale: Southern Illinois UP, 2009. Print.

———. "Before Mina Shaughnessy: Basic Writing at Yale, 1920–1960." *College Composition and Communication* 60 (2008): 12–45. Print.

———. "(En)Gendering the Archives for Basic Writing Research." In *Working in the Archives: Practical Research Methods for Rhetoric and Composition*. Barbara L'Eplattenier, Wendy Sharer, Lisa Mastrangelo, and Alexis Ramsey, Eds. Carbondale, IL: Southern Illinois University Press, 2009: 181-194. Print.

Roberge, Mark, Meryl Siegal, and Linda Harklau, eds. *Generation 1.5 in College Composition: Teaching Academic Writing to US–Educated Learners of ESL*. New York: Routledge, 2009. Print.

Rogers, Paul. *Methodological and Developmental Lessons from Longitudinal Studies of Writing across the College Span*. Working paper. U of California, Santa Barbara, 2006. Print.

Rogoff, Barbara. *Apprenticeship in Thinking: Cognitive Development in Social Context*. New York: Oxford UP, 1990. Print.

Rosaldo, Renato. *Culture and Truth: The Remaking of Social Analysis*. Boston: Beacon, 1989. Print.

Rose, Mike. *Lives on the Boundary: A Moving Account of the Struggles and Achievements of America's Educationally Underprepared*. New York: Free Press, 1989. Print.

———. *The Mind at Work: Valuing the Intelligence of the American Worker*. New York: Viking Penguin, 2004. Print.

Rose, Shirley K., and Margaret J. Finders. "Thinking Together: Developing a Reciprocal Reflective Model for Approaches to Preparing College Teachers of Writing." Pytlik and Liggett 75–85.

Rose, Shirley K., and Irwin Weiser, eds. *The Writing Program Administrator as Researcher: Inquiry in Action and Reflection*. Portsmouth, NH: Boynton/Cook Heinemann, 1999. Print.

———. *The Writing Program Administrator as Theorist: Inquiry in Action and Reflection*. Portsmouth, NH: Boynton/Cook Heinemann, 2002. Print.

Rowan, Karen. "All the Best Intentions: Graduate Student Administrative Professional Development in Practice." *Writing Center Journal* 29.1 (2009): 11–48. Print.

Roy, Alice M. "Alliance for Literacy: Teaching Non-native Speakers and Speakers of Nonstandard English Together." *College Composition and Communication* 35 (1984): 439–48. Print.

———. "ESL Concerns for Writing Program Administrators: Problems and Policies." *Writing Program Administration* 11 (1988): 17–28. Print.

Royer, Daniel J., and Roger Gilles. "Directed Self-Placement: An Attitude of Orientation." *College Composition and Communication* 50 (2002): 54–70. Print.

Ruby, Jay, ed. *A Crack in the Mirror: Reflexive Perspectives In Anthropology*. Philadelphia: U of Pennsylvania P, 1982. Print.

Rude, Carolyn D. *Technical Editing*. New York: Longman, 2002. Print.

Russell, David R. "Writing in Multiple Contexts: Vygotskian CHAT Meets the Phenomenology of Genre." *Traditions of Writing Research*. Ed. Charles Bazerman et al. London: Routledge, 2010. 353-64. Print.

———. "Activity Theory and Its Implications for Writing Instruction." *Reconceiving Writing, Rethinking Writing Instruction*. Ed. J. Petraglia. Hillsdale, NJ: Erlbaum, 1995. 61–78. Print.

———. "Introduction: WAC's Beginnings; Developing a Community of Change Agents." McLeod and Soven 3–15.

Russell, David, and A. Yanez. "Big Picture People Rarely Become Historians? Genre Systems and the Contradictions of General Education." *Writing Selves/Writing Societies*. Ed. Charles Bazerman and David Russell. WAC Clearinghouse, 2003. Web. Accessed 17 March 2009.

Rutz, Carol, and Nathan D. Grawe. "Pairing WAC and Quantitative Reasoning through Portfolio Assessment and Faculty Development." *Across the Disciplines* 6 (2009). Web. 28 Feb. 2011.

Sauer, Geoffrey. EServer Technical Communication Library. 28 Sept. 2009. Web. Accessed 1 March 2011.

Sauer, Geoffrey, David Dayton, and Carolyn D. Rude. "Bodies of Knowledge for Technical Communication: Paradigms and Possibilities." Web. Accessed 1 March 2011.

Savage, Gerald J., and Dale L. Sullivan. *Writing a Professional Life: Stories of Technical Communicators On and Off the Job*. Needham Heights, MA: Allyn & Bacon, 2001. Print.

Saxe, Geoffrey. "Transfer of Learning across Cultural Practices." *Cognition and Instruction* 6.4 (1989): 325–30. Print.

Schaafsma, David. *Eating on the Street: Teaching Literacy in a Multicultural Society*. Pittsburgh: U of Pittsburgh P, 1993. Print.

Schell, Eileen, and Patricia Stock. *Moving a Mountain: Transforming the Role of Contingent Faculty in Composition Studies and Higher Education*. Urbana, IL: NCTE, 2000. Print.

Scribner, Sylvia and Michael Cole. *The Psychology of Literacy*. London: Harvard University Press, 1981.

Schriver, Karen A. *Dynamics in Document Design*. Wiley Technical Communication Library. New York: John Wiley & Sons, 1997. Print.

Scott, Tony Scott. "Creating the Subject of Portfolios: Reflective Writing and the Conveyance of Institutional Prerogatives." *Written Communication* 22 (2005): 3–35. Print.

———. *Dangerous Writing: Understanding the Political Economy of Composition*. Logan, UT: Utah State UP, 2009. Print.

Segall, Mary T., and Robert A. Smart, eds. *Direct from the Disciplines: Writing across the Curriculum*. Portsmouth, NH: Boynton/Cook, 2005. Print.

Seitz, David. *Who Can Afford Critical Consciousness: Practicing a Pedagogy of Humility*. Cresskill, NJ: Hampton, 2004. Print.

Selber, Stuart A. *Multiliteracies for a Digital Age*. Carbondale: Southern Illinois UP, 2004. Print.

Selfe, Cynthia L. "The Movement of Air, the Breath of Meaning: Aurality and Multimodal Composing." *College Composition and Communication. College Composition and Communication* 60.4 (2009): 616-663. Print.

———. *Technology and Literacy in the Twenty-first Century: The Importance of Paying Attention*. Urbana, IL: NCTE, 1999. Print.

Selfe, Cynthia L., and Gail E. Hawisher. *Literate Lives in the Information Age: Narratives of Literacy from the United States*. Mahwah, NJ: Erlbaum, 2004. Print.

Severino, Carol, and Elizabeth Deifell. "Empowering L2 Tutoring: A Case Study of a Second Language Writer's Vocabulary Learning." *Writing Center Journal* 31.1 (2011): 25–55. Print.

Severino, Carol, Jeffrey Swenson, and Jia Zhu. "A Comparison of Online Feedback Requests by Non-mative English-Speaking and Native English-Speaking Writers." *Writing Center Journal* 29.1 (2009): 106–29. Print.

Shamoon, Linda, and Deborah Burns. "A Critique of Pure Tutoring." *Writing Center Journal* 15.2 (1995): 134–51. Print.

———. "Plagiarism, Rhetorical Theory, and the Writing Center: New Approaches, New Locations." Buranen and Roy 183–92.

Sharer, Wendy. *Vote and Voice: Women's Organizations and Political Literacy, 1915–1930*. Carbondale: Southern Illinois UP, 2007. Print.

Shaughnessy, Mina P. "Diving In: An Introduction to Basic Writing." *College Composition and Communication* 27 (1976): 234–239. Print.

———. *Errors and Expectations: A Guide for the Teacher of Basic Writing*. New York: Oxford UP, 1977. Print.

Shor, Ira. *Empowering Education*. Chicago: U of Chicago P, 1992. Print.

———. "Our Apartheid: Writing Instruction and Inequality. " *Journal of Basic Writing* 16 (1997): 91-104. Print.

Silva, Tony. "An Examination of Writing Program Administrators' Options for the Placement of ESL Students in First Year Writing Classes." *WPA: Writing Program Administration* 18.1–2 (1994): 37–43. Print.

———. "Toward an Understanding of the Distinct Nature of L2 Writing: The ESL Research and Its Implications." *TESOL Quarterly* 27.4 (1993): 657–77. Print.

Silva, Tony, Ilona Leki, and Joan Carson. "Broadening the Perspective of Mainstream Composition Studies: Some Thoughts from the Disciplinary Margins." *Written Communication* 14.3 (1997): 398–428. Print.

Slack, Jennifer Daryl, David James Miller, and Jeffrey Doak. "The Technical Communicator as Author: Meaning, Power, Authority." *Journal of Business & Technical Writing* 7.1 (1996): 12–36. Print.

Sledd, James. "Why the Wyoming Resolution Had to Be Emasculated: A History and a Quixotism." *JAC* 11.2 (1991): 269-281. Print.

Smagorinsky, Peter. *Research on Composition: Multiple Perspectives on Two Decades of Change.* New York: Teachers College Press, 2005. Print.

Smagorinsky, Peter, and Michael Smith. "The Nature of Knowledge in Composition and Literary Understanding: The Question of Specificity." *Review of Educational Research* 62.1 (1992): 279-305. Print.

Smagorinsky, Peter, and Melissa E. Whiting. *How English Teachers Get Taught: Methods of Teaching the Methods Class.* Urbana, IL: NCTE, 1995. Print.

Smit, David W. *The End of Composition Studies.* Carbondale: Southern Illinois UP, 2004. Print.

Soles, Derek. "A Comment on the *WPA Outcomes* Statement for First-Year Composition." *College English* 64 (2002): 377–78. Print.

Soliday, Mary. "From the Margins to the Mainstream: Reconceiving Remediation." *College Composition and Communication* 47 (1996): 85–100. Print.

———. *The Politics of Remediation: Institutional and Student Needs in Higher Education.* Pittsburgh: U of Pittsburgh P, 2002. Print.

Sommers, Nancy. "The Call of Research: A Longitudinal View of Writing Development." *CCC* 60.1 (2008). 152-64. Print.

———. "Revision Strategies of Student Writers and Experienced Adult Writers." *College Composition and Communication* 31 (1980): 378-88. Print.

Spilka, Rachel. "Orality and Literacy in the Workplace: Process- and Text-Based Strategies for Multiple-Audience Adaptation." *Journal of Business and Technical Communication* 4.1 (1990): 44–67. Print.

———. *Writing in the Workplace: New Research Perspectives.* Springfield: Southern Illinois UP, 1998. Print.

Spiro, R. J., and J. C. Jehng. "Cognitive Flexibility and Hypertext: Theory and Technology for the Nonlinear and Multidimensional Traversal of Complex Subject Matter." *Cognition, Education, and Multimedia: Exploring Ideas in High Technology.* Ed. D. N. Nix and R. J. Spiro. Hillsdale, NJ: Erlbaum, 1990. 163–205. Print.

Sprague, Jo, and Jody D. Nyquist. "A Developmental Perspective on the TA Role." *Preparing the Professoriate of Tomorrow to Teach.* Ed. Jody D. Nyquist et al. Dubuque, IA: Kendall/Hunt, 1991. 295–312. Print.

Stancliff, Michael, and Maureen Daly Goggin. "What's Theorizing Got to Do with It? Teaching Theory as Resourceful Conflict and Reflection in TA Preparation." *Writing Program Administration* 30.3 (2007): 11–28. Print.

Stenberg, Shari J. *Professing and Pedagogy: Learning the Teaching of English.* Urbana, IL: NCTE, 2005. Print.

Sternglass, Marilyn S. *Time to Know Them: A Longitudinal Study of Writing and Learning at the College Level.* Mahwah, NJ: Erlbaum, 1997. Print.

Strickland, Donna. "The Managerial Unconscious of Composition Studies." *Tenured Bosses and Disposable Teachers: Writing Instruction in the Managed University.* Marc Bousquet,

Tony Scott, and Leo Parascondola, Eds. Carbondale, IL: Southern Illinois UP, 2004. 46-56. Print.

Stygall, Gail, and Kathleen Murphy, eds. *CCCC Bibliography of Composition and Rhetoric, 1995*. Carbondale: Southern Illinois UP, 1999. Print.

Sullivan, Patricia A. "Ethnography and the Problem of the 'Other.'" Mortensen and Kirsch 97–114.

Sullivan, Patricia A., and James E. Porter. "Remapping Curricular Geography: Professional Writing in/and English." *Journal of Business and Technical Communication* 7.4 (1993): 389–422. Print.

Sunstein, B. S. *Composing a Culture: Inside a Summer Writing Program with High School Teachers*. Portsmouth, NH: Boynton/Cook, 1994. Print.

Swales, John. *Research Genres*. New York: Cambridge UP, 2004. Print.

Swales, John, and Christine Feak. *English in Today's Research World*. Ann Arbor: U of Michigan P, 2000. Print.

Taczak, Kara. "The Sixth Knowledge Domain: A Theory of Reflection." Forthcoming.

Tardy, Christine M. *Building Genre Knowledge*. West Lafayette, IN: Parlor, 2009. Print.

Tate, Gary. "Empty Pedagogical Space and Silent Students." *Left Margins: Cultural Studies and Composition Pedagogy*. Ed. Karen Fitts and Alan W. France. Albany: State U of New York P, 1995. 269–75. Print.

Tate, Gary, Amy Rupiper, and Kurt Schick, eds. *A Guide to Composition Pedagogies*. New York: Oxford UP, 2001. Print.

Taylor, Denny. *Family Literacy: Young Children Learn to Read and Write*. Portsmouth, NH: Heinemann, 1983. Print.

Taylor, Denny, and Catherine Dorsey-Gaines. *Growing Up Literate: Learning from Inner City Families*. Portsmouth, NH: Heinemann, 1988. Print.

Taylor, Todd. *CCCC Bibliography of Composition and Rhetoric, 1984–1999*. Conference on College Composition and Communication. Web. 28 Sept. 2009.

Teich, Nathaniel. "Transfer of Writing Skills." *Written Communication* 4.2 (1987): 193–208. Print.

Thaiss, Chris, and Terry Myers Zawacki. *Engaged Writers and Dynamic Disciplines: Research on the Academic Writing Life*. Portsmouth, NH: Boynton/Cook, 2006. Print.

Thatcher, Barry. "Orientation for Teachers of Technical Writing." Pytlik and Liggett 266–77.

Thompson, Isabelle, David Shannon, Alyson Whyte, Amanda Muse, Milla Chappell, Abby Whigham, and Kristen Miller. "Examining Our Lore: A Survey of Students' and Tutors' Satisfaction with Writing Center Conferences." *Writing Center Journal* 29.1 (2009): 78–105. Print.

Thonus, Terese. "What Are the Differences? Tutor Interactions with First- and Second-Language Writers." *Second Language Writers in the Writing Center*. Ed. Jessica Williams and Carol Severino. Spec. issue of *Journal of Second Language Writing* 13.3 (2004): 227–42. Print.

Thorndike, E. L. *Principles of Teaching*. New York: Seiler, 1906.

Thorndike, E. L., and R. S. Woodworth. "The Influence of Improvement in One Mental Function upon the Efficiency of Other Functions." *Psychological Review* 8 (1901): 247–61. Print.

Townsend, Martha. "Re: Writing Intensive Course Criteria." Online posting. WPA-L, 3 Oct. 2010. Web. 14 Feb. 2011.

———. "Re: Writing Intensive Course Criteria." Online posting. WPA-L, 10 Oct. 2010. Web. 14 Feb. 2011.

Tremmel, Robert. "Seeking a Balanced Discipline: Writing Teacher Education in First-Year Composition and English Education." *English Education* 34.1 (2001): 6–30. Print.

————. "Still Loading Pig Iron After All These Years: Tribalism and English Education in the Global Contact Zone." *English Education* 32.3 (2000): 194–225. Print.

Tremmel, Robert, and William Broz, eds. *Teaching Writing Teachers of High School English and First-Year Composition*. Portsmouth, NH: Boynton/Cook, 2002. Print.

Truscott, John, and Angela Yi-ping Hsu. "Error Correction, Revision and Learning." *Journal of Second Language Writing* 17.4 (2008): 292–305. Print.

Tuomi-Groehn, Terttu, Yrgo Engestroem, and Michael Young. "From Transfer to Boundary-crossing Between School and Work as a Tool for Developing Vocational Education: An Introduction." *Between School and Work: New Perspectives on Transfer and Boundary-Crossing*. Eds. Tuomi-Groehn and Engestroem. New York: Pergamon, 2003. 1-15. Print.

Tuten, Nancy. "Writing Intensive Course Criteria." Online posting. WPA-L, 29 Sept. 2010. Web. 14 Feb. 2011.

Valdés, Guadalupe. "Bilingual Minorities and Language Issues in Writing: Toward Profession-wide Responses to a New Challenge." *Written Communication* 9 (1992): 85–136. Print.

Van Mannen, J. *Tales of the Field: On Writing Ethnography*. Chicago: U of Chicago P, 1988. Print.

Villanueva, Victor. *Cross-Talk in Comp Theory: A Reader*. 2nd ed. Urbana, IL: NCTE, 2003. Print.

Volet, Simone. "Learning across Cultures: Appropriateness." *International Journal of Educational Research* 31 (1999): 625–43. Print.

Vygotsky, Lev. *Thought and Language*. Cambridge, MA: MIT Press, 1969. Print.

Walvoord, Barbara E. "The Future of WAC." *College English* 58.1 (1996): 58–79. Print.

Walvoord, Barbara E., et al. *In the Long Run: A Study of Faculty in Three Writing-across-the-Curriculum Programs*. Urbana, IL: NCTE, 1996. Print.

Walvoord, B. E., and L. P. McCarthy. *Thinking and Writing in College: A Naturalistic Study of Students in Four Disciplines*. Urbana, IL: NCTE, 1991. Print.

Ward, Irene, and William J. Carpenter, eds. *The Allyn & Bacon Sourcebook for Writing Program Administrators*. New York: Longman, 2002. Print.

Ward, Irene, and Merry Perry. "A Selection of Strategies for Training Teaching Assistants." Ward and Carpenter 117–38.

Wardle, Elizabeth. "Understanding 'Transfer' from FYC: Preliminary Results of a Longitudinal Study." *WPA: Writing Program Administration* 31.1/2 (2007): 65-85. Print.

————. "Can Cross-Disciplinary Links Help Us Teach 'Academic Discourse' in FYC?" *Across the Disciplines* 1 (2004). Web. Accessed 12 December 2009.

————. "'Mutt Genres' and the Goal of FYC: How Can We Help Students Write the Genres of the University?" *College Composition and Communication* 60.4 (2009): 765–88. Print.

Warnick, Chris. "Locating the Archives: Finding Aids and Archival Scholarship in Composition and Rhetoric." Ramsey et al. 91–101.

Watson, Sam. "My Story of Wildacres, 1983–1998." McLeod and Soven 168–99.

Weiser, Irwin. "Portfolios and the New Teacher of Writing." Black et al. 219–31.

Wesch, Michael. *From Knowledgeable to Knowledge-able: Learning in New Media Environments*. *Academic Commons*. 7 Jan. 2009. Web. 21 Dec. 2009.

White, Edward M. "Re: Writing-Intensive Course Criteria." Online posting. 3 October 2010. Web. Accessed 14 February 2011.

White, Edward M. "The Scoring of Writing Portfolios: Phase 2." *College Composition and Communication* 56.4 (2005): 581–600. Print.

————. *Teaching and Assessing Writing: Recent Advances in Understanding, Evaluating, and Improving Student Performance*. San Francisco: Jossey-Bass, 1994. Print.

Wilhoit, Stephen. "Recent Trends in TA Instruction: A Bibliographic Essay." Pytlik and Liggett 17–27.

Williams, Jessica, and Carol Severino, eds. *Second Language Writers in the Writing Center.* Spec. issue of *Journal of Second Language Writing* 13.3 (2004): 165–242. Print.

Williams, Joseph. *Style: The Basics of Clarity and Grace.* New York: Pearson Longman, 2006.

Williamson, Michael. "The Worship of Efficiency: Untangling Practical and Theoretical Considerations in Writing Assessment." *Assessing Writing* 1 (1994): 147–74. Print.

Winslow, Rosemary. "The GTA Writing Portfolio: An Impact Study of Learning by Writing." Dobrin, *Don't Call It That* 315–36.

Winsor, Dorothy A. *Writing Power: Communication in an Engineering Center.* Albany: State U of New York P, 2003. Print.

WPA Executive Committee. "Evaluating the Intellectual Work of Writing Program Administrators: A Draft." *WPA: Writing Program Administration* 20.1–2 (1996): 92–103. Print.

The Writing Centers Research Project. "Materials Archive." 2010–2011. Web. 16 Nov. 2011.

———. "Oral History Archive." 2010–2011. Web. 16 Nov. 2011.

Wu, Hui. "Historical Studies of Rhetorical Women Here and There: Methodological Challenges to Dominant Interpretive Frameworks." *Rhetoric Society Quarterly* 32.1 (2002): 81–98. Print.

Wysocki, Anne. "Bookling Monument." *Kairos* 7.3 (2003). Accessed 1 May 2009. Web.

Wysocki, Anne Frances, Johndan Johnson-Eilola, Cynthia L. Selfe, and Geoffrey Sirc. *Writing New Media: Theory and Applications for Expanding the Teaching of Composition.* Logan: Utah State UP, 2004. Print.

Yakel, Elizabeth. "Searching and Seeking in the Deep Web: Primary Sources on the Internet." Ramsey et al. 102–18.

Yancey, Kathleen Blake. "College Admissions and the Insight Resume: Writing, Reflection, and Students' Lived Curriculum as a Site of Equitable Assessment." In Asao B. Inoue and Mya Poe, Eds. *Race and Writing Assessment.* New York: Peter Lang Publishing, 2012. 163-176. Print.

———. "Just wondering: FW: Consulting Opportunity for Professors of First-Year Students." WPA-L. January 15, 2011.

———. "The Impulse to Compose and the Age of Composition." *Research in the Teaching of English* 43 (Feb. 2009): 316-38.

———. "Looking Back as We Look Forward: Historicizing Writing Assessment." *College Composition and Communication* 50.3 (1999): 483–503. Print.

———. "Made Not Only in Words: Composition in a New Key." *College Composition and Communication* 56.2 (2004): 297–328. Print.

———. "Make Haste Slowly: Graduate Teaching Assistants and Portfolios." Black et al. 210–19.

———, ed. *Portfolios in the Writing Classroom: An Introduction.* Urbana, IL: NCTE, 1992. Print.

———. "The Professionalization of TA Development Programs: A Heuristic for Curriculum Design." Pytlik and Liggett 63–74.

———. "Reflecting on Portfolios." *Portfolios in the Writing Classroom: An Introduction.* Ed. Kathleen Blake Yancey. Urbana, IL: NCTE, 1992. 102–17. Print.

———. *Reflection in the Writing Classroom.* Logan: Utah State UP, 1998. Print.

Yancey, Kathleen Blake, and Brian Huot, eds. *Assessing Writing across the Curriculum: Diverse Approaches and Practices.* Vol. 1. Perspectives on Writing: Theory, Research, Practices. Greenwich, CT: Ablex, 1997. Print.

Zebroski, James. "Composition and Rhetoric, Inc.: Life After the English Department at Syracuse University." *Beyond English Inc.: Curricular Reform in a Global Economy.* Ed. David B. Downing, Claude Mark Hurlbert, and Paula Mathieu. Portsmouth, NH: Boynton/ Cook, 2002. 164–80. Print.

INDEX

ABOUT THE AUTHORS

KELLY RITTER is Associate Professor of English and Director of Composition at the University of North Carolina–Greensboro. She is the author of *Before Shaughnessy: Basic Writing at Yale and Harvard, 1920–1960, Who Owns School? Authority, Students, and Online Discourse,* and *To Know Her Own History: Writing at the Woman's College, 1943–1963.* She is also coeditor, with Stephanie Vanderslice, of *Can It Really Be Taught? Resisting Lore in Creative Writing Pedagogy.* Her articles on writing pedagogy, history, and theory have appeared in *College English, College Composition and Communication, Composition Studies, Pedagogy, Rhetoric Review,* and *WPA: Writing Program Administration.* She is the incoming editor (2012) of *College English.*

PAUL KEI MATSUDA is Professor of English and the Director of Writing Programs at Arizona State University, where he works closely with doctoral and master's students in rhetoric and composition as well as applied linguistics and TESOL. Previously, he taught at Miami University and the University of New Hampshire, where he directed the composition program. Founding chair of the Symposium on Second Language Writing and editor of the Parlor Press Series on Second Language Writing, he has edited a dozen books as well as special issues of *College English, Journal of Second Language Writing,* and *WPA: Writing Program Administration.* His articles have appeared in such journals as *College English, College Composition and Communication, Composition Studies, Computers and Composition, Journal of Basic Writing, Journal of Second Language Writing,* and *Written Communication.*

LINDA ADLER-KASSNER is PROFESSOR and Director of Writing at the University of California–Santa Barbara and was president of the Council of Writing Program Administrators from 2009 to 2011. She is author of *The Activist WPA: Changing Stories about Writing and Writers,* winner of the Council of Writing Program Administrators Best Book Award. Most recently, she coauthored *Reframing Writing Assessment to Improve Teaching and Learning* with Peggy O'Neill. With Susanmarie Harrington, she is also coauthor of *Basic Writing as a Political Act* and coeditor of *Questioning Authority.* Her other publications include book chapters and articles in *College Composition and Communication, College English, WPA: Writing Program Administration,* and *Journal of Basic Writing.*

ELIZABETH CHISERI-STRATER is Professor of English at the University of North Carolina–Greensboro, where she has directed the Composition Program and is on the faculty in Women's and Gender Studies. She is the coeditor of *Fieldworking: Reading and Writing Research,* 4th ed., *What Works? A Practical Guide for Teacher Research, Academic Literacies,* and articles in *WPA: Writing Program Administration* and the *Journal of Advanced Composition,* as well as numerous book chapters.

CHRISTIANE DONAHUE is Director of the Institute for Writing and Rhetoric at Dartmouth College and member of the Théodile-CIREL research group at the Université de Lille III. She publishes in linguistics, composition theory, and educational sciences in France and the United States; her work has appeared in journals including *Written Communication, College Composition and Communication, Recherches linguistiques,* and *Langage et société.* Her scholarly interests are in cross-cultural research, the study of knowledge and competence transfer, and the study of genre. Her analysis of French and U.S. student writing, *Ecrire à 'Université: Analyse Comparée en France et aux Etats-Unis,* was published in France in 2008, and her current longitudinal study of student writing at the University of Maine–Farmington is exploring questions of transfer and disciplinary knowledge.

DOUG DOWNS is Assistant Professor of Rhetoric and Composition at Montana State University–Bozeman. His and Elizabeth Wardle's June 2007 *College Composition and Communication* article on writing-about-writing pedagogy has fostered widespread conversation and research. With Wardle, he is coauthor of *Writing about Writing: A College Reader*, which supports WAW courses, and he recently published an essay in *Reader: Essays in Reader-Oriented Theory, Criticism, and Pedagogy* on teaching reading in WAW courses. His research interests coalesce around the problem of research pedagogy—how college writing instructors teach research, how that teaching is shaped by cultural conceptions of writing, and how undergraduate researchers in the humanities write with authority. His articles and chapters on related material appear in *CUR Quarterly*, *Teaching with Student Texts*, and *Undergraduate Research in English Studies*.

HEIDI ESTREM is Associate Professor and Director of the First-Year Writing Program at Boise State University. She serves on the CCCC Committee on Assessment and is a member of the *College Composition and Communication* Editorial Board. She is author or coauthor of several publications on the policies and pedagogies of writing program administration and graduate program development, which have appeared in *WPA: Writing Program Administration*, *Rhetoric Review*, and edited collections. Currently, she is investigating TAs' conceptions of their growth as instructors in a multiuniversity, survey-based project with E. Shelley Reid.

LAUREN FITZGERALD is coeditor (with Melissa Ianetta) of the *Writing Center Journal*, and Associate Professor of English at Yeshiva University, where she is also Director of the Yeshiva College Writing Center and was previously director of the YC Composition Program. She has worked in writing centers for over fifteen years and was the Director of the Erica Mann Jong '63 Writing Center at Barnard College. Her publications on writing centers, writing programs, and the teaching of writing have appeared in the *Writing Center Journal*, the *Writing Lab Newsletter*, *Composition Studies*, *WPA: Writing Program Administration* (with Elizabeth Vander Lei), and several edited collections, including (with Denise Stephenson) *The Writing Center Director's Resource Book*. She was a member of the Executive Committee of the Conference on College Composition and Communication from 2007 to 2010.

JEANNE GUNNER IS Vice Chancellor for Undergraduate Education and Professor of English and Comparative Literature at Chapman University in Orange, California. She has been a writing program administrator at UCLA and Santa Clara University, and continues to work closely with the writing program and the rhetoric-composition curriculum at Chapman, where she also teaches undergraduate writing courses. A past member of the Council of Writing Program Administrator's executive and editorial boards, she was co-facilitator of the WPA Summer Workshop in 2001–2 and 2002–3. One of her primary areas of research is the intersections of writing programs and ideology. Most recently she served as coeditor with Donna Strickland of *The Writing Program Interrupted: Making Space for Critical Discourse*. She was editor of *College English* from 1999 to 2006.

SUSANMARIE HARRINGTON is PROFESSOR and Director of the Writing in the Disciplines Program at the University of Vermont. She chairs the CCCC Committee on Assessment and has previously served on the Executive Board of the Council of Writing Program Administrators. She is a coeditor of *The Outcomes Book: Consensus and Debate in the Wake of the WPA Outcomes Statement*. With Linda Adler-Kassner, she has authored *Basic Writing as a Political Act* and edited *Questioning Authority*. Her essays have appeared in *Journal of Basic Writing*, *Computers and Composition*, *WPA: Writing Program Administration*, and *Educational and Psychological Measurement*.

BILL HART-DAVIDSON is an Associate Professor of Rhetoric and Writing at Michigan State University where he directs the Rhetoric and Writing Graduate Program and is Codirector of the Writing in Digital Environments (WIDE) Research Center. He teaches courses in technical and professional writing, interaction design, and research methods. Bill's research interests lie at the intersection of technical communication and human-computer interaction in such areas as visualizing knowledge work processes, information, and user experience design. Bill's writing has appeared in journals such as *Technical Communication, Technical Communication Quarterly, Computers and Composition, Kairos,* and the *Journal of Software Documentation* and in various edited collections. Through his work at WIDE, he produces writing software that incorporates and extends the range of the significance of research in the field of technical and professional writing.

GAIL E. HAWISHER is University Distinguished Teacher/Scholar and Professor Emeritus of English at the University of Illinois–Urbana-Champaign, where she also founded the Center for Writing Studies and the University of Illinois Writing Project. Her work engages literate activity and new information technologies and is reflected in her books with Cynthia L. Selfe, *Literate Lives in the Information Age, Passions, Pedagogies, and 21st Century Technologies,* and *Global Literacies and the World Wide Web* among them. In 2004, she was honored with the Lynn Martin Award for Distinguished Women Faculty and the Illinois Campus Award for Excellence in Undergraduate Teaching. With Patrick Berry, she and Selfe are coauthors of *Transnational Literate Lives in Digital Times,* a study of how people across the world take up literacy and digital media. Her most recent coauthored article, "Globalism and Multimodality in a Digitized World," appeared in the 2010 anniversary issue of *Pedagogy.*

DEBORAH H. HOLDSTEIN is Dean of the School of Liberal Arts and Sciences and Professor of English at Columbia College, Chicago, and she served a five-year term as editor of *College Composition and Communication* (2004–9). Prior to arriving at Columbia College in 2007, Holdstein was Professor and Chair of the Department of English at Northern Illinois University; before that, she was Faculty Associate for Graduate Studies and Research and Professor of English at Governors State University. A past officer and member of the Executive Committee of the CCCC, Holdstein also was for ten years the Director of the Consultant-Evaluator Program of the Council of Writing Program Administrators and served a four-year term on the Publications Committee of the Modern Language Association. She has published widely in composition and rhetoric, technology and the humanities, film studies, and literary studies, and her work has appeared in such journals as *College Composition and Communication, College English, JAC, Jump Cut,* and *Pedagogy.* Her books include *On Composition and Computers, Computers and Writing: Research, Theory, Practice* (with Cynthia L. Selfe), *Personal Effects: The Social Character of Scholarly Writing* (with David Bleich), several textbooks, and *Judaic Perspectives in Rhetoric and Composition Studies* (with Andrea Greenbaum). Her current research interests involve rhetorics of adoption and alternative rhetorical canons, the "global turn" in literary studies and its relationship to composition studies, and challenges to a "scholarship of administration."

BARBARA L'EPLATTENIER is an Associate Professor in the Department of Rhetoric and Writing at the University of Arkansas at Little Rock. Her coedited collection with Lisa Mastrangelo, *Historical Studies of Writing Program Administration: Individuals, Communities, and the Formation of a Discipline,* won the 2006 CWPA Best Book of the Year award. Along with Wendy Sharer, Lisa Mastrangelo, and Alexis Ramsey, she is coeditor of the collection *Working in the Archives.*

ANDREA A. LUNSFORD is the Louise Hewlett Nixon Professor of English and Humanities and past Director of the Program in Writing and Rhetoric at Stanford University. She has designed and taught undergraduate and graduate courses in writing history and theory, rhetoric, literacy studies, and intellectual property and is the author or coauthor of many books and articles, including *The Everyday Writer, Essays on Classical Rhetoric and Modern Discourse, Singular Texts/Plural Authors: Perspectives on Collaborative Writing, Reclaiming Rhetorica: Women in the History of Rhetoric, Everything's an Argument, Exploring Borderlands: Composition and Postcolonial Studies,* and *Writing Matters: Rhetoric in Private and Public Lives.*

RITA MALENCZYK is Professor of English at Eastern Connecticut State University, where she has directed the Writing-across-the-Curriculum Program since 1994. Her work on the politics and rhetoric of writing program administration has appeared in *WPA: Writing Program Administration* and in numerous edited collections, including Shirley K. Rose and Irwin Weiser's *The Writing Program Administrator as Theorist.* She is also coeditor, with Susanmarie Harrington, Keith Rhodes, and Ruth Overman Fischer, of *The Outcomes Book.* She is Vice President of the Council of Writing Program Administrators, and will succeed to President of the organization in 2013.

LISA MASTRANGELO is a Professor of English and Program Director of Women's Studies at the College of St. Elizabeth. With Barbara L'Eplattenier, she coedited the award-winning *Historical Studies of Writing Program Administration: Individuals, Communities, and the Formation of a Discipline.* With Barbara L'Eplattenier, Alexis Ramsey, and Wendy Sharer, she coedited *Working in the Archives.* In addition, her work has appeared in journals such as *College English, Composition Studies, Rhetoric Review,* and *Rhetoric and Public Affairs.*

TIM PEEPLES is Professor of Professional Writing and Rhetoric, and Associate Provost for Faculty Affairs at Elon University. For the past twenty-plus years, he has taught first-year through advanced writing and rhetoric courses, including visual rhetoric, document design, style and editing, composition pedagogy, writing center practices, theories and histories of rhetoric, and publications development and management. In addition to seven years of mid- to senior-level administrative experience in dean, provost, and president offices, he has ten years of WPA experience, serving in directorships of writing across the curriculum, a writing center, and a preengineering writing program and in assistant director positions for programs of both composition and professional writing. Tim's research focuses on examining and influencing the ways rhetorical space is reproduced, particularly through (everyday) practices of rhetoric and management/organization/administration, as well as the intersections of rhetoric and professional writing. His work has appeared in *Composition Studies,* a number of edited collections, and *Professional Writing and Rhetoric: Readings from the Field.*

E. SHELLEY REID is an Associate Professor of English and directs the Composition Program at George Mason University. Her arguments about strategies for educating composition teaching assistants have appeared in *Composition Studies* in 2004 and in *College Composition and Communication* in fall 2009; an article on educating TA peer mentors also appeared in *Composition Studies* in fall 2008. With Heidi Estrem, she has recently completed a three-year, two-site study of TA education. She has published related articles about the need for substantive faculty development in support of various academic endeavors such as the adoption of multiculturalist composition pedagogies and the implementation of large-scale revisions to writing program curricula.

CYNTHIA L. SELFE is Humanities Distinguished Professor in the Department of English at Ohio State University, and the coeditor, with Gail E. Hawisher, of *Computers and Composition: An International Journal.* In 1996, Selfe was recognized as an EDUCOM Medal award winner for innovative computer use in higher education—the first woman and the first English teacher ever to receive this award. In 2000, the CCCC Committee on Computers presented Selfe, along with longtime collaborator Hawisher, with the Outstanding Technology Innovator Award. Selfe is the author or coauthor of *Literacy and Technology in the 21st Century: The Perils of Not Paying Attention, Literate Lives in the Information Age: Narratives of Literacy from the United States* (with Hawisher), *Writing New Media: Theory and Applications for Expanding the Teaching of Composition* (with Anne Frances Wysocki, Johndan Johnson-Eilola,, and Geoffrey Sirc), *Computers and the Teaching of Writing in American Higher Education, 1979–1994: A History* (with Hawisher, Paul. LeBlanc, and Charles Moran), *Multimodal Composition: Resources for Teachers, Gaming Lives in the Twenty-first Century* (with Hawisher), *Technical Communication: Outcomes and Approaches, Global Literacies and the World Wide Web* (with Hawisher, *Passions, Pedagogies, and 21st Century Technologies* (with Hawisher), *Literacy and Computers: Complicating Our Vision of Teaching and Learning with Technology* (with Susan Hilligoss), *Evolving Perspectives on Computers in Composition Studies: Questions for the 1990s* (with Hawisher), *Computers and Writing: Theory, Research, and Practice* (with Deborah Holdstein), *Computers in English and Language Arts: The Challenge of Teacher Education* (with Dawn Rodrigues and William Oates), *and Critical Perspectives on Computers and Composition Instruction* (with Hawisher).

Elizabeth Wardle is Associate Professor, Associate Chair, and Director of Writing Outreach Programs in the Department of Writing and Rhetoric at the University of Central Florida (UCF). With Doug Downs she recently published *Writing about Writing: A College Reader.* She has also published in *College Composition and Communication, WPA: Writing Program Administration, Enculturation,* and *Technical Communication Quarterly.* Her research interests center around transfer and designing curricular structures that encourage transfer. She is currently part of a grant partnership between UCF and AASCU, for which she is working with composition faculty at fifteen schools across the country to introduce writing about writing in a blended format.

Kathleen Blake Yancey, the Kellogg W. Hunt Professor of English and Distinguished Research Professor at Florida State University, directs the graduate program in Rhetoric and Composition Studies. Past president of the Council of Writing Program Administrators, past chair of the Conference on College Composition and Communication, and past president of the National Council of Teachers of English, she is second vice president of SAMLA. She also codirects the International Coalition on Electronic Portfolio Research, which has brought together over sixty institutions worldwide to focus on and document the learning that takes place inside and around electronic portfolios. She is the author, editor, or coeditor of ten books and over sixty chapters and refereed articles. Her edited, coedited, or single-authored books include *Portfolios in the Writing Classroom, Assessing Writing across the Curriculum, Electronic Portfolios, Teaching Literature as Reflective Practice,* and *Delivering College Composition; The Fifth Canon,* which won the Council of Writing Program Administrators' Best Book Award. Her current projects include the volume based on her CCCC Chair's Address, "Composition in a New Key: A Theory and Practice of Composition in the 21st Century" and *The Way We Were: A Cultural History of Vernacular Writing in 20th Century America.* In 2010, Yancey assumed the editorship of *College Composition and Communication,* the flagship journal in the field.